BRIAN ROBERTSON started life in Aberdeenshire, Scotland, and now lives in Queensland. In between, he's had many adventures, including two years in the 1st Battalion Gordon Highlanders in Cyprus. He has also been a teacher, a botanist and an author of children's textbooks.

The Five Mile Press Pty Ltd
1 Centre Road, Scoresby
Victoria 3179 Australia
www.fivemile.com.au

First published 2012

Printed in Australia at Griffin Press.
Only wood grown from sustainable regrowth forests is used in the manufacture
of paper found in this book.

Edited by Julian Welch
Page design and typesetting by Shaun Jury
Cover design and map by Luke Causby, Blue Cork
Cover photo courtesy David Barrett
Internal maps by Kristy Lund-White

National Library of Australia Cataloguing-in-Publication entry

Author:	Barrett, David.
Title:	Digger's story: surviving the Japanese POW camps was just the beginning/David Barrett; Brian Robertson.
ISBN:	9781743007426 (pbk.)
Subjects:	Barrett, David.
	Great Britain. Commonwealth War Graves Commission—Biography.
	Burma–Siam Railroad.
	Changi POW Camp (Changi, Singapore)—Biography.
	World War, 1939–1945—Prisoners and prisons, Japanese—Biography.
	World War, 1939–1945—Personal narratives, Australian.
	Prisoners of war—Australia—Biography.
	Prisoners of war—Thailand—Biography.
	Prisoners of war—Burma—Biography.
	Soldiers' bodies, Disposition of—Thailand.
	Soldiers' bodies, Disposition of—Burma.
	World War, 1939–1945—Registers of dead—Thailand.
	World War, 1939-1945—Registers of dead—Burma.
Other Authors/Contributors:	Robertson, Brian.
Dewey Number:	940.547252

To all those prisoners of war of the Japanese who died before they could be rescued and to those who, on returning home, suffered from the residual effects of their imprisonment and died long before the time nature normally allows us to enjoy life.

Foreword

During the Pacific War, the death rate for POWs under the Japanese was seven times that of those detained by the Germans and Italians. The majority of them were captured by the Japanese in the first three months following the outbreak of war in the region, so most who survived until the end of the war endured more than three years of arduous and painful internment. In fact, the post-war death rate among surviving POWs of the Japanese was four times higher than that of those imprisoned by German and Italian forces. These statistics clearly reflect the brutal treatment of POWs by the Japanese.

This gripping biography, a remarkable joint work by David Barrett, a former POW, and Brian Robertson, a skilled researcher and writer, vividly portrays the cruelty and brutality that Japanese troops inflicted upon POWs and numerous *romusha* (forced Asian labourers). David's honest and straightforward account of Japanese wartime behaviour illustrates how easily the inculcation of malicious ideologies – such as racism, imperialism and Emperor-worship – can lead to barbarous behaviour. We Japanese need to examine seriously how our fathers' and grandfathers' generations were able commit such atrocities as a result of the indoctrination of nationalism. At the same time, we need to educate our fellow citizens – in particular, our politicians – about how Japan as a nation should bear responsibility for such war crimes.

David's compelling testimony is evidence that one can survive such an indescribable, prolonged ordeal with the aid of wisdom, a deep understanding of humanity and a sense of humour. It is truly moving to learn how he maintained humane compassion despite ruthless treatment by the Japanese day after day for three and a half years. Unsurprisingly, his hatred of the Japanese remained with him for many years after the war. Ultimately, though, his profound humanity overcame this hatred, as he gradually made friends with people from this former enemy nation. This experience reminds us that hatred does not permit progress; rather, it destroys the humanity of those who continue to be consumed by it.

David's strong sense of justice is closely intertwined with his humane compassion. His continuous search for justice for former POWs of the Japanese Imperial Forces, even decades after the war, has moved many people, not only his fellow former POWs, but also Japanese supporters, including myself. His warm-hearted and embracing friendship for Japanese people has contributed to a strong and healthy grassroots relationship between many Australian and Japanese citizens. In short, David's life clearly symbolises continuous and powerful resistance to the dehumanisation caused by war, and for this reason he can be called 'A True Digger of Peace Making'.

Toshiyuki Tanaka
Research Professor
Hiroshima Peace Institute

Contents

FOREWORD *by Toshiyuki Tanaka*   vii

ACKNOWLEDGEMENTS   xi

PREFACE   *The Monsoon Drain*   I

PART I   THE YEARS OF LEARNING   5

CHAPTER I   *The Early Years*   7

CHAPTER 2   *To the War*   17

CHAPTER 3   *Retreat to Singapore*   35

CHAPTER 4   *The Fight for Singapore*   43

PART 2   THE YEARS OF SURVIVAL   59

CHAPTER 5   *Life at Changi*   61

CHAPTER 6   *The Officers' Mess*   77

CHAPTER 7   *Journey to the Railway*   89

CHAPTER 8   *Mates and Survivors*   99

CHAPTER 9   *The Return of F Force*   117

CHAPTER 10   *Relative Respite*   133

PART 3   LOCATING THE GRAVES   143

CHAPTER 11   *Freedom*   145

CHAPTER 12   *The On-on Hotel*   157

CHAPTER 13   *Back to the Railway*   169

CHAPTER 14   *The War Graves Commission*   177

CHAPTER 15   *Transition*   197

PART 4   A FINAL ACCOUNTING   205

CHAPTER 16   *The Business Life*   207

CHAPTER 17   *Fighting Again*   219

CHAPTER 18   *The Fight Continues*   233

CHAPTER 19   *The Health of the Ex-POW*   245

CHAPTER 20   *To Geneva*   259

CHAPTER 21   *Reconciliation*   275

ENDNOTES   285

Acknowledgements

David Barrett told this story and I wrote it. We live in a retirement village in Queensland Australia, in the lower and upper units of the same building. Our coming together to produce this book was just by happy chance. David wanted to tell his story and I was indeed fortunate to get the opportunity to write it. I thank him sincerely for willingly risking his life's story to one who until that time had written only school textbooks.

We usually met on Sunday afternoons in David's unit. We sat at his dining room table and I switched on the recorder as he organised a bottle of good red wine. We would then spend an hour or two talking about some aspect of David's life, after which I would stagger downstairs and leave the transcription until the following morning.

David is a collector and hoarder of all letters, artefacts, photographs and the like that he came by throughout his life. There were newspaper cuttings, documents, correspondence, reports and minutes of meetings, all pertaining to activities in David's long life, particularly for the period from 1986 to 2000 in connection with the Reparations Committee. I thank David for being such an archive keeper, although it took me years to sort through everything. There is probably enough material to write at least one other book!

The authors are indebted to Ria Fewster, another resident in our village, her late husband Col, and Barbara L'Herpiniere from Perth, who read each succeeding chapter and reported faithfully the whole way through. Also to the members of the Scribblers writers' group meeting every month at Mary Ryan's bookshop in Springfield. I could not have written the book without everyone's very valuable, encouraging and critical comment. Thanks also to Stanley Sparkes, yet another village resident, who took great care during development of the early chapters to ensure that the authors understood the correct use of the English language. Trevor Tindall, a co-author of mine in the textbook business, also needs a thank you for the application of his skills and knowledge in the Japanese language.

Marjorie, my wife, gave valuable feedback on the presentation of the story, typed all the unreadable documents, and patiently supported me during the whole time the book was gradually emerging – over a long three and a half years. Thank you, Marjorie.

We are also very grateful to our agent Curtis Brown and our publisher The Five Mile Press for taking this book on in these very uncertain publishing times and to our very able editor, Julian Welch, who was particularly helpful in structuring the book.

David also hopes that many young people will read this book and gain some understanding of the kind of things that happen in war. He is also a little worried about the swear words in the story. We both apologise for that, but they were hard times and we judged that it would be best to tell it as it was. David wishes to assure all young people, his great-grandchildren in particular, that he no longer swears and hopes that they don't either.

Brian Robertson

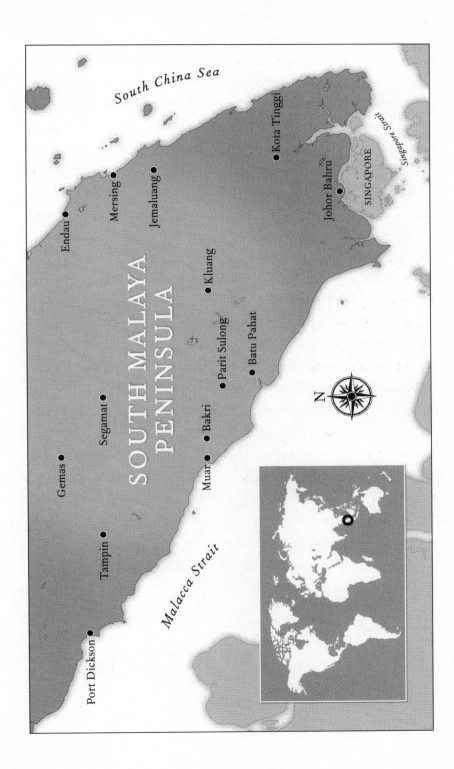

South China Sea

Kota Tinggi

Singapore Strait

Johor Bahru

SINGAPORE

Mersing

Jemaluang

Endau

SOUTH MALAYA PENINSULA

Kluang

Parit Sulong

Batu Pahat

N

Segamat

Bakri

Muar

Gemas

Tampin

Malacca Strait

Port Dickson

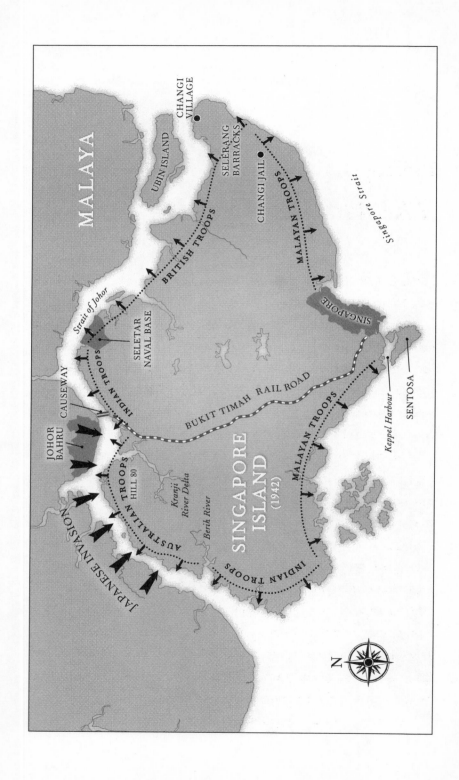

MALAYA

CHANGI VILLAGE

UBIN ISLAND

SELERANG BARRACKS

CHANGI JAIL

Singapore Strait

MALAYAN TROOPS

BRITISH TROOPS

Strait of Johor

SELETAR NAVAL BASE

SINGAPORE

INDIAN TROOPS

CAUSEWAY

JOHOR BAHRU

BUKIT TIMAH RAIL ROAD

Keppel Harbour

SENTOSA

MALAYAN TROOPS

HILL 80

Kranji River Delta

AUSTRALIAN TROOPS

Berih River

SINGAPORE ISLAND
(1942)

JAPANESE INVASION

INDIAN TROOPS

N

Preface

The Monsoon Drain

'WELL, WE CAN'T bloody go anywhere else, can we?' said Private Roy Keily. It was a statement, not a question.

Roy was sitting with Private David 'Digger' Barrett on the lawn just outside the entrance to St Andrew's Cathedral, Singapore, around lunchtime on 15 February 1942. They had their backs against the trunk of a large tropical flame tree and were enjoying their first real meal for several days, which had been supplied by a hastily constructed field kitchen in the cathedral's grounds.

The two men were discussing the latest movement of their unit, the 2/9th Field Ambulance of the Australian 8th Division. They had moved a lot recently, always seeking a safer location for their more than 400 sick or wounded men.

'Back to Australia should be the next move, eh?' Digger replied. 'Perhaps if we —' But before he could complete his sentence a shell exploded at the far side of the lawn, and then another, closer.

Both men hit the ground, their food no longer a concern. Mess tins, biscuits and bully beef went flying. More explosions followed. Digger could hear the whine and whistle of shrapnel above him as he lay flat on his stomach, pressing himself into the lawn, half-choking on the smoke and the pungent smell of burning grass.

Get lower, get lower, he thought. *I'm not dying here.*

When at last he dared to look around, he saw the concrete of the open monsoon drain that surrounded the cathedral; it was barely ten metres away. That was his goal. He knew he had to reach it right now if he was to survive.

Shells continued to explode nearby, despite the large red crosses that were plastered on the roof and walls of the cathedral. Trying to ignore the hell around him, Digger put every ounce of effort into shuffling forward, on his knees and elbows, snake-like towards the drain. Not for a second did he contemplate standing and running.

At the same time he was thinking about his mother. He couldn't understand it. It was as if one half of his brain was remembering his mother and what they did together at home, while the other half was concentrating on getting to the drain. And yet another part of his brain was wondering why he was thinking of his mother at this time.

Exhausted, Digger gratefully reached the drain and dropped into it. He knew that, barring a direct hit, he would be relatively safe here. Gasping for breath, he began to take stock of his situation. The drain was a good eighty centimetres deep and about a metre across. Digger was able to sit in relative comfort, except for his knees and arms, which, he suddenly realised, were hurting like hell. When he inspected them, he discovered burns: he'd been crawling over hot fragments of shrapnel on the lawn.

All Digger could hear was the thunder of shells exploding nearby, and shouting coming from the cathedral and the Adelphi Hotel at the other side of the lawn. Although he knew that keeping his head down was the best course of action, he couldn't resist raising it just high enough to glance at the main entrance of the cathedral, where just two minutes earlier he and Roy had been relaxing. A few ambulances had been parked on the lawn near where they'd been eating. One had suffered a direct hit and was now a twisted wreck. There was no sign of Roy. *So I got here just in time*, Digger thought.

The 2/9th Field Ambulance had been moving into St Andrew's Cathedral for the past day or so. They were gradually vacating their old Main Dressing Station (MDS), which was in the Cathay Building at the end of Orchard Road, and setting up the cathedral and the Adelphi Hotel opposite as their new one. This was just the latest of many moves that the unit had made on its fast retreat south from Mersing, on the east coast of the Malayan peninsula.

As bad as Digger's situation in the monsoon drain was, he was confident that he would survive. He'd always had the ability to look ahead to a positive outcome rather than dwell on a present problem. This had sustained him when the bigger lads beat him up during his first year at Hyde Street State School in Melbourne. Even as he was losing the fight, he had still tried his best to give as much pain as he received, and he knew that as soon as he was able, he would plan revenge.

Despite the occasional bullying incident at school, Digger had thoroughly enjoyed his early childhood and his teen years. He had great mates, who, regardless of the hardships of the times, were together able to create adventures that saw them grow and develop into young men eager to enter adult life.

Perhaps because of the way he had spent his youth, Digger had a perpetual optimism that he was always able to call on, no matter how dire the circumstances. This was to stand him, and his mates, in very good stead over the next few years. They would indeed need all Digger's ability and positive attitude, and much more besides, in order simply to survive.

PART I

The Years of Learning

Chapter 1

The Early Years

DIGGER WAS BORN David William Barrett in Charlestown, New South Wales, on 18 February 1922, the third child of David and Ethel Barrett. Their eldest child was Reginald, and then there was Digger's sister, Iris. From the moment he was born, his father called him Digger, and the name had stuck. Perhaps his father recognised a fighting spirit in his son, or perhaps it was just that he had served in the Australian Army towards the end of World War I. For whatever reason, Digger's nickname endured.

In 1926 the whole family moved to Footscray in Melbourne, where Digger's father went to work in a foundry. He was a good family provider. In 1928 the family moved a short distance to a shop premises in Barkly Street, Footscray. Digger, Reginald and Iris were transferred to the nearby Geelong Road State School.

During the 1920s, most women whose husbands had a job were content to be housewives. However, this move to rent and operate a shop was Ethel's idea. Digger's mother not only took care of the family, but also eventually became the main breadwinner as well.

David Barrett senior, Digger's father, always remained aloof from the children, and it was Ethel who supplied all the love and care. Perhaps the hard foundry work and long hours sapped his strength, as he never seemed to have the energy required for a loving relationship with his wife and children. Even when he was a young child, Digger's father was remote and unapproachable. Digger was never afraid of him, but he was belted for talking back to him on several occasions.

Digger's father was gruff and brutal. As a boy, Digger thought this brutality was because his father was an Englishman. The other men he knew were the fathers of his schoolmates, who were generally good fun and friendly towards their children, and they weren't English. It never occurred to Digger to question this reasoning until he was practically an adult.

His father had deserted from the British army and boarded a ship bound for Australia, subsequently jumping ship in Adelaide – or so Digger understood. He had changed his surname from Barrett to Sowter to protect himself from the authorities. He was David Sowter when he met and married Ethel, and had only changed his name back to Barrett just before Digger's birth, by which time he felt it was safe to do so. As a result, Digger's sister and brother both had the surname Sowter.

The shop Ethel Barrett rented – at 311 Barkly Street, Footscray – was big and airy, although it had only one large display window looking onto the street. The lounge room, dining room and kitchen were behind the shop, and the first floor had two bedrooms and a large landing. Digger, being the youngest, had his bed on the landing. There was a carport and several outhouses in the back yard, which was accessed through the lane at the side of the shop. Digger's father would send him to the nearby Plough Hotel with a billy, which he would put on the bar, asking the barman to 'fill her up, please'.

Ethel was no ordinary woman. Whereas many women would probably have sold children's clothes or groceries, Ethel was interested in and knowledgeable about radio. Her shop sold various types of furniture, but its main product was American Van Ruyton radios. By the age of eight or nine, Digger, encouraged by his mum, was using part of a large storeroom in the shop to build crystal radio sets, which he traded at school.

Financial hardship in the 1920s and 1930s led many people to abandon their dogs. Digger turned this sad situation into another entrepreneurial activity. He rounded up stray dogs, took them home, fed them, washed them and groomed them. After kitting them out with collars and leads, he would take them to the doors of houses in the up-market areas of town and sell them. This gift for enterprise, which was always encouraged by his mother, would serve Digger well in the future.

As he progressed through the grades at school in the early 1930s, Digger got only average marks for most subjects. He was interested in preparing for life after school but could not, at this early age, see the value of subjects such as history and geography. He certainly wanted to learn about people and how they lived and worked, but he considered that the present and his own future were much more important than someone else's past.

Digger and some of his more adventurous friends would occasionally skip school and hitch a ride into town on the horse-drawn beer barrel cart, as it returned to the brewery with the empties from the Plough Hotel and other nearby pubs. He and his mates would then go exploring. When they were hungry, they would ask the nearest greengrocer for any 'spec' – fruit that was unfit for sale. When the time came to go home, they would simply go to the nearest police station and claim that they were lost. Digger's father would come to collect the boys in the family's 1928 Chevrolet. He never seemed to care that young Digger was wagging school.

In 1936 Digger left school. He was fourteen, and he went to work at the Australian Glass Factory in Melbourne. His boss was Tommy Hall, a friend of the Barrett family. Digger learned to stencil product manufacturers' names onto glass bottles; the names were then baked onto the glass in a kiln. He was a good and reliable worker but had only marginally more enthusiasm for glass manufacturing than he'd had for school. However, the company's management was pleased with his efforts, and Tommy Hall soon put him in charge of the stencilling section. Digger now had a few even younger boys working under him.

Digger's real enthusiasm during this period was for rabbit-shooting with his friends on a Sunday. He had acquired a .410-bore shotgun and a .22-calibre rifle and loved to use them.

I really looked forward to the odd weekends I would get off from the glassworks. Arthur Bowden and Charlie 'Tusker' Blewett were my mates at the time. We were about fifteen and would take the train up to Clarkefield, north-west of Melbourne. I remember it well: one pub, a store and a railway station, but plenty of rabbits.

The pub would sell us beer at the back door, and we would get other supplies at the store and then go to our favourite campsite, about a mile away. It was down a steep gully and on a flat area halfway up the other side. One day we started drinking the beer as we walked to the camp, and as we made our way down the steep gully I fell and tumbled nearly all the way to the bottom. Thank God I wasn't carrying my rifle, but I was carrying the food, including a half pound of butter we had just bought at the store, in my inside jacket pocket. By the time I stopped rolling down the gully the butter was through everything. I told my mother the truth when I got home except for the bit about the beer!

We would sit around the fire at our camp in the evening and talk about the war, which we all knew was coming, and tell each other of our plans to join the army or the navy. We all knew that the Japanese had invaded China, and that they had murdered thousands of Chinese. During the day, we would practise with our rifles, firing at tree trunks right next to where one of us was standing. It was just the kind of dangerous stupid thing that young blokes do. We always had a few rabbits to take home on Sunday night. All three of us joined the militia as soon as we turned sixteen.

Digger joined the 16th Field Ambulance, 2nd Cavalry Division, Light Horse. He chose the cavalry because he thought riding horses would be easier than walking. The navy was out because he didn't fancy swimming to save himself, should the need arise, and the air force was just all too dangerous. It was simply chance that he ended up in a Field Ambulance unit.

They were a part-time volunteer force, and most men who had regular jobs, as Digger did, were given time off by their employers to take part in weekend training. They were ridiculed by many members of the regular army, who referred to them as 'chocolate soldiers' or 'chocos' – since they believed these amateur soldiers would melt in the heat of battle.

Despite this, Digger loved the training, which got him away from his father. He spent as much time with the militia as he possibly could and learned a great deal. He particularly enjoyed the company of the older men, veterans of World War I, of whom there were many in his unit.

Our last camp was at Torquay in Victoria in January, February and March of 1940. There were 6500 men and 3000 horses. Most of the country men had their own horses but us city boys didn't. We were given what they called 'remounts'.

I was about the last to get one, and I called him Lop Ears. He was a funny horse, and when we got onto the beach in the sand he would lie down, roll in it and wouldn't get up. An old soldier told me that to get him up I had to piss in his ear. So I took him at his word and, right enough, it worked well!

What I enjoyed most was driving the limbers. They were two-wheeled carts, with one in front of the other, and they were pulled by two or sometimes four horses. Sometimes they transported stores and sometimes they pulled artillery pieces. They were very difficult to drive. There were two drivers if there were two pairs of horses, but I only drove the two-horse limbers, so I was the only driver.

The driver was always mounted on the left horse of the pair. The driver had the reins of his own horse and of the one to his right. You also had a leg iron on your right leg to protect it from getting squeezed between your horse and the shaft. It was great being able to drive them properly, but it took a while to train the horses to do exactly as you wanted.

Not long after this camp, Digger went to the Melbourne Town Hall to enlist as a regular soldier in the Australian Imperial Force (AIF). It was 24 June 1940 and he was eighteen years old. Like most young men, Digger wanted fun and adventure – there was no thought of service to country or any of that nonsense.

At the Town Hall, the sergeant in charge took one look at Digger's slight frame. 'You're too young, son,' he said. 'Come back when you're older and you've been round the block a bit.'

Of course, Digger already was eighteen, although he knew he looked much younger. He decided to take the sergeant literally. He ran round the block and came back to the front entrance of the Town Hall, where he met a different sergeant. This time, he said he was twenty years old and he was duly signed on. His army papers would always list him as two years older than he really was, but that didn't matter – he was in!

Perhaps it was because Digger was in his Light Horse uniform that the very day he joined the regular army, he was ordered to march twenty or so other new recruits down to Flinders Street station, where they were to take the train to Caulfield Racecourse.

I was expected to be in charge of this lot, and I didn't even know where Caulfield Racecourse was. However, there were plenty of local lads in the group and so we were able to make our way there. When we arrived, a sergeant major threw two stripes at me and said, 'Get those on, lad,' but I said no as politely as I could. All I wanted to do was enjoy myself, and I was wise enough to know that responsibility would cramp my style.

My first two weeks in the AIF were spent at Caulfield, and most of us slept in the stables. From there we went to Mount Martha, down the Mornington Peninsula in Victoria. We slept on the floor on palliasses but I didn't mind. The routine was normal drills, route marches, gas drills, keeping fit and first-aid training. I really enjoyed it.

When my sister, Iris, was due to have a baby, I asked for leave to visit her but they wouldn't grant it. So I thought, 'Bugger them!' and I just took off and stayed away a couple of days. When I returned I was charged with being absent without leave, but Colonel Glynn White, the Assistant Director Medical Services of the 8th Division, sorted it out and got the charges dropped. He was a mate of mine because he'd also been in the Light Horse.

I didn't know it at the time but I was being held back, waiting for the formation of the 2/9th Field Ambulance. I should have been sent to the Middle East with the 7th Division because all the guys that joined up with me were sent there. We privates had no idea what was happening. I just accepted it all. I eventually found out that Lieutenant Colonel Dr Hedley Summons, who had been our commanding officer in the Light Horse, had been promised a unit. He had directed that his men from the Light Horse be held back from assignments until his AIF unit was formed.

From Mount Martha, many of us were moved to a camp at Puckapunyal, around sixty miles north of Melbourne. This was where the 2/9th Field Ambulance was formed in July 1940. Medical training was all the go from then on. We were given stretcher and ambulance drills, bandaging drills, procedural drills in the case of a gas attack and so on. I was in A Company. It was great!

Colonel Summons was well liked and respected by his men, many of whom had served with him in the militia. He was a great fitness enthusiast, and so when the unit was required to move from Puckapunyal to Bonegilla, near Albury, he decided that the men would march the 130 miles or so. The men in his unit were also put through a rigorous medical, including an assessment of their mental fitness – although none of the men were aware of this at the time.

Summons was determined to take only the best soldiers with him – wherever it was he was going. By the end of September 1940, fourteen men had been discharged as unfit for various reasons. Those over forty years of age were considered unsuitable for overseas service, two men had physical illnesses, and six were mentally unfit. Colonel Summons wrote somewhat bitterly in his report: 'There were two high grade imbeciles, one moron type, one congenital criminal and two anxiety states (one severe). These might not have been spotted in non-medical units. Several others were irresponsible, uneducated or a general nuisance.'[1]

Digger's physical and mental capacity was never in doubt. In fact, his mind was so sharp that he didn't have to march to the new camp. He was able to organise it so that he went on the train, looking after the unit's supplies and medical stores, all the way to Bonegilla.

Digger and his mate Joe Milledge had organised a couple of days' leave in early November 1940 to attend the Melbourne Cup. While in Melbourne, they met another friend of Digger's, who assured them that a horse called Old Rowley would win the race. Like most punters, Digger and Joe believed that a hot tip from a mate was much better than any other method of choosing the winner, so they put every penny they had on the horse – including their money for the train trip back to Bonegilla. Old Rowley came in at 100/1.

Digger and Joe were at Spencer Street Station a day later, already AWOL and planning to go somewhere else to spend the rest of their winnings, when a railway employee came up to them. 'Are you blokes on embarkation leave?' he asked.

'No, we're AWOL,' Joe explained, in his normal innocent and honest manner.

'Well, all the rest of your mob seem to be on embarkation leave.'

The two decided that their Melbourne Cup holiday was over. On their return to camp, they told their story and received a dressing-down. They were told they would be dealt with later, but in the meantime they were sent on embarkation leave. Six months later, long after they arrived in Malaya, the case of their going AWOL came up. They were fined a couple of days' pay but it had been well worth it.

Chapter 2

To the War

AT TWO A.M. on the morning of 2 February 1941, a little over seven months since Digger joined the AIF, the men of the 2/9th Field Ambulance arrived by truck at Albury railway station. They were off on the greatest adventure of their young lives.

Since the outbreak of hostilities in Europe, everyone expected the eventual involvement of Japan in the war, so troop movements such as this were kept top-secret. Few details of the journey were known even to the soldiers themselves. But somehow everyone from the Albury-Wodonga area seemed to be at the station to see the boys off. Half an hour after this great farewell, all on the train were fast asleep.

By the early afternoon they had arrived at the Pyrmont dock in Sydney, where they were transferred onto a queue of ferries that took them to a huge ocean liner at anchor in the harbour – the RMS *Queen Mary*. As they approached, there was a gentle swell in the harbour. The massive ship was anchored opposite Taronga Zoo and within sight of the Heads.

Digger and Joe could see two ferries on the port side of the ship, loading soldiers onto the *Queen Mary*. As the ferry and the pontoon at the side of the ship moved up and down, the soldiers were required to jump at just the right moment. Their mates still on the ferry threw their kit bags after them onto the pontoon, then the soldiers scrambled up the sea ladder attached to the side of the ship, before disappearing through very small doors about halfway up the hull. The ferry carrying Digger and Joe moved around to the starboard side. They were soon moving up the ship's side and disappearing into its belly.

As they entered they looked around in awe. Despite the masses of young men, the place was strangely quiet. There was carpet on the floor and crew members were holding buckets from which soldiers had to draw a number. This determined where they were to be billeted on the ship. It took Joe and Digger a good half-hour to find their allotted bunks. They had been lucky, drawing a cabin with two separate bunks and its own porthole. The glass was painted to black it out but they kept it open during the day. Many of their mates were in the main hold, they learned, each man with just a hammock to himself.

The *Queen Mary* had undergone a refit in Sydney the previous May. Formerly, she had hosted 2140 well-heeled trans-Atlantic travellers, but now she carried 5500 poorly paid troops. She had also lost her colourful paint job and was now a dull grey. Anti-mine paravanes had been fitted to her in Singapore in late 1940. Despite these changes, the lavish furniture, the carpets and the art-deco interior made the troops feel like they were about to start a luxury cruise.

The next day they remained at anchor while troops from the 2/10th Australian General Hospital (AGH) filed onto the ship. Joe had found some of the ship's old stationery in a bottom drawer in the cabin, and he was busily drawing. This was his way of recording his experiences.

In many ways, Digger and his mate were very different characters. Digger was always up-front and keen for others to know his opinion, while Joe tended to keep his thoughts to himself. Joe worried a bit about Digger's opinions getting him into bother, but Digger's forthright and assertive manner never changed.

Joe always wanted to know how things worked, and when he and Digger saw the paravanes Joe could not rest until he discovered more about them. He questioned members of the crew and met a like-minded individual who, despite the rules about secrecy, was happy to explain the principle to him. Digger, despite his relative disinterest in the topic, eventually found himself in possession of most of the facts about how a paravane worked.

The ship towed two paravanes, one on each side. Each one was attached to the bow by a thirty-metre tether. Because of their fins, the paravanes would travel a metre or two under the surface and pull the tether outwards from the bow as the ship moved forwards – 'just as a kite keeps pulling on the string', Joe explained. If the paravane towing lines encountered mines, they were diverted away from the hull of the ship and collided with the paravane. If the paravane was destroyed the crew simply fitted another.

Joe sketched the ship's paravanes, showing how they were attached and how they would operate to protect it from mines. Later in the voyage he offered Digger a drawing of his choice. Digger chose a drawing of the *Queen Mary*, although Joe thought he might have chosen the paravane diagrams, of which he was very proud.

On 4 February the *Queen Mary* weighed anchor and sailed in convoy with the *Aquitania*, a slow four-funnel coal-burner that had been launched in 1913, and the *Nieuw Amsterdam*, which was loaded with Kiwis. They travelled through Sydney Heads at the speed of the slowest ship, the *Aquitania*, and then began to head south. Two days later, having rounded Tasmania, they were joined by the *Mauretania*, from Melbourne.

The troops knew they were travelling west through the great Southern Ocean. They also knew that the British army had retreated from Dunkirk in May and June of 1940, and that Britain had successfully repelled the German air force later that year in the Battle of Britain, but at great cost to London and other cities on the southern coast of England. Those aboard the *Queen Mary* who took more than a passing interest in international affairs, such as Digger, knew that China and Japan were also at war, and that this European war was very likely to spread to Asia, with Japan on Germany's side.

Anticipation was in the air. All knew they were on a great adventure. They were volunteers, and were ready to fight wherever they were asked to fight, secure in their ignorance of exactly what this meant. The topic of just about every conversation in the cabins, on the promenade decks and in the canteen at the stern was where were they going. To Europe to fight the Germans? Or perhaps to Asia, where the Japanese were becoming more aggressive and talking of the 'Greater East Asia Co-Prosperity Sphere'? Many of the other ranks on the ship were well aware that the Co-Prosperity Sphere was a plan by Japan's prime minister, Fumimaro Konoe, to unite all Asian nations and free them from the influence of Western powers.

The voyage was generally calm. The only time Digger and Joe felt much movement was when they climbed the broad staircase at the stern leading up to the canteen. They never noticed any movement on the way down again after a few beers. And the cigarettes and the booze were almost for free. While the troops enjoyed the old-world elegance, the wood panelling and the plush carpets, they deplored the near constant diet of stewed kidneys. The officers, on the other hand, had printed menus and a wider selection of fare.[1]

The men had several theories about why they were served kidneys so often. One was the strong flavour of the kidneys was to disguise the taste of potassium bromide, which they were being fed to reduce their libido. Another was that the rich passengers who had sailed on this ship had eaten all the good cuts, and kidneys were all that was left. Yet another was that the cost of the officers' menu was so great that the army had to save money somewhere. The most popular theory, however, was that the ship's provisioner and the captain were colluding, to the financial benefit of both.

As it turned out, Joe and Digger didn't have to eat kidneys for much longer. With absolutely no effort on Digger's part, he was about to land butter-side-up again.

The convoy anchored at Fremantle but there was no shore leave. Digger decided that, against all the rules, he would write a letter to his mother and let her know how he was enjoying the trip. He wrote the letter, put it in an envelope, along with a stamp, and enclosed it in an empty tobacco tin. He then joined the crowd at the rail, gazing down at the small boats fussing round the big ship.

Digger waited until a group of likely-looking young lads in a tender was directly under him at the rail. He attracted their attention and dropped the tin down to them. They looked up, waved acknowledgement and soon disappeared towards the shore. Digger was sure his mum would get the letter eventually.

However, the crew of the tender had obviously been well briefed about the rules regarding unauthorised communications, and Digger was dobbed in. After the war, he discovered that his mother did eventually receive the letter – suitably censored – but in the meantime, he was sentenced by his company commander to work for the rest of the voyage in the galley attached to the officers' mess. Joe and Digger lived off the officers' menu for the rest of the voyage. A nightly ritual developed, as they discussed what they might fancy eating the following day.

After leaving Fremantle and pushing out into the Indian Ocean, the convoy was joined by two destroyer escorts. The men were notified that all the ships apart from the *Queen Mary* were going to the Middle East. The *Queen Mary* – which was like a speedboat compared to the other ships – sailed around its fellow boats as everyone sang the 'Maori Farewell' (to the tune of 'Now Is the Hour'). Digger watched the boats lean as people moved from one side to the other as the *Queen Mary* sailed around them.

On 16 February the *Queen Mary* left the convoy and headed for Singapore. Briefings were then given about the Japanese. The men were told, for example, that Japan's pilots were substandard because they were all myopic.[2] This was pure propaganda, of course, and it ought to have been questioned, but the troops took what their officers told them very seriously.

Digger turned nineteen two days later, although the army thought he was twenty-one. During those two days, the *Queen Mary* had sailed through the Sunda Strait and passed many Indonesian islands, then turned north-west towards Singapore. They then sailed past the eastern tip of Singapore and into the Straits of Johor. The men saw the cream-painted Changi Barracks and Changi village on their port side. Few paid much attention, although for many it was to become their home. The ship docked at the Seletar naval base, to a great welcome from the locals.

Within a few hours, the men of the 2/9th Field Ambulance were aboard a train, and as night fell they were on their way to Port Dickson, on the western side of the Malayan peninsula. At sunrise the following morning, everyone was eager to see this new and strange country. Even at this early hour it was already hot and steamy.

The train travelled slowly and the scenery changed frequently: villages, paddy fields, dense jungle. Every time they passed through a village, they could see vertical plumes of wispy smoke rising from what they presumed were cooking fires, and they savoured the slightly sour but not unpleasant smells that penetrated the carriage through the open windows. Adults squatted around the fires as children rushed towards the train and waved.

There was great excitement in Joe and Digger's carriage when the first monkey was spotted in the trees, and gasps of amazement as the train dived through endless green tunnels, where the large-leaved plants formed sheer walls of vegetation. Melbourne lads had never seen growth like this. They soaked it all in, and then noticed that, as they sat back, their shirts were sticking to their backs with sweat. Digger wondered to himself how it would be in the middle of the day if it were this uncomfortable first thing in the morning.

The train pulled into Bagan Pinang and the troops were soon clambering onto open trucks for the last leg of the journey to their new two-storey barracks at Port Dickson. Here they were accommodated in large concrete dormitories, but each man had a very comfortable canvas stretch bed. There was also a good shower area, which was soon full to capacity. The Victorians, although used to the heat of a Melbourne summer, had never experienced humidity like this before.

In due course they had other things to get used to, such as having someone called a *Dhobi-wallah* do all their laundry and ironing, and getting used to the occasional attack of prickly heat and Dhobi's itch, which some put down to the *Dhobi-wallah* not changing his washing water often enough. The soldiers quickly learned to take preventative measures against malaria. They wore long-sleeved shirts and rolled their long 'Bombay bloomer' shorts all the way down over their knees in the evening. All in all, however, they regarded themselves as being very well looked after.

Training soon began in earnest. Dressing stations were set up in jungle areas and rubber plantations around Port Dickson. There was also some time for relaxation, and the men got to know the local people, the Malays, the Chinese Malays and of course the expatriate British.

Digger and Joe took up cycling. They would take off when not on duty, most often at the weekend, to explore the area around Port Dickson. They would stop at roadside stalls for a refreshing drink, and would interact with the local people as much as they could. They were surprised at how many could speak English, and put this down to the fact that many of them worked for British companies or in British households.

Once, when they were on a street of houses with very large gardens, Joe's bicycle had a puncture. He and Digger had turned the bicycle upside down and taken off the front wheel when a young Malay girl, also on a bicycle, came up to them. At first she just stood there and smiled.

'Joe's bike has a puncture,' said Digger, returning her smile and immediately realising that what he'd said was completely obvious. 'And we are going to fix it with this postage stamp. See?' Joe was holding the partially inflated tube up to his face to see if he could feel the air escaping from the hole.

'It would be much better with a rubber patch,' said the girl, whose name was Angela Siawa. 'If you like, I could ask our gardener to fix it for you.'

Within a couple of minutes Digger and Joe were on the veranda with Angela's mother and father, enjoying a glass of homemade lemonade, while she helped the gardener to fix the puncture. It turned out that her father was Superintendant Siawa, the police chief of Port Dickson.

Digger felt immediately that he had made a friend, and lemonade on a Sunday afternoon, followed by dinner, became quite a regular occurrence. After dinner, Angela would teach him to play *mahjong*. Only very occasionally was Digger able to persuade Joe to accompany him. The conversation was often of politics and the coming war, and Joe was never comfortable participating in such talk.

Digger got on well with most people, regardless of their race, profession or station in life. He had friends in the British army whom he met occasionally at the Navy, Army and Air Force Institute – the NAAFI – which was the equivalent of the Australian army canteen. He also chatted with the *Dhobi-wallahs* as well as the language barrier would permit. But he did not like the way most British expatriates treated the Malays and Chinese in general. In Digger's opinion, it was definitely harder to get to know the British in Malaya than any other ethnic or racial group.

Bill Flowers, a friend of Digger's, wrote in his personal recollection of the time that 'the attitude of the British residents caused some resentment, as they treated the newly arrived Australian troops in the same manner as the British troops. They were apparently oblivious to the fact that the Australians were a volunteer force.'[3]

The class system that ruled British society – and the British army, in a way – was little understood by the friendly Aussies. While the resident British expatriates might have entertained the officers of the British army, they would rarely associate with the rank and file, regardless of whether they were volunteers or conscripts. Unlike in the Australian army, the British officers tended to be from the upper classes, while the other ranks tended to be from the lower classes.

Digger learned from one English friend, Private George Lampart, that corporal punishment was still practised in the British army. George insisted that he knew of prisoners who had been flogged. Each battalion had a special sergeant called a 'provost sergeant', who was in charge of troop discipline and the battalion's guardhouse. This was effectively a jail where soldiers – mostly privates – who could not be demoted and who had offended against army rules, would be confined. George knew personally that if the provost sergeant was in a particularly nasty mood, anything could happen.

For example, the provost sergeant could decree that an offender needed a 'regimental scrub'. With his clothing removed, he was put in a bathtub filled with cold water, and the hardest of scrubbing brushes were used on him. Alternatively, he might require that the prisoner run on the spot up against a stone wall while dressed in full army kit. The unfortunate individual would be required to bang his knees on the wall until they bled.

Digger didn't agree with any of this and explained to George how it couldn't happen in the Australian army. He advised his British friend that he and his fellow soldiers should get their act into gear and not put up with such treatment. Fortunately, the authorities never found out about Digger's conversation with Private George Lampart, otherwise he might have been the one facing a charge.

The British ignorance and racial prejudice may even have been a factor in the eventual success of the Japanese army in Singapore. Their racist attitude was epitomised by the dismissal of Japan's capabilities by Henry Brooke-Popham, the commander in chief of the British Far East Command. In a letter to the war office in February 1941, Brooke-Popham wrote:

> I had a good close up across the barbed wire, of various sub-human specimens dressed in dirty grey uniform, which I was informed, were Japanese soldiers. If these represent the average of the Japanese army the problem of their food and accommodation would be simple but I cannot believe they would form an intelligent fighting force.[4]

The Australians of the 2/9th Field Ambulance were drilled in stretcher-bearing, bandaging wounds, marching and tactical manoeuvres, and for the most part they complied willingly. They were all fit and healthy, and they made the best of everything they were asked to do.

Map-reading and tracking was particularly challenging. Digger and a few others, with a corporal in charge, were dropped off at the side of a road a few miles out of Port Dickson with a compass, a map and a *parang* (or machete) each. They had to track and hack their way to a point about four miles through the thick jungle.

The most obvious route through the vegetation – the one that needed the least knocking down – was often nearly, but not always exactly, in the direction they were supposed to travel according to the compass. On one occasion this accumulation of small errors in direction made a difference, and they became less sure of exactly where they were on the map. Within an hour they were completely lost. One of the group then suggested they have a rest, and it was not until they were all sitting down, everyone having had his say about exactly what they should do next – Australian army style – that they heard the sound of a truck in the distance.

Immediately, they all began talking, but they were soon persuaded by the corporal to be quiet, and luckily they heard another truck – or a car, perhaps. That was it. The exercise with the compass and map was abandoned, and everyone began clearing jungle in earnest in the direction of the noise. The men never found the target location they had aimed at, but they were eventually able to hitch a lift back to Port Dickson.

Digger also lost his appendix while stationed at Port Dickson. He and Joe were on one of their leisurely cycle trips in July 1941 when he fainted suddenly. Joe quickly found help and Digger was rushed to the 10th Australian General Hospital (AGH) at Malacca, about eighty kilometres to the south. The 10th AGH was very well set up, complete with well-trained nurses who were loved by their patients for the care they provided. But no matter how much the patients loved them, the nurses were always in charge.

One very warm evening while Digger was at the 10th AGH, Sister Geoffrey came around the ward. She was especially friendly and loved by every patient in her care. As she walked through the ward, Digger was lying there with an erection, which was very obvious under the light sheet that covered him.

Sister Geoffrey did not back away from the challenge. She marched straight up to Digger's bed, smiled sweetly and asked him to close his eyes. Digger did so and leaned back on his pillows, not knowing what to expect but with his imagination running wild.

He suddenly heard a very loud slap and felt a sharp pain in his nether regions as Sister Geoffrey brought both her hands together suddenly and swiftly to create a sandwich. 'Goodnight, boys,' she called out as she turned and walked out of the ward.

The other patients were laughing fit to burst, but Digger lay there gasping, the sheet lying straight across his belly.

Despite this incident, Digger saw his hospitalisation as the highlight of his stay in Malaya. He got to know all the nurses, most of whom were among the sixty-five nurses evacuated on a small coastal steamer, the *Vyner Brooke*, the following year, just before the fall of Singapore.[5]

By August 1941, the men of the 2/9th Field Ambulance knew that Japan would join Germany and the other European Axis powers in the war, and therefore that its Imperial Army would invade Malaya. The Japanese were continually expanding their empire in China, and now, with the agreement of the Vichy French government in Indochina, they landed 40,000 troops in Indochina (the present-day countries of Cambodia, Laos and Vietnam).

Meanwhile, the Australians, under Major General Gordon Bennett, were made responsible for the defence of Johor and Malacca in the south of the Malayan peninsula. The 2/9th Field Ambulance's B Company was moved to Mersing on the eastern coast. Digger and Joe, who were with A Company, went with the rest of the 2/9th to Kota Tinggi, eighty kilometres south of Mersing and just north of the big smoke of Singapore.

The main relaxation activity when we were at Kota Tinggi was the canteen. I guess it is the same for young soldiers the world over. Joe and I would be there most evenings for a beer or three, and for some of the blokes it was a lot more than three. It was strong Tiger beer, served in ten-ounce glasses. Sometimes there would be arguments that ended up in fights.

One night just such an argument broke out. Now, Hec Graham was a big bloke and was always looking for a fight. Joe, the stupid little bugger, kept looking at Hec – why, I've no idea – but Hec naturally asked him what the fuck he was so interested in and grabbed him by his shirt. Without thinking, I shouted at him to pick on someone his own size. He immediately responded with, 'Right, you'll do – outside!'

I followed him outside and down the broad steps of the canteen building. I knew he would thrash me but there was no stopping now, so before we got to the bottom of the steps I threw the hardest punch I could muster at his head. The next thing I remember is being in the barracks with Joe trying to stop my nose bleeding. Hec had belted the shit out of me.

Poor old Hec was eventually part of a group that was moved from Changi to Sandakan, in northern Borneo, to work on the construction of an airstrip. He died there, or on one of the infamous marches from there to Ranau, in early 1945.

There were many well-remembered fights in Singapore at this time that did not involve the Japanese. The most famous altercation was the so-called 'Battle of the Union Jack Club' between Australian soldiers and the fiery Scotsmen of the Argyll and Sutherland Highlanders. It all started when an Australian made a remark to one of the Argyll men that the Scot considered offensive – the Scot had poured beer over his head. Many soldiers on both sides were injured in the ensuing ruckus. Later, an Australian soldier was killed in a brawl that became known as the 'Battle of Lavender Street'.[6]

On the whole, though, Digger found Kota Tinggi to be a great place. Life went on much as it had in Port Dickson, with a mixture of training and relaxation. Having a haircut was one of the great pleasures in Kota Tinggi. The barber shops were all staffed by beautiful girls, and after you got your hair cut, if the girl liked you she would then ask if there was 'anything else' she could do for you. The men very quickly learned that this signalled that she was willing to take you to the back room for sex. The cost was considerably more, but it was well worth it, if the very short hairstyles around the camp were anything to judge by. The troops also had access to Singapore, and so could patronise Miss Lily's and other similar establishments.[7]

'Blue-light centres' were medical establishments that soldiers were encouraged to visit after they had sex with prostitutes, in order to prevent them from getting venereal disease. They were simply rooms in buildings that the army had rented for the purpose, but they were very well signposted. These clinics were manned by Digger and other members of the 2/9th Field Ambulance, and were set up in appropriate areas near the red-light districts, such as Lavender Street, because the sooner treatment was administered, the more likely it was to be effective.

At the blue-light centre, the soldier was given a small tube with a long, thin nozzle at one end. He was required to push this nozzle up the eye of his penis, and then to squeeze the ointment out of the tube and into the urethra. The arsenic and bismuth ointment was supposed to kill the gonorrhoea or syphilis bacteria before they had time to infect the individual. Soldiers were also given antiseptic soap and water and told to wash themselves thoroughly, in order to get rid of any external parasites.

You know, the insight you got working at the blue-light centres around Singapore was really something. Number one, of course, was not to bloody get infected. You very soon noticed that it wasn't the blokes that came to the centre on a regular basis that got infected – it was more likely to be blokes you rarely or never saw. We all knew who had VD because they had to attend special clinics run by the doctors. It never ceased to amaze me what a little arsenic and bismuth could do. I gradually became really interested in the work. Because I talked a lot to the officers – who were the doctors, of course – I began to wonder whether, despite the fact I had left school so early, I might be able one day to become a doctor myself.

Some of the officers of the 2/9th knew that Digger was developing an ambition to become a doctor, and they organised for him to get as much experience as possible at this time. He was seconded to work in the venereal diseases ward at the British army hospital at Tanglin. Some of the Pommies he treated appeared to have no respect for themselves. They would be cured and then within a few weeks they would be back with another dose. Digger also worked for a short time in the cancer ward at the Malayan hospital in Kuala Lumpur; there many of the patients died from arsenic poisoning, which was a common treatment for cancer at the time.

Despite the generally good times the soldiers were enjoying in Malaya and Singapore, the war with Japan was creeping closer. Digger was on guard at Kota Tinggi – complete with his .303 rifle, specially issued just for this duty – on 8 December 1941, the night the Japanese first bombed Singapore.

It was about five a.m. and Digger was on the final round of his guard duty. He was too far from Singapore to have heard the bombing, which had begun at 4:15 a.m. The usual night noises of the tropical jungle and the first calls of birds were shattered by a very loud bang, which was quickly followed by several others a little further away. At the same time, he heard planes flying overhead in a northerly direction.

Bombing was the first thing that crossed Digger's mind, so he called out the guard. But no bombs appeared to have exploded. There was a general flurry of activity around the camp as dawn broke. A 'recce' – a reconnaissance mission – was organised to try to discover what these non-exploding bombs might be.

It turned out that the planes that had just bombed Singapore were dropping their extra fuel tanks, now empty, on their return journey to their bases in southern Indochina. The Japanese knew how important air support would be in Malaya and had taken great care to ensure that their planes could fly distances much greater than their initial designs permitted.[8]

Later this same day, the Japanese bombed Pearl Harbor, the action that would bring the United States into the war. They also landed at Kota Bharu on the east coast of the Malayan Peninsula, about 600 kilometres north of Singapore. By all accounts, the troops of the 8th Indian Brigade had put up a fierce defence here, and yet the British Royal Air Force had abandoned the position, claiming they heard that the Japanese had overrun the defences. This, in turn, caused the Indians to retreat southwards after dark, and thus a pattern of retreat by the Allies was begun on the Malayan peninsula. The Japanese also collected a very valuable airfield.

A day or two after this activity, Digger was sent north to join B Company at Mersing. It had been given the task of building an Advanced Dressing Station (ADS) into the side of a hill. The approach to the ADS was through a swampy area, so it needed what was known as a 'corduroy road', which was constructed of tree trunks laid across the road to form a reliable hard surface. Digger's job was to help to build this road. The men of B Company were saying that this ADS would be like the defensive position which the Australian 9th Division had defended at Tobruk earlier that year.

As the Japanese advanced down the peninsula from Kota Bharu – meeting little resistance – life was still relatively quiet for the men of the 2/9th Ambulance at Mersing and Kota Tinggi. They knew, however, that the enemy was advancing on all fronts, and not just in Malaya. British troops in Burma had been forced to withdraw to Rangoon. The British also withdrew from Hong Kong to Hong Kong Island. On 16 December the Japanese landed on Penang, on the eastern coast of the Malayan peninsula, and on 19 December the British withdrew completely from that island.

Mersing was also bombed by the Japanese on 19 December, and shortly afterwards the Australians at Kota Tinggi, to the south, cheered as formations of Vildebeest and Hudson bombers, escorted by Brewster Buffalos, flew over them in a north-easterly direction. But none of these aircraft, despite their fearsome names, was a match for the Japanese Zeros, and shortly afterwards a few were observed limping back to Singapore. They soon acquired other names. The Vildebeest, which had a top speed of just 160 miles per hour, was nicknamed 'the flying coffin', while the Buffalos were called the 'peanut specials'.[9]

In fact, the British High Command had been relying on air defence as its prime strategy for the defence of Malaya, but the Allied planes were clearly no match for the Japanese aircraft. A further problem was that there were never enough troops on the ground to defend the airbases, so the Japanese inherited several very useful airfields as they progressed down the peninsula. There was no more talk now of the 'myopic' Japanese pilots.

On 3 January 1942 the Australians received a clear notification that the war was creeping ever closer when a patrol of the 2/18th Battalion captured two Japanese airmen who somehow had escaped with their lives when their plane was shot down.

A week or so later, all men of the Australian 27th Brigade – comprising the 2/26th, the 2/29th and the 2/30th Battalions – left Mersing to join three brigades from the Indian 9th Division under Major General Bennett on the western side of the Malayan peninsula. They were to hold the line north-west of Johor and stop the Japanese advance on the west coast. This left only Brigadier H. B. Taylor's 22nd Australian Brigade – comprising the 2/18th, the 2/19th and the 2/20th Battalions – to defend Mersing in the east.

At Mersing, the 2/9th Field Ambulance's B Company now had an ADS built into the side of a hill. Digger and his mates were confident it could withstand a siege by the Japanese. They were all well aware that the serious action was about to start.

Chapter 3

Retreat to Singapore

THE CAPTURE OF two downed airmen on 3 January 1942 by the 2/18th Battalion was a reminder to all the Australians stationed at Mersing that the effort they were putting into the defence of the area was very necessary indeed. Morale had started off high enough, until the British battleship the HMS *Prince of Wales* and the battlecruiser the HMS *Repulse* were sunk off the east coast of Malaya on 10 December by Japanese bombers. This not only confirmed the vulnerability of the 'invincible' British fleet but also demonstrated the efficiency of the Japanese air force.

The troops on the ground in Malaya were determined that the Japanese would not find them such an easy target, and throughout late December and the first half of January defences were prepared around Mersing at a feverish rate. The 2/18th, the 2/19th and the 2/20th Battalions were all fully engaged in defence work north of Mersing. The defences included the construction of fortifications, such as weapons pits and machine-gun posts, as well as minefields and barbed wire on all approaches from the north, particularly along the northern bank of the Endau River. Unfortunately, the mines, laid for the sole purpose of killing the enemy, also led to casualties among those placing them.

The men of the 2/20th Battalion were engaged in laying thousands of mines between the sea and the road running north to Endau, which was about seventeen miles north of Mersing. Mines were laid very carefully and in strict mathematical arrangement, with fine tripwires running between them. Agricultural piping was set in the ground to accommodate the mine, then the wires were attached. When the tripwire was pulled, the mine was designed to rise up out of the ground and explode at about waist height. They were deadly to anyone within a fifty-yard radius.

The mined areas were indicated to the enemy, in accordance with international rules, by rags placed on poles every few yards. But because of monkeys and goats setting them off and the monsoon rains flooding the area, the mines were not very effective. And laying mines was very dangerous. One engineer near the Mersing Bridge literally blew himself to bits. He had to be collected and carried back to camp in a ground sheet.[1]

Around 7 January or 8 January, Digger accompanied an ambulance to the 2/20th Battalion's Regimental Aid Post (RAP) to collect another casualty from the minefield being laid between sea and the road north from Mersing to Endau. This soldier had been laying mines according to the recognised pattern, and had just set the charges when a frightened goat had scuttled across the area and set off a mine. The man received bad wounds to both legs but was lucky it was not more serious.

On 13 January Mersing was heavily bombed, and the ambulances of B Company of the 2/9th Field Ambulance swung into action, rescuing civilians from the raid. The very next day, just as things were beginning to hot up in eastern Malaya, the 2/19th Battalion was called to join western force; the Japanese were apparently advancing faster there. This left only two battalions at Mersing, the 2/18th and the 2/20th. Later, it was learned that the very good defences north of Mersing had persuaded the Japanese to concentrate more of their forces on the west coast of the Malayan peninsula.

However, despite the solid defences, reconnaissance patrols from the 2/20th were reporting increased Japanese activity north of Mersing and had been engaged in several preliminary skirmishes. It was as if each side was testing the other.

On 15 January, a platoon from the 2/20th Battalion, led by Lieutenant Frank Ramsbotham, received intelligence that the Japanese were advancing south down the road from Endau. Ramsbotham moved his men north to set up an ambush at a small bridge crossing a tributary of the Endau River. The Australians knew the Japanese would have little hope of escape because there were minefields on either side of the road on the southern side of the bridge.

The Japanese – riding bicycles three abreast – were given a very warm reception as they crossed the bridge. They suffered many casualties but kept coming. Ignoring the minefields on either side of the road, they tried to encircle Lieutenant Ramsbotham's patrol. Unfortunately, the mines failed to go off, mainly due to the spring tides that had recently flooded the area. However, the platoon understood what the Japanese tactics were and very smartly withdrew before they were overwhelmed.

Three members of this platoon had suffered minor injuries, but they were able enough to regale Digger with exactly what happened as the ambulance took them to the ADS.

Digger was also involved with evacuating another casualty, Charlie O'Brien, a few days later. Charlie, a member of the 2/20th Battalion, had a more serious wound. He had taken at least one bullet in the groin area; it had broken either his pelvic girdle or perhaps his upper femur. O'Brien suffered this wound while in action with Corporal Elliott McMaster, who had been selected as a forward scout on the northern bank of the Endau River.

The patrol was on the north side of the Endau River. The men had just organised their breakfast when a lookout returned and reported that he had seen about fifty Japanese moving down the road towards them. They informed their battalion headquarters by field telephone, and back came an order to attack. Corporal McMaster wasn't too happy about this since they were so few. They only had .303 rifles and one Tommy gun, while they knew the Japanese would be armed with automatics.

Keeping a lookout, they saw six Japanese disappearing behind a house about fifty yards up the road, so they attacked. All hell broke loose. Charlie, who had the Tommy gun, was firing from a standing position in the open but suddenly his gun jammed – he became a sitting target for the Japanese, who were now apparently occupying the hillside above and behind the house. Charlie was hit and put out of action, but he was rescued by his mates, who carried him to cover.[2]

Digger accompanied Charlie in the ambulance to the MDS at Kluang, since the road to Kota Tinggi was flooded. During the journey, Charlie was delirious from the combination of morphine and pain from his wound, but he was conscious enough to insist that Digger see to it that his Tommy gun went to the battalion armoury to be repaired. Digger assured him that he would attend to this.

Charlie was sent back by ship to Australia, and Digger took his Tommy gun to the armoury as promised. Despite his position as a medical orderly – a non-combatant – Digger persuaded the armoury corporal to sign him out a .303 rifle in Charlie's name.

I'd thought about this often. What the hell would I do if, by some chance, I found myself alone and facing an armed Japanese soldier? Would I put my hand up as a halt sign and then try to explain in sign language that I was a non-combatant? I knew it was likely I'd be dead before I got that far. *Bugger it*, I thought. *I'll make my own luck and get myself a rifle.* Nobody seemed to care that I had one.

The Allied forces on Malaya's eastern coast were now more determined than ever that they would put up a good show against the Japanese. They had received minimal casualties and were sure that they had accounted for many Japanese dead and wounded. Morale was high, they were confident of victory, and – despite the disappointment of the flooded minefields – they had created great defences.

However, on 23 January the 2/18th and the 2/20th Battalions received orders to abandon their well-prepared defences at Mersing and withdraw further south to Jemaluang. Japan's successes in the west were now threatening the forces on the east coast. Although never really tested, the strong defences had indeed dissuaded the Japanese from conducting a landing around Mersing, which would have allowed them to take the shortest landward route to advance on Singapore.[3]

Meanwhile, the three battalions of the Australian 27th Infantry Brigade and the 2/19th Battalion of the 22nd Infantry Brigade were having a much harder time on the west coast of the Malayan peninsula. The Japanese forced them to retreat southwards towards Singapore.

The Japanese first experienced the Australians' determination and aggression on the west of the peninsula as they moved between the towns of Tampin and Gemas. An ambush was set up by Captain Desmond Duffy of B Company of the 2/30th Battalion at a bridge over the Gemencheh River, about eleven kilometres west of Gemas. The main force of the 2/30th Battalion was five kilometres to the rear.

As the Japanese approached the bridge in their hundreds, many of them on bicycles, the bridge was blown and the Australians opened fire. Unfortunately, Captain Duffy was unable to contact his battalion headquarters to call in the artillery and B Company was forced to withdraw. In this action alone, however, it was estimated that the Australians killed 600 Japanese for the loss of one of their own soldiers. Following this ambush, a prolonged battle took place nearer Gemas, that lasted for two days, and the Australians eventually had to withdraw to the Fort Rose Estate.[4]

On 15 January the 2/19th and the 2/29th Battalions were sent to the aid of the Indian 45th Brigade, defending the line of the Muar River against the Japanese Imperial Guards Division, at the village of Bakri, about sixty-five kilometres south of Gemas. Japanese forces were able to penetrate between the 2/29th and the 2/19th, which was closer to the main force at Bakri. The men of the 2/29th were isolated but fought their way back to join the main force. Their commanding officer, Lieutenant Colonel James Robertson, was killed in this engagement.

At about this time, the Indian 45th Brigade headquarters was bombed, killing or wounding all its staff. This left Lieutenant Colonel Charles Anderson, commanding officer of the 2/19th Battalion, in charge of all Australian and Indian troops. They were under attack from the Japanese on all sides. Anderson waited another two days for extra Indian troops to arrive, and then decided on 20 January to make a break through the Japanese lines for Parit Sulong.

Anderson's push was successful, despite heavy casualties, and the men reached Parit Sulong on 22 January. A strong Japanese force still blocked their final escape route. Many Australian and Indian troops had been killed, and they were carrying 140 wounded. A British force sent to relieve them could not get through. Colonel Anderson ordered all guns and vehicles to be destroyed, then took the difficult decision to leave the 140 wounded at Parit Sulong. He then ordered his men to form small groups and escape as best they could through the countryside, with the aim of joining the main force further south at Yong Peng.

Some 271 men of the 2/19th Battalion and 130 men of the 2/29th Battalion escaped through the Japanese lines. This was less than a quarter of the Australians' original force in this action. The Japanese murdered all but one of the wounded at Parit Sulong. Lieutenant Colonel Charles Andersen was later awarded the Victoria Cross.[5]

This was in the early days of the campaign, before the Australians understood how the Japanese treated their prisoners. It had to be assumed that they would abide by the international rules of war. But this was not the case; summary execution of prisoners was the rule rather than the exception. These men were simply lined up against a shed and gunned down. Only one survived to tell the tale. The Japanese general responsible for this massacre was Lieutenant-General Takuma Nishimura, who eventually suffered a similar fate as a result of the war crime trials after the Japanese surrender.[6]

Meanwhile, back on the eastern side of the Malayan peninsula, the 2/18th and the 2/20th Battalions of the 22nd Australian Infantry Brigade and B Company of the 2/9th Field Ambulance had been ordered by General Bennett to retreat to Jamaluang, but they were not ready to give up just yet. The retreat was barely completed when, on 26 January 1942, Brigadier Harold Taylor decided that they would prepare a surprise for the rapidly advancing Japanese. Of all places, it would take place at a pig farm on the Nithsdale Estate, just north of Jemaluang.

Three companies of the 2/18th Battalion lay in wait for the Japanese, expecting them to arrive before nightfall. The Japanese walked into the ambush in the early hours of the morning of 27 January. It took them completely by surprise. The Australians suffered too, however; in the confusion, D Company of the 2/18th was trapped behind Japanese lines. Eighty Australian lives were lost but it was estimated that about 2000 Japanese were also killed.

As a result of this action, we went into overdrive during the next few days, trying as best we could to tend to the severely wounded men and ferry them to the MDS at Kluang. After about two days I remember thinking to myself, *Bugger it, I'm going to have a sleep for a bit*. It was evening, so I ate some dry biscuit, drank some water and fell asleep in a thatched hut opposite our unit's temporary headquarters.

I awoke the next morning thinking it was really early, but it was already eight o'clock. All was quiet. When I went outside, the ambulances and the men were gone. I had a good look around and there was no one to be seen. The bastards had left without me! By good luck, there was still some traffic on the nearby main road, so I got my haversack and my rifle and headed over there. Every army truck was headed south so I just hitched a ride. After driving for about three hours, we crossed the causeway into Singapore.

Chapter 4
The Fight for Singapore

BEING A PRIVATE, Digger of course had no say in the organisation of the war, but like all his mates, he knew that so far it had been a complete stuff-up. It seemed to them that those in charge – the British – had spent too much time organising and implementing the retreat, and not enough time planning how to attack the Japanese and win. They seemed to stumble from one retreating position to the next, concerned only with survival. As time wore on, the retreat strategy seemed to become 'every man for himself'.

Digger decided for himself what action he should take, where he was going, where he slept, when and what he ate, and all the time he tried to keep ahead of the Japanese advance. He was more certain than ever that being a non-combatant was not really in his nature, particularly if he were the one making the decisions that affected his welfare. He was very glad that he had acquired his .303 rifle and ammunition.

All the other medical orderlies knew exactly what was expected of them, but they were also aware that the retreat had been so fast that many wounded had been left behind. An injured soldier was treated on the spot, but by the time the medical orderly had organised a mate to carry the other end of the stretcher, their regiment's position had often been overrun and another retreat south was on. Many wounded men were left to be captured by the Japanese. What was not known at this time was that the Japanese army, under strict orders to advance at all costs, simply found it more efficient to kill wounded captives than care for them – just as had happened at Parit Sulong.

Despite the success of the 2/20th Battalion north of Mersing, the ambush at the Gemencheh Bridge by the 2/30th Battalion, the brave resistance and horrific decimation of the 2/19th and 2/29th Battalions as they fought to join the main force at Yong Peng, and the success of the 2/18th Battalion at the Nithsdale Estate, all the Allied forces still had to flee to the island of Singapore. It did not feel good. Scottish battalions of the Argyll and Southern Highlanders and the Gordon Highlanders were the last to cross the causeway, and their sappers blew it up behind them.

This act turned out to be symbolic rather than practical, as the Japanese bombed and shelled the island fiercely; they were also able to repair the causeway in record time. By now, the Allies recognised Japan as a very efficient, ruthless, skilled and able enemy.

But it was not all doom and gloom. After making enquiries, Digger was able to make his way to Hill 80, near Keat Hong, to join his original unit, A Company. He even wrote a very optimistic letter home to his brother Reg and his wife.

VX40463 A Coy.
2/9 Field Ambulance

Malaya
1/2/42

Dear Reg and Peg,
A few more lines to let you know that I am still well and still manage to knock up a bit of fun. All of the Imperial troops are on the island

now but we hope to be on the mainland in the near future. It is now about 2 months since we received our last mail but we are expecting it in the near future . . . We have got some A-A guns near us and do they kick up a row! When I first heard them I thought they were bombs landing . . .

xxxxxx Digger
P.S. Give my love to all at home.

At this time, Japanese aircraft had total command of the air, since there were no Allied planes still serviceable. 'Ack-ack' – or anti-aircraft – guns were deployed against the Japanese planes but were seldom successful. Troop positions were bombed several times a day and during the night, and it seemed as though the enemy always knew where to bomb.

The Allies were also well informed about what was happening in Johor Bahru and along the north shore of the Johor Strait. Lieutenant General Arthur Percival, chief of Malaya Command, had reports from reconnaissance patrols that explained in detail where and how the Japanese were preparing to invade the island. Elliott McMaster could not understand why the Allies did not simply shell the Japanese positions on the north shore of the strait:

Our artillery observed trainloads of Japanese troops unloading at Jahor Bahru station and requested permission from Malay Headquarters to shell the station – they were sitting ducks. Malayan Command refused permission to fire, claiming it would give our positions away. It seemed to be unaware that the Japanese knew our positions as well or better than we did, thanks to Malay collaborators or even Japanese easily passing themselves off as natives and seeing for themselves. We sent our own patrols back over the Straits, under cover of night. One patrol under Harry Dietz, 2/20, moved through all of the Japanese assembly areas. The patrol observed their gun and mortar sites and their tank assembly area. With an almost unlimited supply of ammunition available on Singapore, our excellent Artillery Regiment could have caused havoc in the Japanese assembly area, yet thanks to General Percival's lack of perception, the opportunity was lost, until too late.[1]

The Australians were given a very large area of coastline to defend: from the mouth of the Kranji River at the causeway to the mouth of the Berih River, which was about fourteen kilometres further west. Everyone except General Percival seemed to know that the Kranji rivermouth area was where the Japanese would invade; the British leader thought they would invade to the east of the causeway, near the Seletar naval base, which was where he had placed the British troops.

The area the Australians were given was also very difficult terrain. It had none of the usual defences, such as barbed wire, because the authorities had apparently not wanted to alarm the civilian population by constructing them. There was a coastal fringe of mangroves, and much of the area was a virtual mudflat, crisscrossed with rivers and canals. Percival had insisted that small defended localities should be established in each area to cover obvious approaches such as rivers, creeks, roads and tracks. But it was ideal country for infiltration, particularly for a determined army, many of whom had been raised in the rice paddies of Japan.[2]

For the week after the Allies had retreated to Singapore, the shelling was endless. There were huge numbers of civilian and military casualties, and both the 2/9th and the 2/10th Field Ambulance units did their best to respond to all calls. It was very difficult for the ambulances to move about the island: they never knew which roads would be impassable because of shell holes, and in any case maps were very scarce. In addition, some Field Ambulance personnel, including Digger, were seconded at various times to repair roads and bridges so that they could collect wounded from the various RAPs. The severely wounded were evacuated to the 2/13th AGH at St Patrick's School, or to the 2/10th AGH at Oldham Hall.

One day Digger, with a 2/9th medical officer, took an ambulance to collect two severely wounded men from their position between the mouth of the Kranji River and the causeway. One of the casualties was close to death, having lost a great deal of blood through a gaping shrapnel wound to his abdomen. The other man had lost the lower portion of his right leg.

Digger arranged a drip in the ambulance for the soldier with the abdominal wound and tried to make them both as comfortable as possible for the journey back to Oldham Hall. The seriously wounded soldier was very quiet but the young man who had lost part of his leg kept talking, despite the high dose of morphine he'd just been administered. They learned that his name was Henry.

'You've no idea how fucking dark it is out there, you know,' he said. 'They knew exactly where we were, 'cause we saw their feet marks in the mud yesterday. The bastards were creeping about in the fucking dark.'

'Okay, mate,' Digger said. 'We'll have you in hospital and being looked after by beautiful nurses in no time, so just relax now.'

'And then onto the boat, eh!' said Henry, who seemed oblivious to the fact that he'd lost half his right leg.

By the time they reached Oldham Hall, the soldier with the gut wound had died. He had expired very quietly, as though he did not want to be any bother to those he knew would have a very tough time in the near future. Henry, meanwhile, had constantly been explaining the conditions: the mud, the water-filled trenches, the terrible dark nights that he had never before experienced, and the endless shelling.

Suddenly, he sought confirmation that his mate Robbo would be okay. 'Robbo came out to drag me back into the trench, you know?' he explained. 'That's when he got it.'

'He's doing just fine,' Digger assured him.

The next day Digger heard more about the action of the 2/20th Battalion. It had started a few minutes past midnight on 8 February. The battalion's D Company had sent a runner back to headquarters to inform them that the Japanese had overrun their position and that they had taken heavy casualties. Reinforcements were immediately sent in to retake the ground, but in the dark, through rubber trees in some areas and mangroves in others, it was nigh impossible to know exactly what success, if any, they were having.

In their first action, one section of eleven men, led by Corporal William Parker, had three men killed and four wounded. One lad who was killed that morning was only sixteen years old. The fighting had lasted all day. After dark, they made their way back to headquarters through enemy lines; they had to swim the Kranji River. The next morning the men got a shock when they discovered they were black all over. The big petrol tanks at Kranji were on fire and had filled the river with soot.[3]

As the Japanese invasion went on, it seemed to Digger that the level of organisation and determination on the part of the Allies was continuing to deteriorate. General Percival's theory about the invasion attack point had been completely wrong. The main thrust had come in the most logical area, just west of the causeway where the straits were narrowest. There were no defence structures there, and the defending forces – the Australians – were thin on the ground. The Japanese knew this well.

There was never any front line as such — or perhaps it would be more accurate to say that there were many front lines. The bombing continued, with the added hazard of not really knowing which areas were controlled by the Allies and which by the Japanese. The only certainty was that the enemy was winning more and more ground.

This made the transportation of the wounded a complete nightmare. Stories abounded of ambulances going in one direction only to meet Japanese forces, and turning back just in time. In many instances, wounded soldiers had to be left at the mercy of the enemy. The Allied troops now had more than an inkling that mercy was unlikely to be shown. More than one British soldier remarked to Digger that they would rather have gone through another two Dunkirks than this.

Digger made many rescue trips, including one particularly harrowing one on 9 or 10 February.

We had a message to proceed to the 2/20th Battalion RMS to pick up three badly wounded men and take them to Oldham Hall. We were not sure exactly where the 2/20th headquarters was, because it was continuously changing position. Nothing stayed in the same place for more than a couple of hours. But our driver was marvellous.

We travelled well up Bukit Timah Road and then went off to the left somewhere, and we found the 2/20th headquarters. We loaded three of the most seriously wounded and I made them as comfortable as possible. One had a bad abdominal wound, which was always a worry, and two other blokes had badly damaged legs.

As soon as I had them as comfortable as possible, we turned around and headed back to Oldham Hall. Before we had even got to Bukit Timah Road the shelling started. I doubt if we were the target but we were in the thick of it.

There was smoke everywhere but the driver just kept moving, until suddenly there was a bang and the ambulance lurched forward and stopped dead. All three patients and I ended up in a heap near the front of the ambulance, even though I thought I'd had them strapped in good and tight.

Before I could find out what had happened, one of the leg patients was yelling at me, 'Get your foot off my head, you stupid bastard!' This was Max Wall of the 2/20th, who eventually became a great pal of mine. The driver had taken us straight into a shell hole that he could not see for the smoke. Luckily, he managed to reverse out and eventually we made it back to Oldham Hall.

It was at the end of this trip, just as Digger and Bobby had delivered their patients into the capable hands of the nurses, that shelling and bombing started very close to Oldham Hall. The noise was terrific but the nurses carried on regardless. They were non-combatants and the building clearly displayed red crosses, so they trusted in this and just got on with the job.

Digger thought he had better look for somewhere to shelter. All the able patients were sheltering under beds or anything that might offer some protection if the building took a direct hit. Loathe as he was to hide under a bed, Digger knew it was the sensible thing to do. As he hesitated, he heard a familiar voice say, 'For God's sake, man, get under here!'

This was the first time Digger had seen Joe Milledge since he left Kota Tinggi for Mersing. That seemed like years ago but in fact it was less than two months before. When the shelling and bombing slowed down, Joe and Digger were able to catch up and talk of their experiences. At the end of a rambling but fervent conversation, they had agreed on three points: the British did not know what the hell they were doing; they were all in a very deep hole; but they would survive!

Like all the Allied soldiers, Digger and Joe were much too busy to think about the conflict from the perspective of the Japanese. However, Digger later learned what some enemy soldiers thought of the fighting at this time. Lieutenant Choi Sasaki, aged twenty-three, was a machine-gun officer in the Imperial Japanese Army (IJA). While he was injured and being cared for at Roberts Hospital, some time later, he spoke about his experiences during the siege of Singapore.

It was ver' bad place, Orstralians shoot ver' hard, ver' fast, brr'p, brr'p, so that Nippon soldiers jump down among mangroves, and sweem, sweem in mud, oil and dark. Hoi! Hoi. What beeg mess! We throw off packs, off shirts, off everything except sword and material for fight. Then we fight with glory in mud. Ah! Orstralians! They are for me a grand souvenair of fight for Seenapoor – what you say? a gallant memory.

When morning come we have crawled to railway line past mangroves. When I look up – all quiet! About feefty metres away I see road where like many dead men er . . . er . . . p'raps twenty-seeven Orstralian, ver' sad, ver' sad! I give them salute of honour! Then on to objective; more fight begin, grand fighting but no water, no food! For five days we drink from stream and eat cocoanut; dam' near starve! But on feefth day take Mandai Hill where we rest, ah! beautiful rest. Never I forget Orstralians and grand fighting souvenair they give me at Seengapoor.[4]

The confusion and sadness of the men of the 2/9th Field Ambulance was increased when a much respected officer, Captain John Park, and ambulance drivers Harold Ball and Lewis Park and medic Alf Woodman went missing. They had been making repeated trips forward to collect the wounded. The bodies of John Park and Harold

Ball were found months later; it appeared that they had been executed. The bodies of Lewis Park and Alf Woodman were never found.

Digger was ordered to accompany an infantry lieutenant on a reconnaissance mission in a jeep to the northern end of Bukit Timah Road. He was unsure why he was selected for this mission. They were driving up Bukit Timah Road and eventually turned east onto a rough track through a rubber plantation. They stopped at a large timber shed. The lieutenant pulled back a large sliding door to inspect the contents of the shed, then closed it again and ordered Digger to stay on guard there. He said he would be back in five minutes and took off down the track.

Digger had his trusty .303 with him; it crossed his mind that perhaps this was the reason he was chosen. He kept the rifle close to him as he waited. After a few minutes, Digger's curiosity overcame him and he opened the shed. It appeared that its main contents were large sacks of grain – probably rice, Digger thought – as well as agricultural machinery and, of all things, about ten bicycles that looked new.

Ten minutes passed and still there was no sign of the lieutenant. Digger was beginning to feel distinctly uncomfortable. He could see up and down the track for about a hundred metres each way, and much less than that through the plantation trees. *Right that's it*, Digger thought. *I've done my duty*. He hopped onto a bicycle and cycled back towards Bukit Timah Road.

After about a mile, he reached the main road and glanced to the right. His heart leapt as he saw a platoon of Japanese soldiers approaching on foot – they were less than a hundred metres away, and Digger had the impression that one was down on a knee with his rifle up, ready to fire.

Digger dropped his rifle, knowing that he would pedal faster without it. His legs had never moved as quickly as they did that day.

He did not look back or try to duck and weave, since he knew this would slow him down. All he could do was put distance between himself and the patrol. He was conscious of bullets passing him; at one point the bicycle jerked to the left but he managed to stay on and keep pedalling.

He cycled all the way back to Oldham Hall. When he stopped, he found that a bullet had just clipped the bicycle's back fork. Digger never knew what became of the lieutenant he'd driven with. He didn't enquire too far because he knew that by jumping on the bicycle and leaving the area, he had technically left his post.

As the Japanese attack on Singapore began to succeed, fewer and fewer orders came through to the men. The medical orderlies did what was expected of them; the only thing that seemed to matter was where they were retreating to next, and when. The optimism of Digger's letter to his brother was gradually dissipating in the face of the disasters he was forced to confront. He now knew that defeat was inevitable.

Nevertheless, there were many who were determined to fight right to the surrender. Digger considered the possibility of escape, even taking the time to visit the docks at Keppel Harbour. Sumatra was a very short journey over the Malacca straits, and Digger had heard stories of Australian and British soldiers escaping there on small boats. Yet he feared being sunk by the Japanese at sea, or – what was worse – being captured. Nor did Digger know what sort of reception he'd get in Sumatra.

The docks was also a very depressing place. There were dead bodies everywhere, which were ignored by all. The stink was terrible and there were hordes of people, mostly civilians, getting onto all sorts of vessels. Digger could see British soldiers organising the evacuation. He wondered how many of those civilians were soldiers in disguise. He decided there and then that he would take his chances and stay, whatever happened.

The situation in Singapore during the last days before the surrender was very hard for everyone. There were large numbers of civilian as well as military deaths. Bodies lay in the streets while shells exploded everywhere. Any troop position or other likely Allied asset was being bombed by fighter planes that were shooting at will. The Japanese had no opposition. It seemed as though they would not be satisfied until they had flattened the whole of Singapore and killed everyone. There was very little water, transport was almost impossible, and the Allies were down to the last of the ammunition.

On 14 and 15 February Digger had to ferry patients from the Cathay Building to St Andrew's Cathedral. The Cathay Building had been the last location of the 10th AGH. It was a horrible, stinking place that had no water, no toilets and nowhere to dig latrines. Standing nine storeys, it was Singapore's tallest building.

Although the whole building was plastered with flags bearing red crosses, it nevertheless attracted a full barrage from the Japanese on 14 February – probably because its second and third floors were occupied by the Indian 3rd Corps of Signals. The Australians had objected to combatants being in a non-combatant area but there was no moving them. As with everything in Singapore, the Japanese knew exactly what the situation was.[5]

The next day the bombing of the hospital continued, forcing Digger to take shelter in the nearby monsoon drain. He did not know it at the time, but that afternoon the documents of surrender were signed by General Arthur Percival.

Digger, crouched in the monsoon drain, didn't move. When the commotion died down he remained still, allowing his body to relax. He waited for his breathing to return to normal, then carefully put his head above the edge of the drain and looked across the lawn towards the entrance of the cathedral. Already several men were trying to tip over the wreck of the ambulance, and others were hovering nearby with a stretcher. It dawned on him that there was a body under the ambulance, and very probably it was Roy Keily.

As the barrage had started, Roy had indeed dived under the ambulance while Digger had crawled to the drain. Digger could not stop himself thinking that the drain had been the better choice; then he started analysing why it was the better choice, even as he realised he shouldn't be thinking that way. He had to find out if Roy was under the ambulance and, if he was, what sort of condition he was in.

Digger clambered out of the drain, taking care not to use his burned knees or elbows in the process. He could hear the soft words of his fellow medics echoing off the cathedral wall as they carefully moved Roy onto a stretcher and carried him inside. The back axle of the ambulance had crushed him when it took a direct hit. Roy had suffered head injuries and was unconscious.

Others were emerging from the safety of their hiding places too. They congregated at the entrance to the cathedral, comparing their minor injuries and enquiring about the wounded. Bobby Inman, Digger's driver mate, and Con Ryan had been badly injured in a shelling incident at St Andrew's the previous day. Both were taken to the Alexandra Hospital for specialist attention.

Soon word spread that the Allies were negotiating with the enemy. It was close to the end of a day of anger, confusion and terror, but the prevailing emotion was apprehension for the future. There was relief that the fighting was over but the men of the 2/9th Field Ambulance were angry that they'd had to endure the shelling of their non-combatant area. Now it seemed that those responsible for this mess were now talking about surrender. Digger and his mates, although privates, new damn well that although the Allies were 'negotiating', in reality they would be doing as they were told.

'Perhaps they will call it a draw and we can all go home,' joked one of the medics, but there was little response from his mates.

The Malaya and Singapore campaigns had lasted from 8 December 1941 to 15 February 1942: sixty-nine days. Seven and a half thousand Allied soldiers had been killed in action, and around 11,000 wounded. The Japanese, on the other hand, had lost only 3507 killed and 6150 wounded.

The Australians, whose men comprised fourteen per cent of all Commonwealth forces, had incurred around seventy per cent of the Allied deaths in battle.[6] This amazing and sad statistic puts to rest any accusation that the Australians did less than their fair share – a comment made by General Sir Archibald Wavell in his report of the time, which was released publicly in 1993.[7]

The rest of the afternoon of 15 February 1942 was spent carrying extra beds and bedding from the Adelphi Hotel to the cathedral, where the more seriously wounded men were housed. Digger learned that although the ground floor of the Adelphi was very crowded, there were empty rooms on the first floor. He mentally booked himself in to one for the night.

That evening, after eating what was available, Digger retired to 'his' room, attended to his own minor injuries and got into a real bed – with real sheets – for the first time in a long while. He didn't know what the future held but he knew this would probably be the last bed he would see for a while. In just a couple of minutes, Digger was fast asleep. Still an optimist despite all that had happened, he dreamed of the great times he and his mates had so recently experienced, before the Japanese had arrived to spoil it all.

Digger awoke the next morning at about six a.m. after a very good sleep. He swung his legs to the floor and reached for his tobacco to roll a cigarette. He took in a couple of lungfuls of smoke and savoured his first fag of the day. As a budding medical man, he always wondered why it was that the day's first cigarette always had a tingling effect on his legs. It was not an unpleasant feeling, and he marvelled at the effect of the smoke or whatever was in it that could cause such an effect.

After a couple more puffs, Digger stood and wandered barefoot onto the balcony. As he continued to smoke, he was surprised when someone wished him a crisp 'Good morning' in an unfamiliar accent.

His neighbour in the next room was also out on his balcony, and was engaged in a similar activity. While Digger was half-naked, this man was fully dressed in the uniform of a captain of the IJA. The way each man was dressed seemed to say something about their status – the victor and the vanquished, the master and the slave – but Digger was not yet thinking of such things.

He returned the greeting, and a few pleasantries were exchanged about the weather before they both returned to their respective rooms. *Well, well*, thought Digger. *This might not be so bad after all.*

PART 2

The Years of Survival

Chapter 5
Life at Changi

DIGGER RETURNED TO the edge of his bed and leisurely finished his smoke. All his anguish over the death and destruction that had preceded this day fell away as his thoughts turned to the future. He felt grateful that he had survived the terror and chaos, and resolved that he would also survive whatever lay ahead.

This thought comforted him. No matter how bad the future might look, it could never be as bad as the recent past. With that in mind, Digger had a quick wash, got dressed and made his way down to the ground floor and across the lawn, dodging the shell holes from the previous day's bombardment as he went. Just before he entered the cathedral he looked back at the first-floor balconies of the Adelphi Hotel. There was no sign of the Japanese officer.

The first thing that Digger learned that morning was that Roy Keily had died from his wounds. Poor Roy had never regained consciousness. He was among those – and there were many of them, Digger knew – who had not survived to experience life as a prisoner of war. Thinking about this, Digger decided that, given the choice, he most definitely preferred the POW option.

The Allied surrender had no effect on the work required to look after the hundreds of patients at the cathedral on the morning of 16 February, and Digger busied himself helping patients prepare to face their first day in captivity. Some were dying and accepted the fact; others were still fighting like hell. A great many were simply depressed, especially those who, the day before, believed they had a ticket home. If only the Allies could have held out a little longer. Now, none of them had any idea what was to happen. Being a POW was one thing, but being captive while having a broken leg or a deep flesh wound, which would be very susceptible to infection in this tropical climate, was another thing altogether.

Digger and the other medical orderlies assured their patients that they would all survive, regardless of how close they were to death, how bad their wounds were or the fact they were all prisoners. All the men of the 2/9th Field Ambulance had to remain optimistic in front of the wounded.

As Digger attended to the patients in the cathedral, an order came through that the 2/9th and the 2/10th Field Ambulance units were to proceed immediately with all the sick and wounded to the village of Changi, on the peninsula in the east of Singapore. There they were to set up a hospital. All those who had weapons were ordered to pile them in specific places under Japanese guard, then all the POWs were required to line up in the streets that very afternoon to bow to their captors as they marched past in a victory parade.

By now, the Field Ambulance units were used to transporting their wounded and supplies at a moment's notice, so this latest move was initiated immediately. Many trips over several days were needed. All the officers of the 2/9th Field Ambulance, along with some men from the other ranks – known as 'ORs' – were to accompany the ambulances and patients to Changi. Most ORs, including Digger and Joe, were left to join the other POWs and pay homage to their new masters.

Even though the thought of bowing their heads to the Japanese was bad enough, Digger and Joe were nonetheless very curious to see their captors up close. They hoped to somehow guess at what might be in store for them. They joined the parade that afternoon a few streets away from the cathedral, and stood with their heads bowed as little as they dared.

Some Japanese soldiers walked outside the marching formation; their job was to see to it that all the Allies' held their heads at a suitable angle of submission. They barked at and jostled anyone they thought was not showing enough deference; a blow to the abdomen with a rifle butt would be delivered to anyone showing any hint of defiance. Digger quickly revised his assessment of the enemy. These Japanese privates certainly did not share the politeness of the officer on the balcony.

That night Joe and Digger tried to sleep in a quiet corner of the now almost empty cathedral. The next morning they joined the thousands of men lining up in the streets to march to Changi.

It was more of a walk than a march, taking them north-east across the city, into the red-light district and up Lavender Street. Here, the girls who, a short time before, had done a roaring trade now lined the streets, some crying and some daring to dart into the ranks of the marchers to deliver sweets and other treats. They understood that the trade from the much poorer Japanese soldiers would not be so good.

Outside the city, as they proceeded through small villages and countryside, many Chinese Malays delivered small gifts of food and money to the soldiers. They knew the danger they were in, being well aware of the Japanese atrocities in China. Word was also out that many Chinese had already been executed in Singapore simply because of their relationship with the British colonial administration.

As a condition of the British surrender, the Japanese had promised to spare the lives of civilians, but they did not adhere to this commitment. Soon everyone knew that the Japanese were arresting and executing any Chinese who had cooperated with the Allies. Digger learned years later that his friend Mr Siawa – the superintendent of police at Port Dickson, with whom he had spent many a pleasant evening – was executed by the Japanese at about this time.

The walk to Changi took five hours. Their destination was a huge area of about twenty-five square kilometres surrounded by the sea to the north, east and south. The land was pleasant, green and undulating, with many trees and shrubs. At the eastern end was the village of Changi. Prior to the war, the peninsula had been the British army's principal base in Singapore, and so the site boasted extensive and well-constructed military infrastructure. There were three major barracks – Selarang, Roberts and Kitchener – as well as Singapore's civilian prison, Changi Gaol, and many smaller camps and buildings.

On entering the area, the Australians were ordered to proceed to Selerang Barracks. It was a complex of several three-storey buildings forming a U shape around a concrete barracks square. Joe and Digger grabbed a small area on the ground floor at the end of one of the buildings. There were no beds or anything in the way of furniture, of course, but they knew this was what they had to expect as POWs. They set down their backpacks, which held all they owned in the world, then lay down for a rest and a smoke after the bloody long walk.

For some reason, Digger's parents were notified at this time that he was 'missing in action'. Presumably, the authorities did not know who had been killed in action and who taken prisoner. The last letter Digger's parents had received from him was immediately after the retreat to Singapore. It was not until sixteen months later, in June 1943, that they were at last notified that he was a POW.

Although Digger was accepting of his situation, there were many reasons for complaint. The only problem was that there was no one

to complain to – or at least no one who was going to take any action.
All their gear, for example – where was it? Soldiers kept everything
except for their personal items in a kitbag; Digger's had gone into the
company storerooms when he'd moved from Kota Tinggi to Mersing
a few months previously. Most men at Changi had little more than
what they stood up in. Digger was relatively well prepared, however.
On the morning of 16 February, he'd been able to buy a six-month
supply of tobacco and soap.

Morale was generally very low, and some soldiers were simply
unable to cope with their situation.

There was a great deal of whingeing, and a few could certainly be
described as mentally disturbed. Some refused to or were unable
to speak, some were full of self-pity, and others were perpetually
sullen and refused any order. One bloke was always masturbating
and didn't seem to care that others could see him – it was a truly
pathetic sight.

Some of the men got really very depressed; there were men who
died just because they didn't want to go on. I never got depressed
and nor did many others, but everyone is different. Perhaps it was
the trauma from fighting, or from not getting home. Perhaps it
was just that many people are not meant for war – they are just
not the type. They might think they are when they join up, but
when it comes to killing or risking your life they are just not in
that league. Or perhaps it was because the war was not what they
were expecting.

Possibly a few of them would have gone off their heads at home
anyway. One guy was so disturbed that when the Jap patrol came
through the camp, he would fall in and march behind them. We had
to run and take him back. We eventually made him wear a bell so
we knew where he was all the time.

Another bloke in our unit stole my dixy – or mess tin – and my mess tools. He didn't even deny it when I fronted him and asked for them back. He just shrugged his shoulders, so I floored him there and then and took them back. I guess we were all affected by the defeat.

By the time most of the captives had arrived in the Changi area, they totalled approximately 50,000 troops, including British, Australians and Dutch. While the Australians were housed in Selerang Barracks, the British and Dutch were housed at Roberts, Kitchener and in the wooden huts where the Indian troops had originally been housed. Part of Roberts Barracks was eventually converted into a hospital for the Allied sick and wounded.

The Japanese were completely overwhelmed by these huge numbers, and so the POWs were generally left alone to organise things for themselves. At this time the Japanese guards were usually nowhere to be seen.

When we got to Changi, we had some time to look around. We had time to get to know each other better and to make a few new friends. I gradually became friends with some blokes who, if they were still alive, I'd be friends with today.

You soon got to know who you wanted to have as a close friend. It doesn't take long to decide what a bloke's like. You can pretty much tell after you've spoken to him for a few minutes – at least, I was always able to tell. And we had plenty of time to talk in Changi.

I'd been wondering about Bobby Inman, whom I hadn't seen since coming to Changi, and then one day we heard about the Alexandra Hospital massacre. It had happened on 14 February, a day or two before the surrender. For whatever reason, the Japanese killed every patient there, as well as all the doctors and nurses, even though they were unarmed and it was very clearly a hospital. Who knows why, but Bobby was among them, the poor bugger.

I never found out why he was in the hospital, and they never even identified his body. He was a great mate of mine, and all he has now is his name on the wall at Kranji Cemetery: Private Robert H. Inman of the 2/9th Field Ambulance.

All the fit soldiers at Changi had some sort of job. Digger, Joe and a few other mates volunteered to clean out the swamp, which had been ordered by the Japanese but was organised by the POWs. The swamp was an area in a hollow between the Selerang and Roberts Barracks. The men had to wade up to their chests into the swamp and retrieve everything that had been dumped there during the fighting.

The biggest problem was that the place was alive with snakes that swam on the surface. It was more than a little off-putting but the men tried their best to catch them. In fact, they turned the chore into a sport, competing over who could catch and throw the largest number of snakes to the bank, where the others would kill the snakes and attach them to their belts as trophies.

One of the group was Max Wall, who would march along the bank with his snakes, singing:

We're a' havin a party tonight, tonight
All stayin' healthy cause we're eatin' right
I just wish it was good Aussie steak
Instead of crap rice and bloody fried snake.

But the snakes were white-fleshed and tender, and Digger reckoned they were delicious. Unfortunately, snakes were not the only items in the swamp. In the first couple of days, the men also retrieved unexploded shells and human body parts.

As the weeks passed, the Japanese became more organised and appointed work parties for various labouring jobs around Singapore, from making roads to working on the docks. This afforded many opportunities for the enterprising and resourceful to acquire goods that were fast becoming scarce. Medical supplies and tinned food were at the top of the list.

Elliott McMaster, of the 2/20th Battalion, had to transport supplies for the Japanese from the docks to Tanglin Barracks, where they were sorted.

> We were labour staff for a Japanese Field Hygiene Unit, responsible for supply of all medical stores to the whole South West Pacific area, including the Dutch East Indies, New Guinea, Solomon Islands, etc. Mostly, the work involved loading and unloading supplies from ships, trucking out to Tanglin, where they were checked, counted, re-sorted and re-shipped . . . The boys pinched large quantities of drugs, including M & B 693, very valuable, rare and up-to-date drugs. These were all sent to Changi (Roberts) Hospital by various underground and underhand routes. In fact, Tanglin virtually supplied all Changi Hospital drugs and medicines, such as they were.[1]

Others were made to repair and maintain the roads all across the island. One group was responsible for a road that ran along the side of a golf course. According to a poem, 'The Golf Course Road', which was penned about this time, they were none too concerned about the quality of the work they provided, so long as it looked right for their Japanese supervisors.

> We used to belong to old Aussie
> We joined in the first Aussie Corps

But now we belong to old Tojo
Bloody well prisoners of war.

We're building a road round the golf links
With progress remarkably slow
It's no bloody good on the surface
And a bloody site worse down below

They feed us on rice for our breakfast
We gobble it up with great glee
They feed us on rice for our dinner
Then more fucking rice for our tea

But one day the Yanks will relieve us
Arriving in all kinds of crafts
In a rickshaw I'll ride round our roadway
With a little Jap boy in the shafts[2]

Changi was a reasonable place in which to be held as a POW. Food was scarce and mostly rice, but everything was well organised. Most of the men were employed in some useful activity. There were various clubs and groups, and prisoners were generally free to follow their own interests in their spare time. Vegetable gardens were established, with the aim of supplementing the rice ration, and the hospital at Roberts Barracks was decently equipped. Some of the AIF members were even thinking of starting a university.

Today, most who went to work for the Japanese – either on the Thai–Burma railway or in other places – remember their days at Changi very fondly. All hardship is relative, and many prisoners who were first interned at Changi before going to other locations in South-East Asia looked on Changi as a home away from home.

In March 1942, the survivors of the USS *Houston* and the HMAS *Perth*, both of which had been destroyed, joined the Australians British, Dutch and Indians at Changi. By then it was home to some 60,000 POWs. Digger met and made friends with quite a few of the Americans.

> I became friendly with Bill Tucker, who was a very personable guy. We spent a great deal of time thinking up schemes that we would implement in the United States when the war was over.
>
> 'You come to the States, pal, and we will make a bundle,' Bill used to say to me in his broad American accent.
>
> We became great friends, and when he was called to join A Force in May 1942, we exchanged gifts as a token of our friendship. I gave him a vial of iodoform, a sure cure for tropical ulcers, and he gave me his belt buckle.
>
> Unfortunately, Bill, strong as he was, succumbed to a tropical ulcer at 80 Kilo camp, south of Thanbyuzayat. I reckon he probably gave all the iodoform away to others suffering ulcers when really he needed it himself.

Many years after the war, Digger tried to trace Bill's relatives to return his belt buckle, but he never found anyone who claimed to know him. So he did the best he could. He had the buckle silver-plated and engraved with both their names, and today it resides in the American National Prisoner of War Museum in Andersonville, Georgia.

Coy York was another survivor of the USS *Houston* whom Digger got to know well. Coy was a great talker and a very skilled gambler, and Changi, despite the lack of money, was a great place to gamble. The men had a lot of time on their hands, and the need to spice life up a little was strong. Coy's father was one of the great Mississippi steamboat gamblers and this was how Coy had been raised. His 'lessons' cost Digger plenty, but he regarded them as well worth it.

The Roberts Barracks boiler room, with its pipes and sterilisation equipment, was the ideal place for a party for those with contacts at the hospital and a little knowledge of winemaking and distillation. Making a drinkable spirit took a lot of work and time, what with collecting the vegetable and fruit materials, fermenting the wine and setting up the still. Everything was used – potato peelings, pawpaw skins, overripe fruit – in fact, any vegetable matter that could not be eaten. Bobby Small, another friend of Digger's, had the necessary expertise; Joe Milledge and Max Wall were also involved.

The spirit took a couple of weeks to make. When the time came to taste it, all declared it a great success. By the time the mates had shared all the liquor they could squeeze from the apparatus and had sung every Australian song they knew, they were all beginning to feel a little queasy. When they staggered out into the cool night air, they were barely able to crawl to the showers in order to sober up enough to get back to their respective quarters. The experiment was not repeated!

By mid-1942, the hospital was well set up for the recovering wounded. The POWs even had it organised so that the fifty or so mentally ill patients were also taken care of in a separate building. Digger had volunteered to take care of this ward. One night he was talking with his mates about what a miserable existence these patients had. Digger explained that he was going to play 'imaginary cricket' with them.

'How the hell do you play imaginary cricket?' Max Wall asked.

'Right, come outside and I'll show you,' replied Digger.

They all went outside to the barracks square, where they took up positions on an imaginary cricket field. Digger explained that, just like in normal cricket, the umpire had the last word – but in this version you could defend your interpretation of what had happened. You could argue about whether or not a no-ball had been bowled, or if someone was out or not – this was the fun of it. After the discussion the umpire would give his ruling. Digger made 'Lofty' Cameron the umpire because he was a natural comedian.

Max Wall was first in to bat. He stood in front of the stumps – a backpack – with an imaginary bat in his hands. Digger went to the other end to bowl. Bobby Small and Joe Milledge were fielding. The game started on Lofty's command, and Digger ran up and pretended to bowl a fast one. Max played it away safely and did not take a run. The game continued, with everyone arguing whether or not Max had been bowled, whether a shot had been caught, whether he was out LBW and so on. There was a great deal of argument and banter, and after half an hour or so they had agreed to give Digger a hand playing the game with the patients.

Imaginary cricket was played twice a week with the twenty or so patients on a grassy area outside their billet. It was difficult to organise and enthuse the group at first, but once the patients got the hang of it Digger's cricket games proved very popular.

But it was not all fun and laughter at Changi in 1942. Some men would occasionally sneak out of the camp to trade with the local people, usually at night. But you were much more likely to come across a Japanese soldier outside the camp than in it, so it was anything but a safe practice. By mid-1942 items such as tobacco were becoming scarce, and the men were desperate to supplement their rice with food brought in from outside the camp.

Digger was a risk-taker and a trader by nature. He and Bobby Small started trading with the locals outside under cover of darkness. One night in Changi village they heard a jeep approaching – a Japanese patrol. They only just had time to hide in the dense vegetation at the side of the road.

The truck stopped at the group of locals with whom Digger and Bobby had been trading, and found on them the goods that they rightly concluded had been acquired through trade with POWs. They searched through the roadside vegetation, beating and stabbing at the shrubbery as they progressed. Digger reckoned that he and Bobby escaped that night by good luck alone. They never went outside the fence again.

Security was tightened further following the arrival of dedicated Japanese POW staff at the end of August 1942. The new Japanese commandant requested that all prisoners sign a statement declaring that they would not attempt escape. The prisoners refused, and on 2 September all 15,400 Australian and British prisoners in the Changi area were confined in the Selarang Barracks square.[3]

Most of the men – including the sick, many of whom had dysentery or malaria – were camped out on the black and hot barracks square.

We had to dig trenches through the bitumen for latrines, and you can imagine how fast they filled up, with 15,000 contributors. The whole square just looked like an overcrowded Asian market. The culmination was when Lieutenant Colonel 'Black Jack' Callaghan, our commanding officer, addressed us after a couple of days. He explained that he had been ordered to witness an execution on the beach, but that what he had witnessed was murder.

Two Australians, Corporal Rodney Breavington and Private Victor Gale, had escaped from the Bukit Timah Road POW camp in early May. After stealing a native fishing boat, they almost made it to Ceylon but were recaptured. They were taken back to Changi, allowed to recover from their ordeal in the hospital and then taken down to the beach, along with two Englishmen who had also attempted to escape. There they were shot by some Indian Sikhs, who had by this time joined with the Japanese.

Anyone who did not sign the agreement not to escape was threatened with the same fate, and so the Australian officers ordered everyone to sign. Most forms were signed 'Ned Kelly', 'Mick Mouse', 'Errol Flynn', 'Charles Chaplin' or something similar. Digger certainly didn't sign his real name.

'The Corporal & His Pal' is a poem written in memory of Corporal Breavington and Private Gale.

He stood, a dauntless figure
Prepared to meet his fate.
Upon his lips, a kindly smile
One arm around his mate.

His free hand held a picture
Of the one he loved most dear,
And though his hand was trembling
It was not caused by fear.

No braver man e'er faced his death
Before a firing squad
Than stood that day upon the beach
And placed his trust in God.

He drew himself up proudly
And faced the leering foe.
His rugged face grew stern, 'I ask
One favour ere I go.

Grant unto me this last request
That's in your power to give.
For myself I ask no mercy
But let my comrade live.'

Then turning to the side
Where his sad faced colonel stands
A witness to his pending fate
Brought here by Jap command.

He stiffens to attention
His hand swings up on high
To hat brim, in a swift salute,
'I'm ready now to die.'

They murdered him in hatred,
Prolonged his tortured end,
In spite of all his pleadings,
They turned and shot his friend.

They said 'twas an example
Of what they had in store
For others who attempt escape
Whilst prisoners of war.

Example, yes, of how to die,
And how to meet one's fate.
Example, true, of selfless love
A man has for his mate.

And when he reaches Heaven's gate
The angels will be nigh
And welcome to their midst, a man
Who knew the way to die.

Whilst here below in letters gold
The scroll of fame e'er shall,
The story tell of how they died,
A corporal and his pal.[4]

Chapter 6
The Officers' Mess

IN LATE 1942 the food situation in Changi deteriorated significantly, and by early 1943 there was a growing degree of deficiency diseases among the POWs. This was despite the allocation of 'rice polishings' and grass juice drink.

Rice polishings was the brown outer surface of the rice grain, which contained vitamins but which the Japanese polished off in order to produce white rice. Grass juice was produced at the hospital as a special vitamin drink. It was particularly foul-tasting but very good for preventing deficiency diseases.

Nevertheless, the calorie ration per man per day was again reduced, and the numbers being admitted to the hospital were increasing. Whilst some of the earlier deficiency diseases had been reduced or contained, there were now more cases of beriberi and pellagra. Malaria and dysentery were always present, and the diet of mainly rice did not help at all.[1]

Joe Milledge had succumbed to a very bad case of dysentery. Very often those with bad dysentery lost all appetite, and Digger felt sure that if he could get some meat he would be able to tempt Joe to eat again. But there was no meat available. By this time, there were no cats, no dogs and – Digger was sure – very few rats in Singapore.

Digger wondered if the snake population at the swamp was increasing again, so he and Bobby went down there and had a good look around. They had evidently done too good a job nine months earlier, as there was not a single snake to be roused from the swamp. Digger did notice the huge numbers of large snails in the nearby vegetation and immediately wondered what they would taste like.

That night he, Bobby and Lofty ate cooked snails with their rice. They were a bit hesitant at first, but eventually decided that they tasted not bad at all. As Bobby said, 'If you close your eyes while you're eating, you can tell it's some kind of meat. But no way can you say if it's lamb, beef or chicken.'

'Not much fucking wonder, since it's bloody snails!' replied Lofty.

The next day they made a second journey to the swamp, this time to collect snails. They left them in clean water for the rest of the day – Digger had read somewhere that this is what soldiers had done in France in the last war. He killed the snails in boiling water, separated them from their shells, roughly chopped them so that they resembled any meat, and then fried them in his precious cooking oil. He served them up to Joe as meat that they had 'acquired', and Joe presumed Digger had stolen some tinned meat.

Joe was soon cured of his dysentery and down at the swamp with the rest of them, gathering snails to supplement their own rice rations. Many other POWs learned of the delicacy, and gradually the snails were as extinct as the snakes.

The general deprivation caused much complaint among the men. They knew that they were slowly starving to death, and that those in the hospital – particularly those with deficiency diseases – were likely to be the first of many victims. The men discussed all aspects of this problem. They had plenty of time to talk and no topic was off-limits. Things came to a head in January 1943, when they had endured a particularly bad three weeks of rations. As well as being meagre, their food was now full of maggots and weevils – they had to pick the rice clean before they could eat it.

In his memoir of this time, Bill Flowers notes: 'How we grumbled at the fact that once again the rice ration had been cut. All were never free from hunger – a situation that one never became accustomed to but nevertheless had to be endured.'[2]

Initially, the Japanese were the main target of their frustration and anger. However, the Australians came to understand that the Japanese were also affected by this war, even if they were the cause of it. They knew that the Japanese soldiers were not living off the fat of the land. With the number of mouths to feed on Singapore Island, there simply was no fat in this land.

It did not take too long before the Australians' own officers copped some criticism. As in armies everywhere, they did not eat with the men but had their own officers' mess. At Changi, some of the ORs served as cooks and servants in the officers' mess, and these men now came under a bit of pressure from Digger and his group. It emerged that there was quite often tinned meat or vegetables on the officers' tables.

That very night, in the early evening, Digger visited the officers' kitchen to have a look at what was being prepared. Sure enough, the quality of food was far above what was available for the ORs, and certainly much better than it was possible to serve to the patients in the hospital.

Digger called together all his trusty mates, including Joe Milledge, Lofty Cameron, Bobby Small and Max Wall, and told them what he had learned. The officers may have had access to this tinned food ever since they came to Changi – perhaps it was left over from what they had smuggled into Changi in the ambulances when patients had been transferred to Changi almost a year previously. Everyone had known about this at the time, but they'd assumed that it had been finished long ago. It was also possible that the officers had organised other supplies – perhaps they had stolen it from the docks or from other sources where POWs were working. But whatever the case, they had reasonable food and no one else did.

By chance, or perhaps not, no officer suffered from a diet deficiency disease. Digger knew that this was probably because they were better aware of the precautions to take to prevent such diseases, but there was certainly the other obvious explanation of a better general diet. Some of Digger's pals also held the notion that officers were expected to eat better than the men because they were the leaders; the ORs would be in a far worse situation if their leaders were sick, they argued.

This did not go down well with Digger. 'Okay,' he said to the group. 'Let's just take the food off them and give it to the hospital. We are all POWs, and not one of us should be eating any better than anyone else, no matter what rank you hold. The only people that deserve to be eating better than the rest are the patients.'

'How do we do that, then?' asked Joe.

Various suggestions for how they might transfer the food from the officers to the hospital kitchen were then put forward. Max Wall made the point that what they were considering might well be regarded as stealing, and stealing from officers could land them all in a great deal of trouble. Digger quickly pointed out that the tinned goods they were going to 'steal' had already been stolen from elsewhere. And no matter what crime they might be accused of, it couldn't be worse than eating well while those in the hospital were starving. Anyone keeping food for himself in this situation, officer or not, did not have a moral leg to stand on.

It was eventually decided that at the very first opportunity they would simply go through all the officers' lockers or boxes in their sleeping quarters. Officers were a great lot for having planning meetings, which lasted for an hour at least, and Digger's mates had already established that the food was not stored in their mess or kitchen. They resolved to take the food and deliver it to the hospital kitchen. An opportunity presented itself the very next day.

Digger organised for eight of the group to hold two blankets open under the windows of the officers' quarters, which were on the first floor of Roberts Barracks. The rest went into the rooms, where they broke open and ransacked every box or cupboard that could possibly be holding tinned food. They threw the tins out of the open windows down into the blankets below. About twenty minutes later, all the food was in the small storeroom attached to the hospital kitchen, where it was guarded twenty-four hours a day from then on.

The group was now ready for some reaction from the officers, and perhaps a visit from the military police. Digger actually looked forward to this, but neither eventuated – at least, not immediately. Digger also thought he might hear from Lieutenant Colonel Summons, who by this time was the commanding officer at the hospital. But nothing happened.

Digger and his mates discussed this non-action, concluding that the officers were too embarrassed to take any action. About a week later, Digger noticed that wherever he went, a military policeman was always close by somewhere. Someone was keeping an eye on him, but that didn't really bother Digger.

Despite Digger's part in the food-recovery project, he was still able to maintain the friendship he had with Major Dr Roy Maynard, a pathologist from Melbourne. Digger had known him for many years, first as the Officer Commanding (OC) his company in the Light Horse and subsequently as the OC of Digger's A Company in the 2/9th Field Ambulance. There were unique opportunities for a pathologist at Changi, and so – with the hospital's blessing – Maynard continued his work. He knew that Digger had ambitions at this time to study to become a doctor, so he asked him to work as a technician in the mortuary.

Digger accepted the offer, rightly thinking that whatever he learned in this position would stand him in good stead for his future training. Little did he know how soon the skills he learned would be put to the test. For the rest of his time at Changi, Digger worked in the mortuary's pathology laboratory.

One area in which Dr Maynard had an interest was the effect of vitamin deficiency on the body, and some of Digger's work in the mortuary was connected with this. There were quite a few medical discoveries made at Changi around this time related to starvation and subsequent death. Studies such as Dr Maynard's eventually led to links being discovered between vitamin deficiency and lack of central vision.[3]

Digger soon learned how to extract organs, preserve them using formalin, replace organs, and how to close the body cavity when the body was no longer required. On one occasion he had to extract a brain. Under Dr Maynard's supervision, he removed the skin from the top half of the skull, sawed transversally around the head until the top half of the skull was almost ready to lift off, and tapped the last attachments through with a small hammer and chisel. The skull was then lifted off, and the brain was detached and removed from the skull cavity.

Most importantly, Digger learned to work quickly and neatly. He soon knew what it felt like to cut through bone and stitch muscle and skin together.

We had microscopes and everything in the pathology room. And there were also interns in Changi, younger doctors who were still learning. They would come to the morgue to watch me do the cutting up. Occasionally one fainted – perhaps because I tended to put it on a bit!

I worked in the morgue for months, and one time I discovered what Dr Maynard called a 'horseshoe kidney'. Both the kidneys were joined at the top. I preserved it in formalin – it might still be in a jar in Melbourne somewhere.

We had to keep everything as clean as possible, of course, and this wasn't always easy. I used to empty out the fluids that collected in the body cavity using an old jam tin, and I sewed up the cavity using a bag needle. Dr Maynard wanted me to join him in the morgue at Melbourne after the war, but by that time I'd had enough.

In April 1943, F Force was formed. 'Forces' were work party groups of POWs formed by the Japanese at Changi to work in Java, Japan, Manchuria, Indochina, Formosa and Korea, and on the Thai–Burma railway. Between May 1942 and August 1943, eleven such forces – A to L – were shipped off to work in various parts of South-East Asia.

Digger's great mate Bobby Small was allocated to F Force, which was a mixed Allied force of 7000 men, of which 3666 were Australians and the rest British. The men were not all fit – many had been patients at the Roberts Barracks hospital – but, as the Japanese explained, the unfit men would have a better chance of recovery with good food and in a pleasant location that had good facilities for recreation. There would be no marching except for short distances, and transport would be provided for baggage and for those unfit to march.

Under these circumstances, Bobby was quite happy to go. Digger and his mates organised a small farewell party the night before he left. They all wished him luck as he departed on this adventure.

The men boarded steel railway boxcars for the five-day journey to Ban Pong, Thailand, at the southern end of the Thai–Burma railway. On their arrival, the great gap between what the prisoners had been led to expect and the conditions they were about to experience immediately became apparent. They were marched a mile to a transit camp of *attap* huts, which had been occupied by native labourers but were now a squalid mess. Here they were organised into different huts by a Lieutenant Fukuda and some Korean guards, accompanied by frequent blows and beatings.

The next morning the men learned they would have to march to their respective places of work on the railway. No one told them that the march would be 300 kilometres and would take twenty-five days.

The march was a nightmare for those who were not fit. They rested during the day and walked at night. Naturally enough, they started off with heavy loads of bulging packs, haversacks and rolls of bedding, but as the march continued they were forced to sell items to the locals or to the Japanese soldiers.

The monsoon rains had started and it became increasingly difficult for the sick to walk. Conditions underfoot were slippery and treacherous in the dark. Stretches of the road were flooded; some roads had been swept away altogether. Those who fell behind were liable to fall victim to local bandits, who would rob them and then disappear.

Very quickly the majority of the men became ill with dysentery, beriberi or malaria, but even in such conditions they were forced to keep marching. By the time they reached Konkoita, the end of the march for a portion of the group, cholera had broken out. Even before they started work on the railway, F Force had lost nearly 600 of its original members.[4]

In August 1943 Digger was still working in the pathology lab, becoming quite skilled in the tasks required of him. Then his name came up to join L Force. This was a medical group going up to the railway, and the word was that it was to work in the so-called 'hospitals' set up there for the native forced labourers, known in Japanese as '*romusha*' or in English as 'coolies'. Originating mainly from Java, Singapore, Malaya and Burma, the *romusha* made up the main labour force on the railway, numbering far more than the POWs. They too had been lied to about the conditions; some had even been kidnapped to work on the railway.

It is estimated that up to 250,000 *romusha* were pressed into service on the Thai–Burma railway. This labour force was in addition to the over 60,000 Allied POWs working there. Due to the depletion of the *romusha* numbers by death and disease, the Japanese made the decision to send medical teams to Thailand and Burma in an effort to maintain them as part of the slave labour force.[5] L Force was the second such team, having been preceded by K Force, which had left Changi in June 1943.

In February 1942 there had been 15,000 Australians at Changi; now there were less than 2500. All those who had left were working for their Japanese captors from Japan to Formosa, with a great many on the Thai–Burma railway.

When Digger heard that he was on the list for L Force, he immediately thought that it might have something to do with his taking the food from the officers' quarters, since some Australian officers were involved in the decision, although he wasn't sure who they were. By now, everyone knew of the hardships that awaited those who were recruited for such groups.

Digger knew that there were a limited number of medical personnel at Changi, however, and that some people had to be chosen to go. He realised that perhaps it was as simple as the fact that he was a fit, trained medical orderly.

He was called up in front of Lieutenant Colonel Summons, who had been his commanding officer since he was sixteen years old, and who certainly knew about most of the exploits Digger had been involved in. Summons explained to Digger that going with L Force would not be any sort of holiday camp. He advised Digger to refuse the invitation and stay where he was, doing useful work in the pathology laboratory at Changi. Summons left him in no doubt that he could fix it so that he did not have to join L Force.

Digger thanked him and said that he was quite content to go. So many of his mates had gone on other forces before him, and anyhow, he was well aware that if he didn't go then someone else would have to go in his place. Lieutenant Colonel Summons thanked him, and Digger saluted and left the office. Digger knew that for men like Summons, it was anything but easy to decide who should go to the railway. He was very grateful that he had at least been given the chance to stay if he wanted to.

Digger also had other reasons for wanting to leave Changi. As a result of his activities in the camp, he was now very well supervised by the Allied officers, which of course he disliked. The optimist in him reasoned that there would be more opportunities outside Changi.

So Digger packed up his gear, such as it was, making sure that he had as large a supply as possible of quinine, iodoform and M&B 693 – an antibacterial drug that was widely used before the discovery of antibiotics. He knew that these supplies could mean the difference between life and death, and he had no intention of dying.

He said goodbye to his mates and joined the march to the station in Singapore, which took about half a day. He didn't know anyone in L Force well, although he recognised several faces. The commanding officer of this force was Lieutenant Colonel H. C. Benson, a British officer of the Royal Army Medical Corps (RAMC). With him were eleven other British medical officers and three Australian medical officers, Majors H. L. Andrews, P. J. Murphy and T. Crankshaw, as well as a hundred ORs, all medical orderlies and mostly Australian.[6]

But Digger knew little of this detail at the time, as he climbed aboard a small steel truck with about thirty-five others. As far as he was concerned, he was off on another chapter of this adventure. As he was shoved into a corner of the truck, the thought passed through his head that he would likely get to know those around him rather well before the journey ended. He was right.

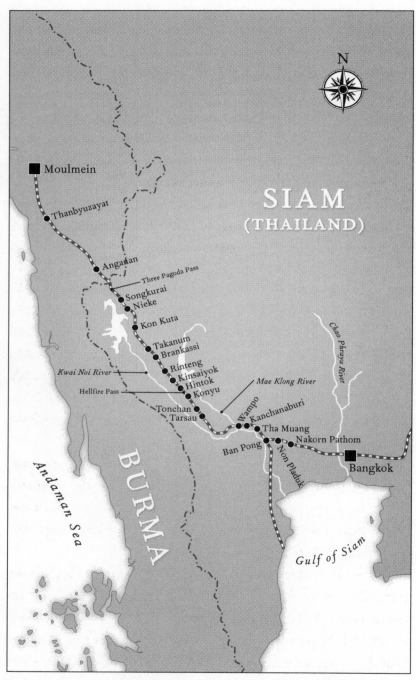

N

Moulmein

Thanbyuzayat

Anganan

SIAM
(THAILAND)

Three Pagoda Pass

Songkurai
Nieke

Kon Kuta

Takanum
Brankassi

Kwai Noi River

Rinteng
Kinsaiyok
Hintok
Konyu

Chao Phraya River

Mae Klong River

Hellfire Pass

Tonchan
Tarsau

Wampo
Kanchanaburi

Tha Muang
Nakorn Pathom

Ban Pong
Non Pladuk

Bangkok

Andaman Sea

BURMA

Gulf of Siam

SIAM TO BURMA RAILWAY   The railway is 421 km from Ban Pong in Thailand to Thanbyuzayat in Burma.
It was built in only 16 months and completed on 17th of October 1943.

Chapter 7

Journey to the Railway

MID-AFTERNOON ON 23 August 1943, the men of L Force felt the movement that signalled the start of their journey. It was relatively dark inside the steel rice truck, and ventilation was poor. Cracks around the door let in a few rays of sunlight but little precious air. Within a few minutes the temperature inside the truck soared, and it was little better even when the speed increased. The men had to stand or else sit with their knees pulled up to their chests. There was much jostling for a half an hour or so, until everyone realised that there was no comfortable position to be had and they would just have to put up with the situation.

No one knew how long the journey would take. They all knew they were heading north to some railway project; the estimates of how long they might be enclosed in these torturous conditions ranged from a day to three days. The men cursed and wished the worst on their captors.

As the day progressed and the sun began to set, the complaints gradually became fewer. The moaners had been told to shut up several times. As Digger and others had explained to them, since no one had the power to change anything they just had to accept what they were experiencing. Gradually, all resigned themselves to enduring the conditions. Finally the unbearable heat of the day gradually gave way, but the temperature at night in August in Malaya was not much lower.

And then suddenly the situation got worse. One man in the carriage was no longer able to control his bowels. He had given everyone fair warning for more than an hour, bemoaning the lack of a toilet stop. Now, with a cry of 'Sorry, fellas,' he finally let it all go.

While the men of L Force were all relatively fit and healthy, diarrhoea or even dysentery was never very far away. The man was sworn at, of course, but many soon realised that without anywhere to relieve themselves they had better not say too much. Who knew who would be next? Those in the corner with Digger became conscious of urine sloshing about the floor before it escaped through cracks at the side of the floor.

The first stop was early in the morning the next day. The men were allowed to step down onto the side of the track to relieve themselves. They were also fed a very meagre ration of cold rice. It was then back into the rice truck and on their way again.

Some days they had only one stop and some days two. Digger soon realised that where and when they stopped had more to do with the needs of the steam engine than the passengers. During one stop, the Japanese guards allowed the men to have showers under the engine water supply pipe at the side of the track. They were quick to strip off and avail themselves of this luxury. A group of about fifty villagers gathered to watch the spectacle. After showering, the men then did their best to wash down the inside of their carriage.

In the end, the journey from Singapore to Ban Pong took five days and four nights. Their destination was situated about fifty miles east of Bangkok. They arrived at midday on 28 August 1943 and were marched a short distance to a landing on the banks of the Mae Klong River. After the most minimal of meals, Japanese style, the men boarded two large barges.

'Well, well, a river cruise,' remarked Vic Kearns as they boarded. 'Who would have thought the Japs could be so considerate? This is exactly what we need after that fucking train journey!'

Vic was one of the seven POWs including Digger, all medical orderlies, who had stuck together – almost literally – in the corner of that steel rail car for the past five days. In such a situation you heard every word that was spoken. There were no secrets, and all one-on-one conversations were shared. It was the kind of situation in which you either became friends very quickly or decided to opt out of the group as soon as possible. In this corner, the bonds that had been forged between these seven men lasted for years.

Along with Digger and Vic, there was Jim 'Mick' Burroughs, a stocky, muscular man, even if he was lighter than he should have been after his time in Changi. He had been a bit of a wrestler and a boxer. Bob Sims was known as 'Yabba' because he would never stop talking – mostly about women and sex. Jack Sansom said little but was always worth listening to when he did speak, while Reg 'Pudding' Young was the quietest of the men. At forty-two years old, Russ King was the daddy of the group, although the army thought he was much younger. Russ had reduced his age when he'd enlisted so that he would be accepted for overseas service.

Their first day of cruising ended at sundown. It had rained heavily in the late afternoon, as it always did during the wet season. The 'Filthy Seven', as the group of mates began calling themselves, were soaked but happy. They were disembarked into a large 'go-down', a sort of warehouse on the riverbank, where they spent the night. The next morning they boarded the barges again, and by the afternoon of 29 August they had arrived at Kanchanaburi, a small *kampong* or village at the confluence of the Kwai Noi and Mae Klong Rivers. This was where the Filthy Seven would spend the next year and eight months.

The streets of this small village and the surrounding area were packed with thousands of Japanese soldiers and their equipment. The village consisted of just a few streets but there was hardly a local to be seen. Thousands of small, wiry men in drab Japanese military uniform were everywhere, manhandling artillery pieces and carts packed with goods. It was an unexpected and disconcerting sight for the men of L Force.

What was this build-up for? The only possible explanation was that they must be headed for Burma, even though that would mean walking on jungle tracks for at least 400 kilometres, following the route of the planned railway. Sure enough, a day later, as the members of L Force were doing their best to settle in to their new camp, the Japanese soldiers, with their heavier equipment on ponies, began heading north.

While the last couple of days had been bearable enough, the Allies' arrival at what they would call the No. 2 Coolie Hospital (or the Dai Ni hospital, as the Japanese referred to it) was anything but pleasant. The area that was to be home to Digger and his friends became the hospital area of a very large *romusha* camp.

Kanchanaburi and the surrounding area contained several camps, most of which served as hospitals both for sick POWs and for sick *romusha*, who were transferred there from work camps further up the railway. Around 35,000 POWs, including F Force and H Force, had now been sent up from Singapore to build the railway. The numbers of *romusha* recruited or shanghaied to work there probably amounted to at least 250,000 men.

When L Force arrived at Kanchanaburi, it was split by the Japanese command into groups of medical officers (MOs) and men of other ranks (ORs), who were then sent to various hospitals. Lieutenant Colonel H. C. Benson kept a record of the movements:

4 MOs and 30 ORs to Ban Pong coolie hospital, Major Crankshaw
in charge.

2 MOs and 10 ORs to Wang Yai coolie hospital, Capt. Lennox in
charge.

4 MOs and 20 ORs to No 2 coolie hospital Kanchanaburi, Major
Andrews in charge.

5 MOs and 40 ORs to H Force hospital Kanchanaburi Lt. Col.
Benson in charge.[1]

Over the next twenty months, there was much movement of K and
L Force personnel up and down the railway camps between hospitals,
but Digger and his six mates remained together at the No. 2 Coolie
Hospital.

It was opened as a base hospital in June 1943 for sick *romusha*.
A coolie *mandor* (a Malay term for foreman) was in charge of
discipline, cleanliness, feeding and general administration. A Japanese
captain, assisted by a medical lieutenant, was in overall control of
the hospital, but they only visited once a week. In charge from day
to day was a non-medical corporal, who would prescribe treatment
for everyone. Requests for drugs were usually met with abuse and
often with physical violence. Digger knew that the Japanese could
get a good price for their quinine from the Siamese traders, and so
the fewer drugs they used the more there was to sell. The Siamese
prostitutes who visited the Japanese officers weekly were paid in
quinine.[2]

The No. 2 Coolie Hospital sat between the newly constructed
railway line and the service road that ran parallel to it. It was built
on old paddy fields. The whole area was level and flat, so there was
no significant fall for drainage.

When the men of L Force were assigned to the No. 2 Coolie
Hospital, the conditions were chaotic and revolting. Digger couldn't

see how anyone in his right mind could have regarded this place as a hospital. Hygiene and sanitation were non-existent. The latrines were open and swarming with flies, and the camp was flooded with their contents every day when it rained. The sick *romusha* defecated where they lay.

Hundreds of men were housed in just twenty huts, each about twelve metres by five metres. The patients lay side-by-side on bamboo platforms that ran along both sides of each hut. Dysentery was rife but there was no isolation areas. Patients who were unable to walk to the 'latrines' were carried into the death house, which was always full.

Here there were no sleeping platforms; men were left to lie on the bare earth, in their own filth. No medical treatment was given, and the Japanese did not considerate it efficient to provide food for them either. The *romusha* were dying at a rate of forty to fifty a day, in the most squalid and miserable conditions imaginable.

The accommodation for L Force members consisted of huts built with bamboo and *attap* palms, like those of the patients. The men's first task was to clean them up as best they could, but Digger and his mates only had time to claim their place at the end of one side of their hut, away from the latrines. A low split-bamboo platform was to be their home for many months. Each man had just enough space to lie down.

The next day the MOs and a few of the orderlies were assigned to medical work, but most of the ORs joined manual work parties. The lucky ones were making roads around the camp. The not-so-lucky – including Digger and Yabba – were digging latrines.

The daily routine never changed: get up at dawn, queue for breakfast outside the cookhouse, eat your allowance of rice pap, parade in front of the Japanese guards and officers, get allocated to a work party and proceed to place of work with your guards.

Members of L Force were frequently bashed by the Japanese guards, especially during the first month or so after their arrival at the No. 2 Coolie Hospital.

Almost everyone got bashed in the first few weeks. Mostly it was for doing the wrong thing. No matter how the guard shouted at you – and they shouted at you constantly – if you did what you thought he was asking but had misunderstood, then invariably you got bashed, usually about the face and head with a thick bamboo pole.

You had to stand there and accept it. You did not complain or call out, if you could help it, and you most certainly did not retaliate. If you were knocked down, then the rule was that you stayed down, just curled into a ball, while doing your best to protect your vital areas, because then you'd be kicked hard. The general opinion was that it stopped sooner if you remained standing.

There were always a few men in the work parties who returned to the huts at night with swollen faces and black eyes. Certainly there were many who suffered broken noses and jaws. Sometimes they would order you to kneel and then pretend to chop off your head with a wooden sword, so you'd suffer a severe beating about the neck or upper back.

Some of the men just took the beatings and gradually became more and more withdrawn and depressed. But the Filthy Seven – or six of us, at least – were not like that. We talked about it at night and we fantasised about taking revenge. We had a bloody good go at thinking up what we could do about it. The obvious answer was to learn more of the language. Reg Young got beaten up several times and he stopped talking altogether, but we always included him in all the discussions and kept asking him questions and such, and eventually he came around.

I got to know one decent guard who spoke quite good English, Takeo Harada. He had worked for an Australian company with an office in Japan, so I got some Japanese language lessons off him – just casual like.

He explained that the word for 'Don't understand' was '*Wakaranai*', but when I used it with other guards I still got beaten up – and sometimes worse than normal. It took a few more lessons to learn that what I should really have said was '*Watasi yoku wakarimasen*,' which says the same thing but in a more polite or formal way that shows respect. I guess '*Wakaranai*' was all that Takeo Harada required when I addressed him, but he forgot to make allowances for the other bastards!

We also learned to say thank you: '*Arigato gozaimasu*,' or – even more politely – '*Domo arigato gozaimasu*.' We were determined to survive at all costs.

Major Kudo, of the Malayan Command, was in charge of all the hospitals around Kanchanaburi. He was not a medical man but he still overruled most of the suggestions made by Lieutenant Colonel Benson and his medical team, with regard to how the hospitals should be run, who would attend to the sick and who would carry out the manual work. This just added to the overall inefficiency of the organisation.

Most of the workers on the railway were the responsibility of Japan's Thai Command, but F Force, H Force, K Force and L Force were under the Malay Command. While inadequacies of food and medical supplies undoubtedly contributed to all deaths of POWs and *romusha*, this was much greater under the Malayan and Singaporean Command, while the Thai Command was better. No doubt this was to do with the distance from their respective IJA headquarters.[3]

These inefficiencies were the cause of the waste of L Force's medical skills, since most of its members were forced to carry out manual tasks around the hospital such as digging latrines, constructing huts, carrying water and firewood, making roads, building air-raid shelters for the Japanese, plucking grass and burying the dead.

Before long, Digger and his mates were carefully observing how the camp was organised and supervised. They talked continually about how to survive, and about the opportunities they could find to get extra food or make money. The food in the camp was the very least that men could survive on. It was rice alone or rice cooked in onion water; very occasionally it had a smell of fish about it. They would also get 'tow gay', a mung bean, with their rice for the evening meal.

The Filthy Seven knew the value of sticking together, looking after each other and above all sharing what resources they had. They were all determined to survive these conditions, which were much more severe than those at Changi had ever been. As Digger looked around, he could see that opportunities were indeed gradually appearing.

Digger had learned during his time at Changi that following certain rules helped to ensure survival under these conditions: take chances whenever they are presented; look for opportunities to volunteer; work outside the camp if possible; get to know the guards; know their behaviour, attitude and habits; test them, befriend them, ingratiate yourself with them, flatter them, bribe them, blackmail them. In short, do whatever is necessary to take advantage.

It was not long until such a prospect presented itself. After parade one morning, Mick, Yabba and Jack Sanson were ordered to join the guard Takeo Harada, who marched them out of the camp. They buried the dead *romusha* in a jungle clearing about 150 metres outside the camp. When they reported this to the rest of the Filthy Seven that evening, Digger smelled an opportunity. He determined to join them the following morning if they were again detailed. He planned to simply volunteer, using as friendly a manner as he could muster.

Volunteering for a task organised by the Japanese might at one time, earlier in the POWs' captivity, have been looked down on as a kind of betrayal. Very soon, however, all were well aware that the name of the game was survival, and you therefore did almost anything to survive.

Digger had volunteered for many tasks at Changi in the past, and his motive now, as it had always been, was purely selfish. It did not in any way diminish the anger or hatred in his heart but he knew, as his mates did, that their first objective was survival. They discussed this frequently and at great length. All agreed that the Japanese would be beaten in time, and then their chance for revenge would come. Until that day they would concentrate on survival.

Chapter 8

Mates and Survivors

BETWEEN 15,000 AND 20,000 sick coolies passed through Kanchanaburi, and from August 1943 to March 1945 total deaths were around 11,000. These figures are fairly accurate, as members of K Force and L Force were constantly associated with this hospital and were also responsible for burials.[1]

As it turned out, Digger had no trouble in joining the burial detail. A week or so later, Mick, Yabba, Jack and Digger were getting used to the routine. It was hard and unpleasant work and it stank, but it was outside the camp, and for the present they had a reasonable guard supervising them.

The first five or six hours of every day would be spent digging a new grave. It had to be big enough to hold fifty bodies, because they never knew how many there would be for that day. The grave had to be about 1.8 metres square and about 1.6 metres deep. It was hard pick and shovel work, but it was on the alluvial plain of the Mae Klong River and so the top soil usually went down the full depth of the grave. Each day's grave was less than half a metre from the previous one. Digging was the hardest work but not the worst.

After the grave was dug, the bodies would start arriving from the death house at the No. 2 Coolie Hospital. They would be carried on stretchers made from two stout bamboo poles and potato sacks. The dead were so thin and light that two *romusha* labourers could carry two or three bodies at a time.

As the bodies arrived they would be tipped into the grave. One of the gravediggers would be inside, packing the bodies, placing them in the most suitable position so that each body took up as little room as possible. When the daily supply of bodies had been packed into the grave, the earth was piled high on top of it, to allow for settlement over time. On many days the bodies came to within a foot or so of the top of the grave. Quite often the first task the following morning was to rebury the arms and legs dug up by the dogs during the night.

At first Digger and his friends had to face some harsh realities about death in the Japanese hospital camp. But they were practical and realistic, and they got used to the tasks relatively quickly. They knew that the Japanese expected total compliance from their POW workers. Digger also knew that if they were able to provide such compliance, then any additional activities they might engage in would be less likely to be discovered.

One day, a couple of weeks after they'd begun the burial work, Mick was packing bodies into a grave. 'What the fuck!' he gasped, staggering back against the grave wall. The body that he had been trying to tuck into position had suddenly groaned, and a hand had moved in unison. 'This poor bastard's still alive,' Mick shouted to those above him. 'Give me a hand!'

Seeing the situation, Digger jumped into the grave to help his mate. They gently untangled an emaciated but living body from among the dead, then lifted it gently up towards Yabba and Jack at the surface.

Takeo Harada approached to see what the commotion was about. 'No, no,' he ordered in English, pointing to the bottom of the grave. 'All body must bury – orders, orders!'

'But he's alive!' shouted Mick.

'Must bury all body.' Talking in an uncharacteristically strict tone, Takeo again pointed down, this time menacingly with his rifle, at the bottom of the grave.

The Japanese army did not allow for any initiative on the part of men of the lower ranks. A private daring to countermand an order for humanitarian reasons – especially in relation to a *romusha* 'work unit' – was unthinkable. Takeo Harada knew that his life would become unbearable, as would the lives of the gravediggers, if they were to return from the burying site with a live body.

Digger and the others realised they had to bury this man, whether they wanted to or not, otherwise their own lives would be on the line. They very carefully laid him back in the grave. A kind of rationalisation went on within each member of the group. They quietly continued their work, piling more bodies on top of this unfortunate fellow.

They knew that this man, even if he was still alive now, was very close to death. Had they been allowed to return him to camp, his best bet would be the death house again anyway, and no one ever survived the death house. If they didn't bury him today they would be burying him tomorrow. The burial ground was his only way out. There was absolutely nothing they could do. The poor bugger was as good as dead, and it wasn't their fault.

This was all the comfort that the four gravediggers could have – that and the fact that they did not hear any sounds coming from below. Digger began filling the grave. They all had enough experience of the ways of the Japanese military to know that this was all they could do. An hour or so later, the earth was piled on top of all fifty or so bodies.

That evening nothing was said about the incident. No one was brave enough to bring up the topic for conversation. They slept that night, because hard work always made them sleep. They knew that the *romusha* bloke's worries were now over.

This experience was repeated on several occasions over the next year or so.

One Korean guard – known as 'Scummadore' and nicknamed 'Ted' by the POWs, because it rhymed with 'shithead' – was perhaps the worst of all who regularly worked at the No. 2 Coolie Hospital. Occasionally he was in charge of the *romusha* burial detail, which was unfortunate for Digger because he'd already had a run-in with him. Scummadore was ugly as well as sadistic. He had obviously been involved in some accident, or perhaps it was a birth defect, but his arms were curved and came from his shoulders at a curious angle. This did not stop him using his rifle or a bamboo baton whenever he wished.

On the burial detail one morning, Digger asked Scummadore if he could *'benjo-e'* – go to relieve himself in the nearby jungle. Scummadore had taken some delight in laughing and signalling him to carry on working. Digger had to ask again, of course, and Scummadore angrily granted the request and sent Digger on his way with a rifle-blow to his back.

Digger might have taken his time, as everyone did in that situation, but Scummadore was for none of it. He was yelling at Digger as he came back out of the jungle growth. The guard pushed a rock, about the size of a football, towards Digger and signalled for him to hold it above his head. Digger was required to stand in that position in front of Scummadore, who sat himself on a tree stump and waited ready to thump Digger on the back the moment his arms tired. This was a favourite punishment of some guards. When Digger's arms could no longer hold the stone above his head, he had to suffer a beating about the face, and then it was back to the gravedigging.

Digger dared not retaliate against any guard, though, no matter how badly he was mistreated. Those who retaliated were sent back down the line under escort, and were mercilessly beaten at each camp along the way, no matter what their condition. Many POWs died in this way.[2]

There was a hierarchy at the No. 2 Coolie Hospital camp, just as there was at all camps on the line, imposed by those who sat at the top of the hierarchy, the senior Japanese officers. Young Korean men were bullied and pressed into joining the Korean Prison Guard Corps. The rank of guard was below that of army private and they could never aspire to be soldiers, so all members of the IJA looked down on the Koreans. But they were still a rung higher than the POWs and the *romusha*.

Japanese army culture maintained discipline through informal means: the more senior meted out harsh physical punishment to those below them. The training of the Korean guards was basically three months of bullying by their Japanese masters, and they were encouraged to treat those inferior to them – the POWs – in a similar manner. Even food was allocated in accordance with the hierarchy. The higher you were, the better you ate.

But it was not all death and beatings at the gravesite. Occasionally, a small group of Japanese would march to a special timber shrine that was built right next to the gravesites. The Japanese party would then stand to attention as an officer ceremoniously placed an offering of food in the shrine. There was a short religious ceremony or incantation or prayer of some sort, and the party saluted, about turned and marched off again.

During this procedure, the four gravediggers were ordered into the grave so that they were mostly out of sight; Takeo Harada was required to stand to attention. At these times, the Australians generally talked quietly amongst themselves about what was happening, enjoying the short rest.

Five minutes after the ceremony, Digger would ask Takeo if it was okay to eat the sweet rice cakes that had been left for the gods or the *romusha* spirits or whoever. Takeo would signal assent, and he and the gravediggers would then share the sweet treats.

On another occasion a very scrawny dog, so scrawny that no one had bothered about claiming it for the pot, wandered too close to the gravediggers. They promptly bumped it on the head and threw it into the pit with the bodies. They hated reburying bodies that dogs had dug up in the night. Unfortunately, two Japanese officers arrived and went mad when they saw the body of the dog in with the *romusha*.

'*Demi dana, gura gura!*' they yelled at Digger, who was in the grave, packing the bodies. Digger knew immediately that they wanted the dog's body out of the grave, so he threw it up to the others.

The actions of the Japanese – making offerings at the shrine and worrying about the dog in with the bodies – were difficult to reconcile with the way that they treated the *romusha* in life. But the gravediggers gave it little thought. Gruesome as the burial process was, like all routines it got easier as their skills increased.

Rations at the No. 2 Coolie Hospital were particularly poor. Breakfast consisted of rice pap – a sloppy porridge consistency. Lunch brought more rice and the day's vegetable ration in a watery stew. Dinner was rice alone.[3]

If the food had been adequate to keep the men in reasonable health, they might have survived without resorting to trading or stealing. As it was, Digger knew that they had to have additional medicines and nourishment. Everyone was always ravenously hungry. Rice and vegetables were in very short supply, and meat or fish were almost unheard of.

The pap that they ate in the mornings invariably had weevils and even maggots in it, but the consistency was such that they could not be easily picked out. But so great was the men's hunger that it all went down the same way. Knowing the benefits of protein, they never complained.

All the POWs were also subject to bouts of diarrhoea and, at times, to what they suspected was amoebic dysentery. They all suffered from malaria, and they all got the occasional tropical ulcer. In general, the Filthy Seven managed to escape the worst of the nutritional diseases — such as beriberi — because they were aware of how to avoid it. They chewed on grasses, ate specific leaves and fruits, such as the wild passionfruit that grew in many places.

Above all, they never reported sick. If one member of their group was sick, the others took on most of the workload until he recovered. Officially reporting as sick was always regarded as a last resort, because camp policy was that the sick were only entitled to half their usual rations, making recovery all the harder.

Digger still had his own small supplies of M&B 693, quinine and iodiform, but he and his mates were gradually using them up. They were always asking questions, listening to the talk around the camp, getting useful information from some of the guards — anything that might help them acquire extra food and drugs. Trading with the locals was strictly forbidden. A severe beating would be the minimum punishment, and it could even cost you your life. If somehow the POWs did have money, they could buy food at the store camp, which was owned by Major Buto, one of the Japanese commanders.

After being at the No. 2 Coolie Hospital for about a month, Digger heard about Boon Pong, a Siamese trader who traded at camps along the railway. Boon Pong was apparently eager to do business with those at the No. 2 Coolie Hospital.

I can't remember exactly how I first met Boon Pong, but he likely knew or made himself aware of our routine of burying the *romusha*. What I do know is that in no time at all he and I were great mates. It's no exaggeration to say that my meeting that man probably saved the lives of the Filthy Seven and many more in our camp. He and I would meet at least once a week. We always arranged our next meeting but he knew that if I didn't turn up then it wouldn't be my fault.

Boon Pong could get just about anything we asked for – quinine, M&B 693 and iodoform. I used watches, fountain pens and cigarette cases to trade with him. Boon Pong would also exchange money for us – Australian pounds, Dutch guilders or American dollars for the local Thai *tical* – so that we could buy food from other locals.

This was very risky work. It was dangerous for Boon Pong and very dangerous for me also, so both of us made money from it. I charged a commission on the trades I did for everyone in the camp, except for those in my own group.

I needed the help of my gravedigging mates to organise the meetings. We would be busy digging the graves but also listening for a special bird call from the nearby jungle – the signal that Boon Pong was there waiting for me. I would then ask permission from Takeo to go to relieve myself: *'Benjo-e?'* Takeo would always just say, *'Benjo-ka?'*, and I would take off into the jungle.

The other workers would carry on digging but would be ready to signal with a special noise if the coast was no longer clear – if an officer or more guards arrived, for example. I was pretty sure that Takeo knew what I was up to but I never took it for granted.

One morning, when Boon Pong brought a cup of coffee to their meeting, Digger decided to test Takeo's attitude. Coffee was completely unknown in the camp, and this coffee also had sugar in it. On returning to the gravesite, Digger asked Takeo whether it would be all right if, by some strange power, he was able to drink some coffee. Takeo signalled okay, and Digger bent down and recovered the coffee from behind a nearby rock.

'Ah, magic!' said Takeo, smiling as Digger shared his coffee with his mates.

Over the months, this unspoken agreement developed into a reliable business. On many occasions Takeo was not the only guard in the vicinity, and there were sometimes even Japanese officers, but Digger and his mates believed that these risks had to be taken if they were to survive.

Despite all the hardships, life was still very much worth living. Trading enabled the Filthy Seven to acquire supplies of food and medicine that allowed a standard of living that was just a notch above survival. They could treat their malaria, arrest the growth of tropical ulcers and eat the occasional duck egg.

'What more could one ask for?' Vic Kearns would say, as they added a little extra tow gay (mung beans) to their evening rice.

Yabba and Digger were also involved in other food-stealing ventures. Digger knew that if there was one thing they could rely on the Japanese for, it was that they abided by a strict routine. The morning parade was held at exactly the same time each day, and the sequence of events during the parade never changed. The POWs lined up in front of their huts and the storage area and faced the Japanese flag. The guards would initially face the POWs, with their backs to the flag.

The first activity was for the POWs to number off in Japanese – *ichi, ni, san, shi, go, roku* and so on. Woe betide the man who failed to learn his number and shout it out at the right time. This might be followed by an announcement from the IJA. Generally it would be about how badly the war was going for the Allies or some such nonsense.

For the final part of the parade, the Japanese turned to face the flag. With their backs to the POWs, they said their morning prayers and incantations to the Emperor. Yabba and Digger worked out that this took exactly five and a half minutes. At the end of this ceremony, the soldiers and POWs alike would be dismissed. The

Japanese would usually move away from the area, and the POWs would have about fifteen minutes to gather their tools and assemble in their work groups.

And so, after very careful preparation, Yabba and Digger and their mates went into action. They determined to steal what they could during the five and a half minutes in which the guards were making their prayers to the Emperor. First, they made sure they were in the right position within the ranks of POWs. They learned the proper rank numbers, as did those who had volunteered to swap places with them, and then spent at least two mornings conducting dry runs.

Once they decided to act for real, Yabba and Digger stole food such as tow gay and cooking oil from the storage rooms. They would return to the ranks with their haul, and on dismissal others would crowd around as they carried the food into their hut. They were very careful to steal amounts that were likely to go unnoticed. They continued stealing during the rest of their stay at Kanchanaburi, and to their knowledge they were never even suspected.

Another enterprise organised by Yabba and Digger did not go so well. Major Buto owned the camp canteen. The POWs had long suspected that he kept their rations short so that he could be sure of selling food from his canteen. The officer POWs earned up to fifty *ticals* a month but the privates received just five *ticals*, of which a certain proportion was deducted for accommodation and rations. No wages were paid if a man was sick.[4]

Major Buto sold the same goods that were supposed to be available as regular rations: rice, vegetables, tow gay, dried fish, tobacco, eggs and so on. Yabba, Digger and the rest of the Filthy Seven had no qualms about stealing from his canteen. As with the store, they figured that taking small amounts would be the way to go.

They knew they could get into the canteen easily enough. There were no locks on any of the buildings because none of the buildings were built to be secure. Whether it was intentional or not, the lack of food, the overwork and the disease combined to have a debilitating effect on most prisoners. This, together with the fear of the consequences, was more than enough to protect the canteen.

While many POWs took no risks if they could avoid it, Digger and the Filthy Seven did. They knew that life was miserable if you gave in and toed the line, so they devoted themselves to beating the system. They talked about this all the time, and they fantasised about the forms that their revenge would take. Stealing was just part of the survival plan. It kept them busy and alive, and it was one more way they could get one over on the Japanese.

On a very dark night, they went ahead with the raid on the canteen. They knew what they would steal — a small amount of dried fish and a small parcel of local tobacco — and they were familiar with the layout of the canteen. They believed they could be in and out within a minute.

It was easy getting to the canteen in the dark. We had practised walking there during the day with our eyes shut. And getting into the canteen was no bother either — we just opened the door, very quietly. But then we got the fright of our lives. All I heard was a quiet 'Fuck!' from Yabba, immediately followed by grunting and a struggle — but not loud. Then I heard what I later found out was the Korean guard's rubber boot drumming on the hard earthen floor as he died with Yabba's hands around his throat. Yabba had walked straight into him sleeping in a chair. He was probably strangling the poor bugger before he was even awake.

We knew immediately that the only way out of this predicament was to burn down the canteen. I hated this because it was not what we had planned. I had failed in the planning and should have known about the guard.

We quickly helped ourselves to a bit of tobacco. I knew where the lamp usually hung and used its kerosene to soak a pile of dry bamboo leaves taken from the roof, which I set against the bamboo wall. I lit it and we quickly got out of the building. I also checked that the guard was dead. If he had suddenly come to life then we'd be dead, of course.

By the time Digger and Yabba reached their hut, the building was well alight. No one had yet raised the alarm.

'How did it go?' asked Mick when he heard them returning.

'Not good – tell you tomorrow,' Digger replied. 'Just shut up and sleep.'

Mick knew to say no more and they all pretended to sleep. Digger could now hear the alarm being raised.

Luckily, the Japanese believed that the guard had fallen asleep while smoking. The canteen was rebuilt and operating again within two days, but Digger and Yabba decided that they would not steal from it again.

The Filthy Seven also did what they could to get additional protein. They soon learned that an excellent source of this were the local rats. But there was competition for them, of course, so – like the snakes in the Changi swamp – they became quite scarce.

Rats were very easy to cook. You simply threw the dead rat into the dying embers of the evening fire for a few minutes; being small, they would be cooked in no time at all. They could then be opened up along the belly, and the gut would come out in one piece, leaving the tender white flesh intact. This was shared out between members of the group.

One-seventh of a rat was not a large portion but it was always appreciated. As Vic Kearns never tired of saying, 'it all goes to make a turd'. Food and eating was such an important part of their lives that there was a spate of turd jokes that went around the No. 2 Coolie Hospital, such as:

Officer: 'What's your most important job today soldier?'
Soldier: 'To build a turd, sir!'
Officer: 'Correct! And remember, soldier, a turd a day is the healthy way.'

Vic Kearns created these jokes mostly because he was a natural comedian, but they also boosted the men's morale and delivered an important health message.

There were so few opportunities to get any meat that when two Japanese officers came and asked a small group, including Digger, whether there was anyone who knew how to butcher a pig, Digger immediately saw the possibilities. No one said anything initially so Digger volunteered for the job, even though he had never butchered anything bigger than a rabbit.

That night, all the talk amongst the Filthy Seven was about butchering pigs. Mick, who was a country boy from Queensland, actually knew a bit about it and taught Digger the theory. Dave Powrie, the camp cook, was also brought in on the discussion.

A few Japanese arrived the next day with a pig that weighed around seventy kilograms. Digger, Mick, Dave and a few others were ready. With great difficulty, they hung the pig from a roof strut and cut its throat. They tried to catch the blood in a large *kwali* – a very large cast-iron cooking pot – knowing how nutritious it would be, and soon they were covered in it. Under Mick's supervision, the carcase was then lowered down and plunged into a large *kwali* of very hot water, before it was slung up again and all the hair was scraped off.

They gutted the pig, and Digger persuaded the officers, who were watching closely, to allow him to keep the offal. Before the officers realised it, Dave and a couple of helpers whisked the liver, kidneys, lungs and all the other bits and pieces to the POWs' kitchen. They then laid the carcase on clean banana leaves and the proper butchery began.

Digger persuaded the officers that they would not require the trotters or the head, and Mick quickly cut them off and handed them to Dave, who took them away quickly. Digger and Mick had earlier agreed where the trotter ended and the shoulder leg meat began, and they made sure that they would have the best of the bargain.

The pig was then cut up into reasonably sized joints of pork, and the Japanese officers left with about twenty banana-leaf parcels. Yet their basket looked very small, given that the pig had originally been all of seventy kilograms. All the POWs enjoyed pork that night, and brawn made from the head the following night. Each man had very little each, of course, but it was the tastiest their evening rice had been for a long time.

On some occasions, Digger managed to acquire the duty of going to the IJA command post in Kanchanaburi village to collect supplies for the camp. He rode in the back of the truck with another POW while two Japanese officers and the driver rode in the front.

There was a permanent arrangement between the POWs on this duty and Dave Powrie that, if possible, anything that could be stolen would be thrown from the truck at a particular spot. Few were prepared to steal, however, because of the risks involved. Digger was always up for such activity. The goods brought back to camp were checked on arrival; for example, the number of sacks of jointed meat had to be the same at the delivery point as they were at the loading point. Any discrepancy would cost all those concerned very dearly indeed. However, it was known that only very rarely were the sacks weighed or the joints of meat counted.

Once, on the return journey from Kanchanaburi, conditions were very favourable for the acquisition of at least one large joint of meat.

The Japanese had picked up a young Tamil girl in the village, and she was riding back to camp – in the cab, of course. The officers and even the driver spent the entire journey flirting with her. This allowed Digger time to get into one of the sacks containing the meat and select a reasonably sized joint.

When the truck approached the arranged spot, he could see Dave Powrie waiting for the delivery. With a quick check to see that the girl still had the full attention of those in the cab, he heaved the lump of meat towards Dave. He caught it full in the chest, and the impetus knocked him backwards. Digger's impression, as the truck flew past, was of Dave on his back – but he was still holding fast to the meat.

Mostly, the relationships between the POWs at the No. 2 Coolie Hospital were good. But just occasionally an individual would get up someone's nose and an argument would result or a few punches would be thrown. Some of the British officers in L Force were a constant source of annoyance to the Australian ORs.

One in particular, Captain W. B. Young, tried very hard to get the Australian ORs to behave towards him as the British ORs did, saluting and standing to attention when addressing him and so on. The Australian ORs called this 'Pommy officer idiocy'. Most of the British officers had the sense to accept the attitude of the Australian ORs and so relationships were generally reasonable, but Captain Young just would not or could not.

The situation got so annoying that, one evening, the Filthy Seven drew straws over who should take Captain Young aside to teach him some manners. Yabba drew the short straw. The next day, Yabba was able to get Captain Young on his own. No one found out exactly what happened, but Captain Young had a black eye the next time he was seen. As Vic Kearns remarked, it was like he'd been born again.

The Japanese were the only authority that had to be obeyed and it became difficult for the British and Australian officers to retain their authority over their men. It was doubly difficult for the British officers because of their authoritarian approach. Generally, Australian ORs were happy to take orders from Australian officers because their normal relationships were always more relaxed.

Digger was annoyed by Colonel Benson, who used the very British custom of referring to privates by their surname only. He ordered Digger around and always called him 'Barrett'. Digger could stand it no longer.

One day, he just stopped what he was doing and approached Colonel Benson. 'Look, mate,' he said, looking the officer in the eye, 'my name is David, my nickname is Digger and my rank is private. You can call me David, Digger or Private Barrett, but no more "Barrett". Understand?'

Finding himself a little out of his depth with this Australian private, Colonel Benson hummed and hawed a bit before saying, 'Well, that seems perfectly reasonable.'

Arguments sometimes occurred even among the closest of mates. Occasionally violence erupted. On one occasion Digger even threw a punch at Yabba. They were digging a grave at the time, and he'd just had enough of Yabba's constant chatter about women that he had known. It was only one punch. Yabba, who was bigger and heavier than Digger, got such a surprise that he didn't even retaliate.

Yabba suffered a broken tooth, and Digger immediately regretted what he had done. Ever afterwards, Yabba's broken tooth was visible when he smiled, and it was a permanent reminder to Digger that he should not have lost his temper. But like all good mates, Yabba just accepted what had happened and never even mentioned it again.

As the months went past, Digger and his mates got used to their life. Hard as it was, Digger always looked forward to the next day and thought about what opportunities it might bring. His optimism rubbed off on his six closest mates. Together, they regarded their lot as temporary, not as bad as it might be, and they looked forward to the small rewards they could scrounge.

No L Force POWs were ever given new clothes or boots, not to mention soap or toothpaste or anything like that. Despite even their minimal pay, most men had no footwear and were reduced to wearing only loincloths.[5]

Nevertheless, Digger took as much care with his appearance as possible. He was always clean, smart and polite, particularly to the Japanese guards. He went out of his way to present an unafraid and confident persona, even though the Japanese officers were always trying to bully and intimidate the POWs. Although Digger was dressed in rags, the guards who knew some English called him 'Dandy'.

The Japanese officers came to the work sites quite often. They talked with the POWs but the conversations were always one-sided. While the Japanese were contemptuous of the prisoners and the Allies in general, the POWs could not retaliate at all.

During one such encounter, Digger and his mates were reminded, as they frequently were, that one Japanese soldier was worth ten Australians. The goading continued for so long that some were brave enough to mutter some words of dissent. This is what the Japanese had counted on. They asked whether the Australians were brave enough to put up their champion against a Japanese wrestler.

The officers kept looking at Digger, expecting a reply. Digger knew they would not let up until they received a reply, so he looked across at Mick, more or less dobbing him in for the job, which he immediately regretted.

Mick stared daggers at Digger as a makeshift circle was marked off in the bare earth. One of the older Japanese officers threw Mick a loincloth, and another fixed it around his waist like a Sumo wrestler would. The older officer seemed to be generally in charge of the event. He stated the rules of the fight, all in Japanese, and then simply signalled for it to begin.

The Japanese fighter was shorter than Mick. No one at Kanchanaburi was fat, not even the Japanese, but he clearly weighed more than Mick, who was pure muscle and bone, courtesy of the very poor diet and the daily gravedigging.

The two men circled each other and then locked together, each struggling to get an advantage. The Japanese fighter, having a lower centre of gravity, began to push Mick towards the edge of the ring. The Japs were shouting to their man, while the Australians were encouraging Mick.

Although he was being pushed back, Mick had a firm hold of his opponent's cloth belt. He heard the advice being shouted out by his close mates, who did not care if the Japanese understood them or not: 'Lift the bastard off the ground . . . Throw him out of the fucking ring!' Mick hoisted the Japanese wrestler up and threw him out of the ring.

A huge cheer went up from the POWs. In the confusion of that moment, Mick was whisked off by the Japanese. Digger doubted very much that it was to award him a prize.

When Mick finally came back to the hut, his face was badly bruised. He clearly felt murder in his heart for Digger. But Digger was not in his usual place, having decided that it was better not to see Mick that night. He spent the night regretting his part in the arrangements.

The next day at the *romusha* gravesite, Digger tried to apologise to Mick. All he got in return was: 'Just shut up and keep fucking digging.' That was good enough for Digger. He assumed that eventually he might be forgiven.

Chapter 9
The Return of F Force

ON 17 OCTOBER 1943, the railway was finally completed when the lines from the north and south met near Konkuita. This was a railway camp 262 kilometres north of Nong Pladuk, Thailand, and 153 kilometres south of Thanbyuzayat, Burma.

By November, F Force was gradually being evacuated from camps up the line to Kanchanaburi and then to Singapore. Its men had probably experienced the worst conditions of any force working on the railway. By the time F Force arrived at Kanchanaburi, its 3600 Australians had lost about one-third of their number, while the British had lost almost two-thirds of their 3400 men. Many were not in any condition to travel any further, and so there was a huge influx of patients into the Kanchanaburi hospitals. The original H Force Hospital was soon overcrowded, and so four additional huts were taken over from the No. 2 Coolie Hospital.[1]

Hundreds of F Force men died of cholera, but many more died of dysentery, malaria, beriberi, strongyloides or other parasitic diseases, all brought on or exacerbated by overwork and lack of food. In many cases, men just gave up and died in misery.[2]

As soon as Digger heard that F Force was returning, he was on the lookout for Bobby Small. Digger was used to living and working with men who were underfed and overworked, but nothing prepared him for the condition of the men of F Force. The worst of it was that they were quiet. As bad as conditions were at Kanchanaburi, the Filthy Seven were at least able to joke about them. They knew they would survive and they talked about it constantly. This was not the case for the men of F Force. Many had given up hope and were simply waiting to die. Some, even when they were on the way to recovery, were unable to drag themselves out of their depression.

Digger soon found his mate. Bobby was very ill, and not the man Digger remembered. Digger found him lying on the ground in a corner of the camp. Bobby had no firm and friendly handshake for Digger, who soon learned that he had dysentery and bad malaria at the very least. All that Digger got was a quiet 'Hello, mate . . . it's great to see you again'. Bobby was literally half the man Digger had known at Changi.

Digger quickly organised for Bobby to join the Filthy Seven in their hut. Bobby still slept on the floor at night, but during the day he slept in Digger's place on the bamboo platform. Digger and his mates provided Bobby with medicines and much better food.

Over the next few days Bobby rested as the Filthy Seven went about their gravedigging and other work duties. They would eat together in the evenings, and everyone encouraged Bobby to talk. They spoke about Changi and what a terrific time they'd had there. They reminisced about the snakes in the swamp, collecting the snails to feed and cure Joe Milledge of his dysentery, about how they got one up on the officers by taking their tinned food, and above all about getting drunk on the booze that Bobby had made in the hospital's boiler room.

They also talked of the future: what they would do when they got home, how soon it would be before the war ended, and what they would do to the fucking Japs when that day came. They all agreed that they would go to Japan and bite the balls off all the breeders!

If willing someone to get better had any effect, then Bobby should have been improving. All Digger's mates could see how he did everything possible to aid Bobby's recovery. Bobby had all the quinine he needed and the healthiest and most tempting food that it was possible to acquire in the circumstances, but he showed little improvement. His bouts of malaria fever did not abate.

Digger woke one night to find that Bobby was missing from his usual place on the floor next to him. He found him sitting outside on the ground next to the hut. Digger sat down beside him. The two men leaned against the wall with their feet in the drainage ditch.

'I thought it might be cooler out here, mate,' said Bobby, 'but right now it's getting a bit cold even.'

'No worries, I'll get my blanket,' Digger replied, knowing well the effects of the malaria.

When he returned, the two sat together with the blanket around them. They talked of how they would get home, and the places they would pass through on their way. Digger did most of the talking and Bobby eventually drifted off to sleep. Digger didn't have the heart to wake him. Eventually, he too slept.

Digger awoke to a cool dawn breeze on his skin and the first birdcalls from the surrounding jungle. He was aware of Bobby's head on his shoulder and gently supported it as he attempted to manoeuvre him into a better position. At that moment he had a terrible feeling. He was suddenly conscious that Bobby's body was as cold as the early morning air. Bobby had already left for home.

The hate that burned in Digger's heart for the Japanese – for what they were responsible for – was as real as the grief he felt for his dear friend. For the next few days, Digger hated everyone as he grieved both for his friend and for his own predicament. Whose fault was it that his friend had died and he was stuck in this hellhole? The Japanese. It was their plans for the Greater East Asia Co-Prosperity

Sphere, and the way they went about achieving them – men working to death on starvation diets and with no medical supplies. Everything for the fucking Emperor, no matter who died in the process.

Bobby would not have died if that mouse mouth, General Percival, and the other superior Pommy bastards had done the right thing and fought for Malaya and Singapore instead of surrendering. What a fucking balls-up that had been. Never mind the British officers – the Australians couldn't even trust their own bloody officers, who seemed to think they were entitled to more food than those in the hospital at Changi. Christ!

Most of all, Digger thought about his own part in all of this. Why the hell had he volunteered? How stupid had he been? He'd thought it would be bloody marvellous to be one of the boys, off to the war, seeing far-flung adventurous places, fighting for King and country. What a load of ignorant, nationalistic crap!

Here he was, twenty-two years old, and what had he achieved in his young years? Absolutely bloody nothing. It seemed like this wouldn't change for a while yet.

After a few days, Digger's feelings of grief and self-pity lessened, particularly as he thought more and more about taking revenge against his present masters. He had no concrete plans yet, just a few ideas, but the bastards would pay for Bobby's death, one way or another. Of that he was sure. By the end of the week, Digger had recovered and was back to his old self again.

H Force also passed through Kanchanaburi on its way back to Changi. Among its men was one outstanding officer, Major Dr Kevin Fagan. It was no exaggeration to say that the men whose lives he saved worshipped him. He was praised by all men in H Force, and others – such as Digger and his mates – who got to know him during his time at Kanchanaburi. Above all, he was admired for his courage during the long 150-kilometre march from Bam Pong north to Tonchan and Konyu, where H Force worked on the line. Years later, Russell Braddon paid tribute to him:

> Above all, there was the extraordinary courage and gentleness and the incredible endurance of the medical officer, Major Kevin Fagan. Not only did he treat any man needing treatment to the best of his ability; he also carried men who fell; he carried the kit of men in danger of falling, and he marched up and down the whole length of the column throughout its entire progress. If we marched one hundred miles through the jungle, Kevin Fagan marched two hundred. And when, at the end of our night's trip, we collapsed and slept, he was there to clean blisters, set broken bones and render first aid. And all of it he did with the courtesy of a society specialist who is being richly paid for his attention and the ready humour of a man who is not tired at all.[3]

Dr Fagan, who was quite sick himself with malaria when he arrived in Kanchanaburi, continued to perform operations. Digger determined to support him as much as he could by donating the substantial sum of money he had accumulated through his trading activities. He also organised to purchase drugs ordered by Dr Fagan through Boon Pong.

Dr Fagan was particularly skilled in treating bad tropical ulcers, which included performing the amputations that were frequently required. Digger learned a great deal during the brief periods he could assist Dr Fagan, when he was not required to be at the *romusha* gravesite.

Dr Fagan later wrote of the relative luxurious operating conditions he experienced in Kanchanaburi.

The facilities available for surgery in the Thailand prison camps were not elaborate. My operating theatre, for example, was at first the open air, later a tent fly, and still later, when we returned to the plains at Kanchanaburi, a luxurious affair of palm leaf with a mud floor, but completely fly proofed with American Red Cross mosquito netting. Sterilising of towels, instruments and dressings was done in a four gallon 'dixie' on an open fire outside the operating theatre. Under these conditions, in addition to excisions of ulcers, such operations as appendectomy, mastoidectomy, craniotomy, 'pinning' of the tibia and skin grafting were performed with a minimum of septic complications. This fact was due to the skill and devotion of the theatre orderlies, who fortunately had received their training in better circumstances and earlier in our captivity.[4]

Another person Digger met through Dr Fagan was Ronald Searle, an artist who later became known around the world for his St Trinian's cartoons. He was a member of H Force and stayed at Kanchanaburi while he recovered from beriberi and tropical ulcers. He later wrote:

When most of H Force was eventually shifted from Kanchanaburi to be taken back to Singapore and returned to the authorities that owned us, I had to be left behind. I have one or two memories of a great hut in Kanchanaburi in which I lay, no longer able to move. High, endlessly long and crammed with skeletal looking bodies sprawled on raised bamboo platforms, it was a luxury hotel compared with what we had just left in the jungle. I was adopted by a cheerful bunch of Australians and two Dutch officers, all of whom were still in rather a mess themselves. They nursed me, spent their money on eggs and extras from the natives for me, washed me and, of all unlikely things, procured some sulphur drugs from somewhere for me. Anything was possible for the Australians — even the impossible. They saved my life and got me back on my bare feet again.[5]

Digger and Yabba had many conversations with Ronald, who described to them the conditions under which H Force had worked. They were expected to work at 'speedo time', whether they were sick or not, as they cut through solid rock at Konyu on the bank of the Kwai Noi River. As Ronald wrote:

Needless to say the 'speedo' order did not decrease the casualty rate, nor did it speed the advance of the railway. Parading for the count at dawn we were a sorry looking lot. Most of us were suffering from something colourful or dramatic that made it a misery to exert ourselves or stand for long periods. Nevertheless we went through the motions. As the first thin rays of sunlight appeared through the vast canopy of trees above us, the order to stand to attention was yelled. It was regularly answered with whoops from the families of gibbons that gazed down on us as our guards bared their shaven heads. Then the signal was given and we faced the east, bowing low five times as we chanted as best we could after our guards the soldiers' 'prayer' to the Emperor.

Hitotsu: Grunjin wa chusetsu o tsukusuo honbun to subeshi!
Hitotsu: Grunjin wa reighi o tadashiku subeshi!
Hitotsu: Grunjin wa buyu o toutobu beshi!
Hitotsu: Grunjin wa shinghi o omonzubeshi!
Hitotsu: Grunjin wa shisso o mune to subeshi!

And translated it means:

A soldier must honour loyalty as his most important virtue
A soldier must be impeccably polite
A soldier must be courageous
A soldier must treasure his principals
A soldier must be frugal

Our dawn chorus over like good Japanese soldiers we politely, courageously and ever so bloody frugally, pushed off for ten hours or so of Imperial rock-breaking down by the muddy Kwai.[6]

As the men of H Force recovered, they were transported back to Ban Pong and then all the way back to Changi. When it was Ronald Searle's time to go, he took Digger aside and presented him with a few of his drawings as thanks for how Digger and his mates had looked after him.

By April 1944, Japanese medical officers – and even other officers and privates who had no medical qualifications – were staffing the hospitals in the Kanchanaburi area. They provided little treatment and interfered with the treatments recommended by the POW medical officers. In some cases, the prisoner MOs had no more status than a dresser.

By this time, the L Force medical orderlies were all on manual work: digging latrines, construction work, road-making, constructing air-raid shelters for the Japanese, felling, cutting and carrying wood and bamboo, and plucking grass. Major Kudo's reason for assigning the medically qualified POWs to manual work was very likely so that he could pocket the money he had been allocated to feed *romusha* labourers for these tasks.[7]

This state of affairs made little difference to Digger, Mick, Jack and Yabba, who continued as the gravedigging team. They were by now very familiar with the routine and totally dedicated to doing all they could to make money, to enable them to buy extra food and drugs. Two events then occurred to upset their routine.

First, Takeo Harada was transferred. He was the one and only decent guard whom Digger ever encountered. The two were never friends – that was impossible – but trust had built up between the two. Just before he left the camp, Takeo gave Digger a large box of Japanese cigarettes.

Second, the Japanese had neglected to pay any attention to the camp hospitals' sanitation and hygiene. All suggestions in this regard by POW medical officers were resented. New latrines were not dug until the old ones were full and overflowing, and the Japanese never took advice about where these should be. The *romusha* were defecating everywhere, flies swarmed and dysentery was rife. Colonel Benson stated that 'conditions could not have been worse than in the dirtiest of Indian Bazaars'.

These conditions were certainly in evidence at the No. 2 Coolie Hospital. Not surprisingly, cholera broke out in May 1944, and immediately the Japanese replaced their own dressers in the cholera wards with Allied medical officers and orderlies. Sanitation was then immediately attended to.[8]

When cholera broke out, Digger was ordered to report to a sergeant in the guards' quarters, between the camp and the railway. The sergeant quickly and forcefully explained to him that he was now '*sanski* boy' for Major Buto and the other Japanese officers who lived there. This meant he was now their house boy, cleaner, servant and general dogsbody, and he did not like the idea.

Digger was not too sure why he was chosen for this job, but it probably had something to do with the fact that he was always clean in appearance and habits, polite and – on the face of it – willing in all his work. He knew he would loathe it, however, and he also knew he could not steal anything from them without being immediately suspected.

> I didn't want to be a *sanski* boy for these bastards but I could see it offered me opportunities to get back at them. Getting away with it would be the trick. It would be a bit like using the snakes against them. The lads that worked outside the camp were always on the lookout for snakes. Usually they caught them for the pot – the bigger, thicker ones such as pythons. But the smaller snakes were often the nasty poisonous little beggars, and the men used to capture them alive if they could.
>
> They would smuggle these snakes into camp and pass them on to any POW who had access to the Japanese guards' quarters. The snakes were surreptitiously released into the drainage ditches that surrounded all the Japanese dormitories. These ditches were built quite deep and wide so that if an air raid came during the night, the Japs could just sort of roll out of their bunks and into the ditch. They'd then get bitten by one of our snakes – that was the theory, anyway! I don't know if it ever happened but it was worth it just thinking about it.

Although the opportunities for revenge were good, Digger did not enjoy his new job. He might have appreciated the relatively easy life but the respectful demeanour that had to be maintained at all times, along with the ever-so-polite and ingratiating conversations he was forced to conduct with the Japanese officers, began to get him down after a week or two. Eventually, all that he could think of was how to get out of this job.

The only thing he could do was contrive to somehow get sacked. Asking for a transfer was not an option. One of Digger's daily tasks was to fill and heat a large drum of water for Major Buto to bathe in.

One day Digger built a larger than usual fire under the bathwater. Strangely, it was not really an intentional decision on Digger's part. He knew perfectly well what he was doing, but while one part of him was telling him to stoke the fire, another side was thinking about the likely consequences of this act. They weren't pleasant.

By the time Major Buto arrived for his bath it was too late to stop what was about to happen. Digger simply braced himself.

Major Buto was short-legged and obviously well fed, not at all like the majority of the lower Japanese ranks. He always looked very smart in his uniform, complete with belt, sword and scabbard, leather knee-length boots, cap and badges of rank, but as he climbed up the timber steps to get into the drum, he looked a little ridiculous and decidedly vulnerable in his nudity.

Digger felt dread at his impending bashing, but this was somewhat offset by the sight of the major confidently plunging his right leg into the water, right up to his testicles. He then let out a huge roar and scrambled out, trying to escape the pain. That brought other officers out of the nearby house.

Buto grabbed a bamboo pole from another guard and, with both hands, smashed the pole into the left side of Digger's head. This fat little Japanese officer, completely nude, with one red leg and one white leg, continued to shout and bash Digger about the head for what seemed to Digger like an eternity. He only just managed to remain standing. Major Buto threw the pole down and barked an order to an officer, who dragged Digger to the gate of the small compound, threw him to the ground, kicked him repeatedly and told him to be on parade the next morning.

Digger dragged himself to his hut. As he approached, he was conscious of Yabba and Vic helping him inside and gently laying him onto the sleeping platform. Within half an hour Digger's eyes had almost disappeared amid his swelling face, and his jaw, which may have been broken from previous bashings, was certainly broken this time. He was fed a thin soup through his swollen and bruised lips, but Yabba swore he could see the beginnings of a smile on Digger's face.

'What the fuck have you been up to?' asked Vic. 'No, don't answer that. I can see you can't, so just shut up for now and swallow the soup.'

Despite the considerable pain Digger was in, he went over the scene in his mind. God, how he wished he could tell the story now. But he couldn't speak, so he took Vic's advice and concentrated on getting the soup down.

The next morning at parade, Digger was not surprised to find himself allocated to the cholera ward. This was probably the worst job that Major Buto could think of, as a suitable punishment for this fool who was unable to get his bathwater to the correct temperature. It probably never entered Major Buto's mind that Digger had intentionally made the water too hot. If Buto had thought that, Digger knew, he would not be alive now.

Digger was happy in the cholera ward because he knew that the last thing he would see there would be a Japanese guard. The Japanese were terrified of cholera. Most of them carried around a small bag filled with herbs of some kind, which they believed increased their body temperature and thus protected them from the disease. Digger and his mates knew how to protect themselves from cholera – you simply didn't drink water that was likely to be unclean – and as he recovered slowly he concentrated on keeping himself out of bother.

Both the death house and the cholera ward had split-bamboo walls and *attap* palm roofs. The *romusha* patients lay on the bare earth down one side of the hut; down the other side, inside the hut, was the latrine. This was so that those who were otherwise unable to walk far could relieve themselves close to where they slept. Many patients were actually past walking, so the conditions inside these huts for all whose misery ended here was utterly appalling.

Digger never once saw any *romusha* patient receive treatment for his condition in the death house or in the cholera house. As a medical orderly in the cholera ward, all that Digger was permitted to do was to get the patients, if they were fit enough, to kneel with their bare backsides facing him in a row, and he would spray their arses with a liquid given to him by the Japanese. Digger expected this was just salt water. No *romusha* ever recovered in these wards. The cholera patients all had other complicating and debilitating conditions, such as dysentery, malaria and beriberi.

It took Digger a good two weeks to recover from the bashing. His jaw was still painful and tender when he attempted to chew, but since there was no steak on the menu this didn't trouble him too much. He knew that as the bones mended this would come good over time. His hatred for the Japanese had only grown.

Digger had three things going for him as he planned his revenge. He knew the routine in the officers' quarters back to front. He also knew and trusted the new *sanski* boy POW who was employed there. Finally, he had twenty-four-hour access to the cholera house.

Digger still had a large syringe in his kit that he had acquired in his days working in the mortuary at Changi. One afternoon, he filled it with liquid from the latrine trench that was laden with cholera bacteria; it was a relatively clear liquid. He went to the officers' bathhouse and gave each toothbrush on the rack a good soaking straight from the syringe.

Major Buto survived this attack of biological warfare, and Digger was unable to find out whether any other officers had succumbed. If officers did get sick, they were always immediately removed from the camp. Still, Digger felt much better to have taken some revenge. He resumed his usual activities of stealing and dealing.

In fact, opportunities for this expanded while Digger was working in the cholera ward, mainly because no Japanese guard or officer would come near it. Digger was free to deal with the local Thais through the back fence. He was able to buy food and sell old clothing; woollen clothing, in particular, was in great demand. The Thai women would unravel the wool and make the most wonderful new garments with it. An old sock, no matter how worn, would get Digger a few bananas; a pair would get him a duck's egg.

By late 1944, the cholera epidemic had subsided. Digger and most of the Filthy Seven were back at their manual labouring jobs around the camps at Kanchanaburi. They knew the area very well by this time, and through their stealing and dealing they were able to provide themselves with the necessities of life. They still got malaria and dysentery occasionally, but they were able to survive.

In early 1945, the bridge over the Mae Klong River was bombed. This was the famous 'bridge on the River Kwai' – the river was later renamed to fit the famous story.

I was in Kanchanaburi when the bridge over the Mae Klong was destroyed. I don't remember the time, but twenty-one Lancaster bombers appeared and an ack-ack battery opened up on the formation. One Lancaster peeled off to take care of the ack-ack battery. It disappeared but reappeared seconds later. The ack-ack battery was silenced. Three Lancasters then peeled off and knocked out the three middle spans of the bridge. The remaining seventeen Lancasters pattern-bombed the Japanese stores depot. We were ordered to clean up the mess the next day. There were Japanese bodies everywhere.

On 6 April 1945, all L Force and K Force personnel were transferred from Japan's Malaya Command to Thai Command. They were

Digger proudly shows off his Light Horse uniform, about 1938. *(Chapter 1)*

Joe Milledge (left) and Digger at Port Dickson, 1941. *(Chapter 2)*

A sketch of the *Queen Mary* as drawn by Joe Milledge, Digger's mate, at the time of departure from Sydney in February 1941. *(Chapter 2)*

Digger with two Malay servicemen.
(Chapter 2)

Angela Siawa outside her parents' house in Port Dickson, 1941. *(Chapter 2)*

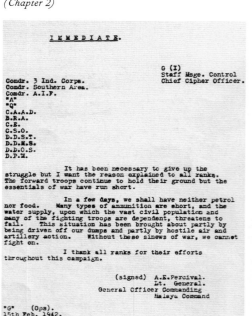

A copy of General Percival's letter of surrender in February 1942.

(David Barrett collection) (Chapter 4)

Digger and Max Wall photographed in late 1945 in Melbourne. *(Chapter 5)*

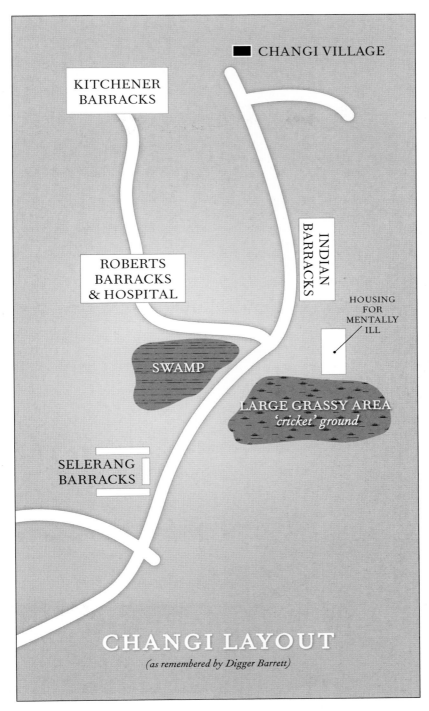

CHANGI VILLAGE

KITCHENER
BARRACKS

INDIAN
BARRACKS

ROBERTS
BARRACKS
& HOSPITAL

HOUSING
FOR
MENTALLY
ILL

SWAMP

LARGE GRASSY AREA
'cricket' ground

SELERANG
BARRACKS

CHANGI LAYOUT
(as remembered by Digger Barrett)

Sketch map of the Changi area as Digger remembers it in 1942/3.
(Chapter 5)

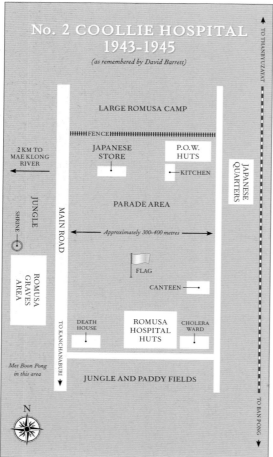

No. 2 COOLLIE HOSPITAL
1943–1945

(as remembered by David Barrett)

TO THANBYUZAYAT

LARGE ROMUSA CAMP

⊦⊦⊦⊦FENCE⊦⊦⊦⊦⊦⊦⊦⊦⊦⊦⊦⊦⊦⊦⊦⊦⊦⊦⊦

2 KM TO
MAE KLONG
RIVER

JAPANESE
STORE

P.O.W.
HUTS

JAPANESE QUARTERS

←— KITCHEN

JUNGLE

SHRINE

MAIN ROAD

PARADE AREA

←— Approximately 300–400 metres —→

FLAG

ROMUSA
GRAVES
AREA

CANTEEN ——

TO KANCHANABURI

DEATH
HOUSE

ROMUSA
HOSPITAL
HUTS

CHOLERA
WARD

Met Boon Pong
in this area

JUNGLE AND PADDY FIELDS

TO BAN PONG

N

Above: Selerang Barracks square on 4 September 1942. *(AWM 132940)* *(Chapter 5)*

Left: This is the layout of No 2 Coolie Hospital at Kanchanaburi as Digger remembers it in 1943/4. The river was about two kilometres away. *(Chapter 7)*

A drawing by Ronald Searle of elephants hauling logs on the railway somewhere near Hintok in 1943/4. *(Chapter 9)*

A drawing by Ronald Searle of POWs working in a cutting near Hintok in 1943/4. *(Chapter 9)*

This bund surrounds Chungkai POW camp just North of Kanchanaburi. It is deeper than the bund the POWs had to build at most camps including at Lop Buri camp. Machine guns were strategically placed to cover these bunds, and there is evidence that the Japanese intended to use them as mass graves after a massacre of the POWs occupying the camp. Such massacres were, it is believed, set to take place towards the end of August 1945, in anticipation of an Allied invasion of the Thailand-Malaya area. *(AWM P00761.019) (Chapter 10)*

Feeding time at Nakhon Nayak, late August 1945. *(Chapter 11)*

Digger, centre, with a few friends.
(Chapter 11)

Nakhon Nayak camp buildings, late August 1945. *(Chapter 11)*

All 16 members of the War Graves Commission Survey party. Left to right – Back row: Sergeant T. Lee (8 Division Provost Company), Private G. H. Kindred (1st Fortress Signals), Sergeant Jack H. Sherman (2/4th Machine Gun Battalion), Acting Warrant Officer 2 Les Cody (in dark glasses; 2/4th Machine Gun Battalion), Padre H. C. F. Babb (ex POW British), Lieutenant J. Eldridge (British), Captain J. Leemon (Australian War Graves Unit), Captain R. K. A. Bruce (Malayan Colonial Force), Sergeant Lloyd Rankin (Australian War Graves Unit); Front row: Leading Aircraftman (RAAF) S. O. Simpson. R. McGregor, E. S. Wheeler, Private D. W. Barrett (Australian Army Medical Corps), Lieutenant G. H. Schroder (Dutch Force), Privat H. R. Lees (2/20th Battalion) and Captain A. R. White (2/26th Battalion). *(AWM P01910.001) (Chapter 13)*

Japanese rail trucks used by the War Graves Commission survey party. The cars had *attap* roofs. *Attap* is the woven leaves of the Nypa palm that grows in coastal areas all over South-East Asia and the Pacific. This was the standard building material used in most POW camps for walls and roofs. *(AWM P00761.049) (Chapter 13)*

Left to right, Eddie Wheeler, Digger and Les Cody at Rinteng in the first week of October 1945. *(AWM P00761.031) (Chapter 14)*

Result of the fishing trip at Brankassi. Sos Simpson holding the largest fish with Mac McGregor and the Japanese train crew. *(AWM P01910.016) (Chapter 14)*

Group portrait of Japanese war crime suspects who may have had information about an Australian POW who was killed by a hammer blow to the head in July 1945. Photograph taken September 1945. *(AWM P01910.004) (Chapter 14)*

The two girls who made Digger and his friend Vern Hansen welcome to Australia when their ship put in to Albany, Western Australia on their return journey in November 1945. If anyone recognises them, please get in touch with the authors. *(Chapter 15)*

APEX CAR RALLY WON BY D. W. BARRETT

FOUR drivers lost their way in the closing stages of the Apex 500 car rally which finished in Maryborough yesterday afternoon.

Cars driven by D. Corser, MacDonald, H. Fittharpe and A. McAuliffe, missed a turn on the last section.

The cars went off course in the stretch through the State Forest near Gympie. Two of these cars abandoned the rally after this mishap.

Provisional winner, with a loss of 22 points, was car No 14, driven by D. W. Barrett.

Barrett said he considered this trial to be the best that Apex had conducted.

It was the first time he had had an opportunity of all night driving in a rally and to both him and his navigator.

He said credit for his car's win must go to W. Siller, his navigator, as it was the navigator who contributed most to any rally.

The innovation of night driving earned praise from all drivers who considered it in-

drivers who survived a loss of points on a stretch of bitumen which proved to be the route's main "hazard" and demanded a low speed limit.

Their "go slow" tactics paid off when other drivers were penalised for exceeding the limit.

Most cars had additional minor mechanical features such as extra speedometers and lighted charts for the benefit of navigators.

A couple of drivers seemed proud of the fact that the only additional "equipment" they had was their navigators.

A small crowd gathered at the starting point on Saturday and again yesterday to see the cars return.

Ken Baynes' red Austin-Healy attracted a good deal of attention from onlookers. This low-slung sports car, hoodless and with sump guards as the

Maryborough Chronicle 4 March 1957 p1

Above: David took part in many car rallies funded by Campbells, his employer. From the *Maryborough Chronicle*, 4 March 1957. *(Chapter 16)*

Above right: The inside front cover photograph of David that appeared in a small booklet published by the Industrial
Public Relations of Australia (Queensland) after the 1966 Ideal Home Show. It was designed to encourage businesses to take part in the 1967 show. *(Chapter 16)*

FOREWORD . . .

Exhibitions of this nature have played their part throughout the world in developing industries and so have fulfilled their role in expanding the economies of these countries.

The Brisbane Ideal Home Show 1966 has created, overall, a good impression. It is in keeping with the impression of a healthy State making tremendous strides in all fields of endeavour.

To all exhibitors who have supported I.P.R. in Queensland, I would like to say, "Thank you". To those who have not yet participated, this booklet is an invitation to join us in helping to develop your own business and the State of Queensland.

D. W. BARRETT,
Queensland Director,
Industrial Public Relations
(Q'ld) Pty. Ltd.

FRONT COVER shows Mr. Joe Box, Past President of the Queensland Master Builders' Association, presenting the Best Stand Award for the 1966 Ideal Home Show to Mr. Hunter Perkins, General Manager of Besser Vibrapac Masonry (Qld) Ltd.

VANCOUVER SUN, JUNE 20, 1986.

Ex-PoWs file claim against Japanese

By NANCY KNICKERBOCKER

Canadian survivors of Japanese wartime prison camps have filed a $13-million claim with the United Nations, charging the Japanese government is bound by international law to make "war crimes" reparations for "gross violations of human rights."

The claim, filed Thursday with the UN sub-committee on human rights in Geneva, has been lauched by the War Amputations of Canada on behalf of the roughly 900 surviving Hong Kong prisoners of war and 200 widows.

Clifford Chadderton, chief executive officer of the War Amps, said Friday that the suffering imposed on the 1,900 Canadians captured by the Japanese violated Geneva Convention principles on treatment of prisoners of war. He added that PoWs held by the Nazis were not treated as badly.

The war amputees are holding their annual general meeting this week at Harrison Hot Springs.

Richmond resident Donald MacPherson was 21 years old that Christmas Day in 1941 when Hong Kong fell and 44 hellish months began.

In an interview, he recalled that during his years of internment his weight fell from 170 to 103 pounds.

Chadderton said $10 per day of incarceration per man would be fair compensation. Most PoWs were held for about 1,000 days.

After Canada and Japan signed a peace treaty in 1951, the vets received $1 per day compensation paid from liquidation of Japanese government property in Canada. The Canadian government later paid them a further 50 cents per day.

DONALD MacPHERSON: veteran holds "lunch bucket," chopsticks used during imprisonment

STEEVE BOSC

A cutting from the *Vancouver Sun* that got David and George Stevenson so interested, 20 June 1987. *(Chapter 17)*

Barbaric, says ex-POW making $500 million claim

Move to sue Japan for war atrocities

by HEDLEY THOMAS

A GOLD Coast group is leading a move to sue the Japanese Government for more than $500 million for atrocities to Australia's estimated 21,000 former prisoners of war.

And the move is tipped as likely to be approved at federal level.

The Gold Coast branch of the Australian Ex-Prisoners of War Association started proceedings in the wake of a similar Canadian claim which is now before the United Nations.

Ambition

Mr David Barrett, 65, chairman of the association's war claim committee, said yesterday he could never forgive or forget the Japanese for the way they treated their captives.

And he warned that the huge amount of Japanese investment in Queensland was part of the Japanese race's ambition to one day control the world.

When Mr Barrett was 19 he was captured by the Japanese and remained a prisoner of war for 3½ years. He worked on the Burma railway line.

"Even if we got $1 million each, it still wouldn't justify what went on," he said. "The actions of the Japanese in the war were barbaric."

Mr Barrett said he and thousands of fellow Australians suffered bashings, starvation, untreated dysentery and numerous untreated fevers.

And he believes the Japanese Government would rather pay the reparations claim than risk renewed and damaging international publicity over the atrocities.

"We think we might shame them into paying," he said.

A successful claim would give veterans $20 for every day spent incarcerated.

On that scale Mr Barrett would receive about $25,000. Widows of former POWs would also be compensated.

A motion submitted by the Gold Coast branch and carried by the Queensland State Council was prepared by Mr Barrett, fellow POW George Stevenson and Surfers Paradise solicitor Peter Collas, who was a prisoner in Germany.

Mr Collas said the issue could not be properly pursued until passed at federal level. However, Mr Barrett said he was certain that would happen 'in the near future'.

"Both the local and state bodies have approved the motion unanimously and it becomes a goer if the federal body approves," said Mr Collas.

"Then we would have to go to the United Nations with evidence.

Brutal

"It is my belief that there is no legal obligation (which would force Japan to pay if the United Nations so directed) but it is a matter of losing face.

"It is a matter of diplomatic concern when a country ignores the United Nations."

The motion says in part:

"This association of ex-POWs is concerned that the heinous, inhuman, brutal and completely unlawful treatment imposed upon Australian POWs by the Japanese military authorities during World War Two has not received recognition or acknowledgement by way of compensation or in any other way on the part of the Japanese nation.

"This association is of the opinion that the bashings, tortures and murderous atrocities imposed upon Australian POWs, which brought about the premature death of 7700 and broke the health of the remaining 13,800 who managed to survive, deserves condemnation of the Japanese by the world community of nations.

"With this objective in mind, this association does on behalf of all Australian POWs who underwent captivity by the Japanese in World War Two — or who have died since — embark on the necessary action to claim compensation from Japan for the unlawful acts so wilfully perpetrated."

Former POW David Barrett with a copy of the World War Two Japanese surrender document ... 'Even if we got $1 million each, it still wouldn't justify what went on'.

ALLIED EX-JAPANESE
P.O.W.

The Qld. Ex P.O.W. Reparation Committee is seeking compensation from the Japanese Government on behalf of ex P.O.W., their widows or next of kin, by submission to the United Nations Commission on Human Rights.

Any person who believes they have a claim, should contact the committee as claims can only be made on the official form obtainable by sending a stamped self-addressed envelope to the address below.

ALL CLAIMS MUST BE SUBMITTED BY 31 APRIL 1989.

Qld. Ex P.O.W. Reparation Committee P.O. Box 1548 SOUTHPORT QLD. 4215

Donations to help the committee in their submission would be gratefully appreciated.

L9546C 0712

Above: An example of the publicity organised by the Reparations Committee, *Gold Coast Bulletin*, 26 March 1987. *(Chapter 18)*

Left: An advertisement that appeared in the *Courier Mail* and other papers on 15 October 1988. *(Chapter 18)*

REPARATION CLAIM FORM

QUEENSLAND EX. P.O.W. REPARATION COMMITTEE

FOR EX. P.O.W.S. THEIR WIDOWS OR IMMEDIATE NEXT OF KIN

NAME. *STATHAM Née* .... *Vivian* ......
   BULLWINKEL
    surname   christian names

ADDRESS .... *32 TYRELL ST NEDLANDS W.A. 6009* ......

RANK *Sister (Lt)* REG.No. *VFX 61330* UNIT. *2/13 Aust. General Hospital*

1. WHEN CAPTURED *16.2.42* WHERE CAPTURED ... *Banka Is.* ......

2. COUNTRIES OF IMPRISONMENT ... *Sumatra & Banka Is* ......

    ....

3. DID YOU EXPERIENCE:
   TORTURE, BASHINGS OR OTHER CRUELTY .... *Yes*
   IMPRISONMENT UNDER IMPROPER CONDITIONS .... *Yes*
   SLAVE LABOUR ON ENEMY WORKS OR OPERATIONS .... —
   EXPOSED TO GUNFIRE, BOMBINGS OR OTHER HAZARDS .... *Yes*
   TRANSPORTATION UNDER IMPROPER CONDITIONS .... *Yes*
   FAILURE TO SUPPLY PROPER MEDICAL CARE, FOOD, CLOTHING, QUARTERS.
   .... *Yes*

4. DID YOU SUFFER ANY DISEASES .... NAME SAME ....
   ... *Malaria, dysentry, tinea* ......
   ... *Banka Is Fever, malnutrition* ......

5. STATE ANY SADISTIC TREATMENT RECEIVED ... *Shot in back.*
   ... *Only survivor of massacre of 21 nurses on*
   beach, Banka Is. Japanese machine gunned
   us from behind as we were forced to wade
   into the sea.

6. FURTHER COMMENTS IF NECESSARY ....
   ....
   ....
   ....

WIDOWS AND NEXT OF KIN NEED ONLY FILL IN SECTION 1.

I AUTHORISE THE QUEENSLAND EX. P.O.W. REPARATIONS COMMITTEE TO FILE
A CLAIM WITH THE U.N.O. FOR REPARATIONS FROM THE JAPANESE GOVERNMENT
ON MY BEHALF.

A PROCESSING FEE OF $10.00 MUST BE REMITTED WITH THIS FORM $. *10* ....
DONATION TO REPARATION COMMITTEE FOR SUBMISSION TO THE U.N. $. *20* ....

SIGNATURE .. *P. Statham* ..... WITNESS *Mr R Carter* ....

DATED AT *20th* THIS DAY OF *December* 19̶8̶8̶ 89
PLEASE RETURN WITH COPY OF DISCHARGE/RECORD OF SERVICE TO:

      THE SECRETARY,
      QLD. EX. P.O.W. REPARATIONS COMMITTEE,
      P.O. BOX 58,
      EAGLE HEIGHTS, QLD. 4271

Vivian Bullwinkel's form claiming the right to reparations from the Japanese,
December 1989. *(Chapter 19)*

Japanese feel unwanted

From STEVE ROUS
in Tokyo

THE Australian Government was yesterday urged to clear up the confusion about whether Japanese investment was still welcomed.

The International Transport and Tourism Bureau's public relations director, Mr Kosuke Shibata, said an anti-Japanese sentiment had become visible a year ago and was persisting.

"It is up to your Government to clarify the matter and make it clear to all investors," Mr Shibata said.

"The Australian Government has given us the impression that they welcome Japanese investment, but we see a very different story in the newspapers.

"It's getting to be very vague now what Australia wants."

Mr Shibata said he had felt that Australia needed more capital investment from overseas and would benefit from it.

"Some Australian people, we gather, object to Japanese investment.

"Just recently there was a very big newspaper article about the Nara resort planned for Sydney Harbor having been turned down by Australia.

"The situation has become awkward and it's not clear."

The Nara Construction Co Ltd announced last week it was reconsidering two projects it had planned for Queensland after the Treasurer, Mr Keating, rejected Nara's planned Woolloomooloo Bay hotel project.

Mr Shibata said Australia was attracting 50-70 percent more Japanese tourists each year.

"But they must feel welcome if you want them to tell other Japanese to visit Australia."

In approximate Australian dollars it costs $1.40 for a daily newspaper, $5 for a loaf of bread and $8 for a stubbie of beer. The flag fall in a Tokyo taxi is about $4.70 and a breakfast of bacon and eggs with coffee and toast costs $21.

SECRET CONFIDENTIAL

PROPOSAL

to

ASIA-PACIFIC FOUNDATION

for

THE
TROPICAL MEDICAL
AND
HEALTH INSTITUTE

at

JAMES COOK UNIVERSITY OF NORTH QUEENSLAND
TOWNSVILLE

Contact: Professor R M Golding
Vice-Chancellor
Phone: (077) 814375
Fax: (077) 251594

Above: Japanese investors were confused about the message being sent to them by Australia and in the long run this probably influenced the Australian Government's decision to pay out the POWs. From the *Courier Mail*, 15 March 1989. *(Chapter 19)*

Left: David received this document in early 1993 from a friend who still had contact with the Reparations Committee. *(Chapter 20)*

PoWs lose court fight

TOKYO — A court yesterday rejected a lawsuit by World War II prisoners of war and civilian internees demanding an apology and compensation from the Japanese Government.

The decision by Tokyo District Court on a lawsuit by six groups representing thousands of Australian, New Zealand, British and American prisoners of war was in line with past rulings in favor of the government.

"I spit on the doorstep of the Diet (Japanese parliament). There's no justice in this country," British former POW Arthur Titherington said minutes after the ruling.

In a short judgment Judge Shigeki Inoue rejected a 1995 suit demanding an apology and $34,540 compensation for each detainee.

Representatives of the POWs, who travelled to Tokyo from around the world to hear the judgment, vowed to fight on.

"We will review and respond to this case. It is not unexpected," Martin Day, a former detainee, said.

If the ruling had gone in favor of the POWs it would have cost Japan about $707 million in compensation.

Japan has held it is not liable for compensation because all World War II claims were settled in 1951 under the San Francisco peace agreements.

Dutch POWs launched a separate lawsuit in 1994, demanding the same

Above: The Australians mentioned in this law suit against the Japanese were civilian internees not the Reparations Committee. 27 November 1998. *(Chapter 20)*

Right: David always saw it as his duty to keep all the claimants informed about how their money was being spent regardless of the wishes of the Reparations Committee, *Gold Coast Bulletin*, 16 August 1993. *(Chapter 20)*

Funding switch triggers outburst

by TRENT PORTER

THE Queensland Ex-Prisoners of War Association yesterday was accused of diverting funds raised to finance a reparations claim to a proposed tropical medicine institute.

The flak came on Peace Day, the memorial day held for comrades in arms who died in Japanese captivity during World War Two.

Former Reparations Committee chairman David Barrett said $160,000 raised between 1986-1990 to fund a personal reparations claim against the Japanese Government were diverted without members' consent to a proposed Japanese-funded research unit at James Cook University.

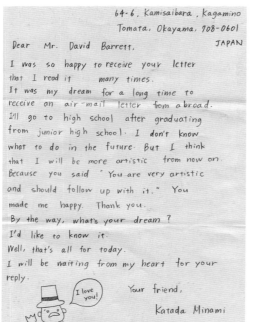

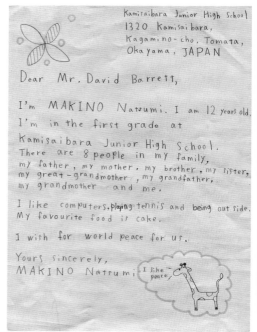

Letter to David from Kitada Minami, a student of Mariko Matsuo's, in reply to a letter from David, December 2011. *(Chapter 21)*

Letter to David from 12-year-old Makino Natrumi, a student of Mariko Matsuo's, December 2011. *(Chapter 21)*

Drawings such as this one were done by second or third year primary school children, students of Mariko Matsuo, on their visit to Thailand and upon meeting with David in 1995. *(Chapter 21)*

moved twelve kilometres south, to a large camp at Tha Muang. Unfortunately, this meant the end for the Filthy Seven as well as the two forces.

Digger was sent east to Lop Buri, in Thailand. He was to serve as a medical orderly for a group of about 200 POWs who were building an airfield.

Chapter 10
Relative Respite

LOP BURI WAS a full day's journey by truck from Tha Muang. It took a convoy of several trucks to transport the 200 POWs east to their new destination in central Thailand. It was a long journey but much easier than the last one Digger had experienced – from Changi to Kanchanaburi.

The men were carried over very rough roads, through thick jungle interspersed with paddy fields and villages, past lakes and over slow rivers in the flat lowlands of Thailand. Lop Buri was a small town in central Thailand with the occasional permanent material structure, but most of its buildings had the ubiquitous split-bamboo walls and thatched *attap* palm roofs.

Their destination was a few kilometres out of Lop Buri, in a large area that had once been paddy field. The men saw a small group of very dilapidated huts, which the Japanese guards indicated was to be their new home.

In this group of prisoners there were no commissioned officers and no medical officers, although there were some non-commissioned officers (NCOs). When K Force and L Force were disbanded, all commissioned officers were separated from the other ranks, and most of the medical officers were sent to other Japanese-occupied areas. It turned out that Digger was the only man left in the group who had any real understanding of things medical. His job, it seemed, was to look after the health of the group.

In general, conditions at Lop Buri appeared to be a lot better than at Kanchanaburi. The Japanese organised everything through the prisoner NCOs, and this system worked well. It was quickly discovered that these Japanese guards acted very differently from those at Kanchananburi. They were not overly aggressive and gave reasonable orders. While the humiliating bowing, scraping and saluting was still insisted upon, these guards' actions demonstrated more empathy for the plight of the POWs.

Over time, the Allied POWs learned that these Japanese guards had served as soldiers at the front in locations such as Papua New Guinea, the Philippines and Burma. Serving in battle had obviously bred a little more tolerance and understanding into them. The guards on the railway, on the other hand, had never served on the front. Digger reckoned that many probably regretted missing out on the kudos associated with being in battle, and so took their frustration out on the POWs.

The guards at Lop Buri listened to the men's requests for materials to fix up the huts, and to Digger's for basic medical supplies. They did what they could to help. The rations were by no means luxurious, but food was available in greater quantity and better quality than it had ever been since the surrender in 1942. Gradually, most POWs even put on a little weight.

The routine in the camp was very similar to that at the railway. There was a morning parade, then large work parties went off to labour on the nearby airfield. Other work parties were engaged in digging a large 'bund' around the camp – a trench more than a metre deep and a metre wide, with the earth thrown up on the outside. Still others were constructing storerooms, guard posts, latrines and the like. The Lop Buri POW camp grew very quickly.

Although the food was better and malnutrition diseases less of a problem, malaria and tropical ulcers were still rife. Digger lacked the rank and the qualifications to be called 'doctor', but he had everything else that was required. He had patients with very genuine diseases, he had access to basic medical supplies, and most importantly he was the only medical help they had. All the POWs regarded him as the camp doctor; some even began calling him 'Doc'.

Prisoner of war or not, Digger began to enjoy his existence at Lop Buri. He had a job to do; he had quinine and M&B 693; he was his own boss — as much as one could be, in the circumstances; the food wasn't too bad; and he was now certain that he would survive the war, no matter how long it took. The Japanese sometimes even took him into Lop Buri and provided him with money to buy the drugs and supplies that he needed.

Perhaps Digger's most important work was in treating tropical ulcers. If left untreated, a tropical ulcer could grow from something the size of a pinhead to a large open and infected sore in no more than a few days. The usual treatment was to clean out the ulcer with a curette, a special scraping tool. Not having one of these, Digger used a small sterile spoon, which he sharpened for the purpose. Once the wound was cleaned, a dressing of crushed M&B 693 tablets and a sterile bandage would be applied.

Digger did his best to educate the men, stressing that prevention was the best treatment. If they could not avoid breaking the skin during work, then treatment with M&B 693 must be undertaken immediately. Only this would avoid the very painful scraping procedure with Digger's curette. But there were always a few cases of men who left the treatment too late, and no matter how Digger tried the ulcer still grew.

Occasionally, more drastic measures were required. One man had an ulcer between his smallest two toes; the scraping treatment was not working well because it was so difficult to get at. Digger told him straight that he could remove the small toe at the joint, and it was likely the wound would heal up well after that. He explained that he could probably get the anaesthetic novocaine, which he would inject around the base of the toe to eliminate the pain.

As he explained this to the poor bloke, Digger appeared much more confident than he felt. He well knew the necessity for the 'doctor' to present a confident and calm presence. As for the surgery, well, he knew he had to give it a go. The last person he had 'operated' on was a corpse in the mortuary at Changi, but he did not tell his patient this.

Digger explained the situation to the Japanese, and within a day he was shopping in Lop Buri for what he needed: a scalpel, some suturing thread, a suitable curved sewing needle, a new injection needle and of course some novocaine. The Thais with whom he did business were very sympathetic. In fact, Digger had to insist that they accept payment for the materials he was buying.

Digger organised for an operating table to be built by a few POWs, who also agreed to help with the operation. Digger explained very clearly to the helpers – out of the patient's earshot – that he was unsure of just how well the novocaine would work. Their one and only job was to hold the bloke still on the table, no matter what happened.

When the time came for the operation, Digger explained to the patient that he had to be held down because the table had been so badly made that it was unstable; it had to be steady for him to work. The poor bloke probably didn't understand, or perhaps he didn't care at that point. He was as white as a sheet and just nodded his agreement.

The helpers took hold of him, and Digger began to sterilise the skin around the toe. He injected the novocaine, and soon was removing the toe at the bottom joint.

The operation went perfectly. The bloke never said a thing or even attempted to move. It took Digger more than half an hour, but he was able to thoroughly clean the ulcerated area. He didn't know how long it would have taken a real doctor, but he was glad it was over. As the patient explained to Digger afterwards, all he felt during the operation was movement. He had felt no pain whatsoever.

Digger told him that all that was required now was to ensure that they kept any infection at bay. This also went successfully and the patient healed in no time.

About a month later, towards the end of June 1945, Digger faced a more serious problem. A patient had an ulcer on the top of his foot and well into his ankle, and no matter what treatment Digger tried it just got worse. Eventually, despite all Digger's efforts, the wound turned gangrenous. The smell was terrible as Digger removed the latest dressing.

'Am I going to die?' the man asked Digger.

'No, not if I can help it, mate,' Digger replied. 'But you know what we have to do, don't you?'

The patient nodded.

Digger set about gathering all the materials he needed for his second operation. He dreaded it, and felt that he had just about had enough of doctoring. This was the last straw. Handing out quinine and temporarily curing bouts of malaria was all very well, but sawing through a bloke's leg was another thing entirely. What if he died? Digger swore that when he got home he would do anything other than doctoring.

In his earlier days in the army, Digger had hoped eventually to become a doctor, but he had seen so much pain, suffering and death that this ambition had dissipated. He was quite happy to do what he could for his fellow prisoners in the meantime, but studying medicine was no longer his long-term plan. *Perhaps something with more immediate reward*, he thought.

Again Digger went to the supplier in Lop Buri, who this time refused point blank to take any money for the materials. He made sure that Digger had everything he could possibly need, including more novocaine than he thought would be required. Best be on the safe side, he advised, and Digger tended to agree. Digger got a suitable carpenter's saw from the Japanese at the camp and had it sharpened.

From his experiences in the mortuary at Changi, and in helping Dr Fagan in Kanchanaburi, Digger knew exactly what he had to do. He knew what peeling back skin actually felt like, what it felt like to cut through bone and sew up skin. He knew he had to keep enough skin to cover the stumps of the two leg bones. With Dr Fagan he had learned what to do with the blood vessels and nerves.

Digger had watched two similar operations at Kanchanaburi. One bloke had lived and one had died from infection and shock. His patient was reasonably healthy and in relatively good shape, having lived at the Lop Buri camp for the past two months.

This time, Digger needed to tie a tourniquet around the patient's leg. He had a few more helpers for this operation, including one whom he trusted enough to hold the ends of the blood vessels as he tied them off, but apart from that and the massive doses of novocaine he injected into the patient's leg, the procedure was very similar to the toe operation.

And, like the previous operation, this one went according to plan. The patient was moaning a lot but Digger was able to shut the noise out and concentrate on what he was doing. He removed the lower part of the man's leg, made sure the blood vessels and nerves were safe, and sewed the skin together to form a stump.

Once the anaesthetic wore off, the patient was in a great deal of pain. Nevertheless, he seemed to be very pleased to be rid of his 'stinking foot', as he called it. Digger treated him very carefully with M&B 693, ensuring that no infection was allowed to take hold, and the man improved daily.

As good as life was at Lop Buri, all the men really thought about was the end of the war and home. They all knew that peace was very close, but there was a great deal of uncertainty about how the war would end. Would the Americans invade Thailand and free them? Or would they continue to bomb the camps, as they had been doing, ever more frequently? Would the Japs give up? Everyone knew they were taking a beating in Burma and in the Pacific, and that bombing in Japan was also now very heavy.

Late in the afternoon of 16 August 1945, Digger had occasion to visit the latrines. As he carefully lowered his skinny frame into a suitable position over the hole in the bamboo slats above the pit, his thoughts turned to home and the relative comfort of a real toilet seat. What would such a seat feel like? He suddenly realised that it had been so long since he had used one that he was unable to conjure up the memory of it.

Would they ever escape this bloody existence? For a second Digger felt hopelessness well up within him, but he quickly brushed aside these desperate thoughts and his more natural analytical and optimistic response to adversity kicked in.

A Japanese surrender must be possible, he knew. But even the more reasonable guards at Lop Buri would do exactly as the Emperor ordered, and so all in the camp lived with the knowledge that their captors were capable of anything. A Japanese surrender would bring escape, but many believed that it might not be in the form they were all hoping for.

Most of the men had been POWs for more than three and a half years. Until their time at Lop Buri, they had all endured regular beatings and daily humiliation; many had experienced torture of a more specialised nature. Everyone knew of at least one summary execution. Those who had survived to this point also knew individual guards and camp officers in the railway camps guilty of carrying out, or of ordering, such treatment. Would they be allowed to live with this knowledge when the war ended?

The men knew that jungle would soon reclaim the camp area once it was shut down. The earth of the bund would fill in the trench and cover their bodies. In time, a circle of bones would be the only evidence of the terrible crimes committed here. There would be no one to carry their story home, to tell of the bravery, the deprivation, the humiliation or the sacrifice, because they would all pay the highest price.[1]

Well, not while I'm still alive and producing a turd, thought Digger. He smiled as he reminded himself of his mates' survival humour at Kanchanaburi, and he started to use the handful of grass he had carefully chosen and carried into the latrine.

Digger was interrupted by a Japanese voice coming from behind the latrine. In imperfect but clear English, it delivered a simple statement: 'War finish.'

This was not the first time Digger had heard such a message. Some guards had taken a sadistic pleasure in making such announcements, particularly six months previously, when they were all in the railway camps. Many guards revelled in the momentary delight on the faces of the prisoners who had not experienced such deception before, or who were so desperate and ground down from illness, torture, starvation and sheer hard work that their minds had suspended any notion of reason.

This time, however, Digger knew that the timing was right. The plain message delivered by one guard at the latrine was very different from the same announcement made by a group engaged in brutal mockery.

'Is that right?' he asked from his side of the screen.

'True,' came the reply.

Perhaps the attitudes of the guards had changed because they knew the war was coming to an end. They seemed less confident. Many now tended to ignore minor breaches of discipline, such as a failure to salute, whereas that would once have earned you a severe bashing. It therefore seemed most unlikely that this was a trick.

But why had the guard told him this? It was either a sign of impending disaster or of imminent release. There was only one way to check for sure.

PART 3

Locating the Graves

Chapter 11

Freedom

FIVE GUARDS WERE on duty at the entrance to the Lop Buri camp. They were sitting on a three-tiered hardwood terrace-like structure, complete with an *attap* palm roof and open sides. They all held rifles, with the butts resting on the step below. The terrace was four or five metres long, with access steps up one side. Similar structures served as the guardhouses at the entrance of almost every Japanese camp on the railway.

Digger walked from the latrine to the camp gate, all the time looking directly at the guards. He knew they had seen him before he drew level with them, and he expected to hear the usual Japanese command: '*Kora!*' The word could mean 'stop' or 'come here', depending on the speaker's body language. In the railway camps it was usually followed up with a rifle butt in the gut. But now he heard nothing, and the guards didn't move.

Digger slowly walked to the gate, and then kept on walking. When he was ten yards outside the gate, he stopped and turned around. He looked directly at the guards, who were still lounging on the 'terrace' as though they were at a cricket match. All of them avoided his gaze.

This could only mean one thing. Digger didn't know if it was worry or relief that he felt, but he felt his heart flutter a little as he walked back into the camp.

A small group of men was waiting for him outside the huts. They had seen what had happened and were now as excited as he was. There was no need to explain or analyse what had happened. Everyone knew instinctively that the war was over, although their fears of what might happen next weren't yet allayed.

For the past few months, as rumours of the end of the war had spread around the camp, the men had been busy preparing. A decision had been made that if the worst happened, they would not go quietly. If ordered to stand by the bund to be executed, they would fight. They would be armed with the weapons they had become so expert in handling: picks, shovels, hammers and crowbars. If it happened during the night, when the tools were locked away, then they'd take up the sharpened bamboo spears that they'd secreted around the camp. The POWs were much fitter now after six months at Lop Buri. They would be no pushover.

There was an eerie calm about the camp. In deep but quiet conversations, the men theorised about what would happen next. The guards stayed in their quarters; it was as if they were avoiding the men. There had been no arrivals of vehicles or extra troops that might have heralded danger. But the homemade weapons were at the ready, just in case.

Very gradually, and without letting ridiculous thoughts such as home or loved ones enter their heads, the men continued to talk late into the afternoon. A quiet but recognisable excitement spread among them. As darkness came, another thought surfaced. Rumours had circulated that when the war ended there would be opportunities for revenge. It was understood that for a period of twenty-four hours after the surrender, Australians would be immune from prosecution if they beat up a few guards. As much as many of them would have liked to take advantage of this opportunity, the Japanese were still armed. At this camp, everyone wanted simply to get home. The truly sadistic guards had all been left behind on the railway.

Some Australians elsewhere did take advantage of this supposed gesture from the authorities, whether or not it was real. In Saigon, for example, the celebrations were great when the POWs heard about the two atom bombs being dropped on Hiroshima and Nagasaki. Jack Noel Taylor of the Royal Norfolks 4th Battalion, 18th Division, wrote the following in his diary:

> When the realization came that the Japs had surrendered, a few tears were shed by us, but not the Australians, they went in search of our guards. The beatings and abuse were too fresh to be forgotten, and all the pent-up emotions of the last few years were let out, many guards lost their lives over the next few days.[1]

At Lop Buri that night, the men did not head to bed as they normally would. Lights could be seen from the Jap quarters, and they knew all the guards were talking. Suddenly there was a burst of activity.

'What the fuck are they up to now?' said a voice in the darkness, echoing what they were all thinking.

'Right, let's get the bastards,' said another.

Hearts beat faster and hands all reached for the weaponry.

'Hold on, hold on,' said Digger. 'Just let's see what they're up to.'

Suddenly, the guards emerged from their buildings. They were not carrying their rifles but boxes of papers. The Allies' hearts returned to their normal rhythm. After some toing and froing, the guards started a large bonfire. They were obviously destroying the camp records. This proved beyond doubt that the war was over.

'I thought we'd had it for sure,' said one guy. His voice expressed the relief they were all feeling.

Gunfire was heard in the distance. Initially, the Australians thought that the poor buggers at a nearby camp were copping it, but these were just single shots. There was no machine-gun fire. It took a further few seconds for the men to work out what they were hearing.

'Jesus! They're shooting themselves,' someone said. 'Fucking great! I hope the bastards burn in hell!'

At Lop Buri, however, the guards were still preoccupied with burning their paperwork. Digger and a few mates headed towards the camp storehouse. The mood had very quickly turned from apprehension about the future to celebration of the present.

The storehouse was on short stumps, about half a metre off the ground. It was a relatively easy matter to crawl under it, from where they could prise up the bamboo flooring. They climbed inside. The grog was in small demijohns, and the men manoeuvred a couple down under the floor and carried them back into the welcome arms of their excited mates. In the centre of their compound, they made up a bowl of 'punch' using the grog and some coconut water.

To the sound of the intermittent distant gunfire, the men at Lop Buri camp got very drunk for the first time in three or four years. The pain from their ulcers, the cramps from their diarrhoea and the fever from their malaria were now more bearable than ever before. They would soon see home again.

> You have no idea the feeling of relief that we experienced, knowing that our term of imprisonment was over. It was like a whole load of worry had been lifted off our minds and been replaced by this feeling of great anticipation about the future. We weren't very sure about what was going to happen but we just knew it was going to be great.

These feelings got stronger over the next few days. There was no more work – it was the first holiday we had had in years! We no longer had to salute the bastards. In fact, some of the blokes would get some amusement by making the Japanese salute them. It was funny, but I – who had been so determined to get revenge – didn't really feel like it. That may have been because, in relative terms, these particular guards had been good to us. It was the bastards at Kanchanaburi who I would have liked to put on the spit.

It was amazing how the guards' demeanour had changed. They became deferential and completely obedient. You could ask them to light your cigarette. In fact, I tried it out and was able to order one guard to hand his cigarettes around our group. I just knew in the back of my mind that this ability we victors now had would come in handy very soon. I was even able to order around Japanese officers.

On the third day, the Japs received orders and provided transport for the 200 or so men who were at the Lop Buri camp. With their meagre possessions in hand, they clambered onto the trucks amid much jostling and joking. It was like a Sunday bus outing only hundreds of times better. They were taken two hours south to a large transit camp at Nakhon Nayok, about 120 kilometres north of Bangkok.

At the Nakhon Nayok camp, chaos reigned. There were at least a thousand Allied men and very few officers; if there were any, they were certainly taking no responsibility for camp organisation or discipline. And anyway, the men were all so exhilarated to be free that any expectation that they would respond to an order was futile.

Previously, at the Kanchanaburi camp, many of the officers had been doctors, and there had been few officers other than doctors on the railway too. The reason for this was probably that the Japs had generally observed the part of the Geneva Convention that said officers should not be required to do physical work. Digger's view was that the Japs probably considered Allied officers more bother than they were worth; they had their own engineers and supervisors. Digger also suspected that the Allied officers had been transferred out of the camps so that it was easier to manipulate and kill the men, if it came to that.

Then came another American air raid. For years prior to the end of the war, the Americans had been bombing the railway and the work camps in central Thailand. As soon as the men heard planes approaching, they ran for the ditch they had so carefully prepared around the camp. It was impossible to think that they might have survived life in hell for three and half years only to die from an attack by the American Air Force. Many men had died from similar attacks in the recent past; as much as they welcomed the strife the raids brought to the Japanese, they feared for the deaths they inevitably inflicted on the POWs.

But this air raid was different. As the two four-engine planes came in low, their bomb bays opened. The crowd of men panicked, and everyone scattered or hit the ground where they were. Hands covered ears to protect against the expected deafening explosions. But there were no explosions.

Heads were cautiously raised, and they realised that what had been dropped were 'storepedoes' – supply containers. Constructed from timber, these were cylinders about six feet long and fifteen inches or so in diameter. They were designed to slide along the ground when they landed, but more often they burst open on impact and all sorts of goodies were strewn across the ground.

The men were soon gathering up these American gifts, which included food and drugs. Over the next couple of days there were more drops. One particularly intriguing piece of technology that came floating down from on high was the self-heating milk drink. This was a tin of milk that had two lids. When you took the first lid off, the whole can began to get warm, and after a minute or so you took off the second lid and could drink it. Closer inspection revealed that a clever chemical reaction powered the heating.

'Well, well,' said Digger. 'I wonder if they'll deliver these to the door every morning!'

While scrambling for food, Digger bumped into Max Wall. Digger hadn't seen Max since Changi. They shook hands and clapped each other on the back. They did not hug, nor did they cry, but neither could they find any words. It was a full two minutes before they could congratulate each other on their survival.

Later that evening, having recovered from their initial emotion, Max and Digger spent a good two hours talking about their many common friends whom they would never see again. They talked of when they died, how they died and where they were buried. These were hard stories to tell, and this time both men had tears rolling down their faces in the dark. They were safe. They were so relieved that they had survived, and yet glad that they could hide this emotion. All over the camp, friends from the past were meeting and similar stories were being swapped, some happy but most sad. And all over the camp the crying was done quietly.

The next day, Digger, Max and a few other mates were sitting in their open-sided hut and talking of how they might be rescued when there was a sudden crash above them. They jumped aside as an American soldier – still attached to his parachute – burst straight through the *attap* palm roof.

This was the first Allied military person the prisoners had seen since their capture. They were delighted, even if the American was a little shaken. He carried news of their imminent departure to nearby

Bangkok. Billets had been organised, and apparently all Australians from the Nakhon Nayok camp were to be transported to the Chamber of Commerce building.

'Who cares about where,' Max said. 'Just set me down anywhere in Bangkok and I'll be fine.'

'That costs money, my friend,' Digger replied. Already his thoughts were turning to how to solve this problem.

The American was carrying a camera that had been slightly damaged in the landing. Digger persuaded him to donate his camera to the group. The POWs, having lived with so little over the years, were inventive and self-sufficient in all manner of things; Digger knew that fixing a camera would be easy for them. Digger realised it was a little late to begin a photographic record, but he was determined to document their existence.

In addition to the 'storepedoes', there were also parachute drops of food over the next few days. Almost immediately a trade in parachute cloth started up with the locals. The men dismantled the parachutes and the locals bought the cloth, the cords and every other part. They used them to manufacture very handsome nylon shirts.

The next visitor from above turned out to be doubly profitable for the men at the Nakhon Nayok camp. As soon as the American landed, a number of laughing and happy ex-POWs surrounded him. They had his parachute almost totally cut up before he could even take it off, and he panicked. He drew his revolver and fired it into the air. 'This parachute is American GI equipment,' he declared in a Southern accent. 'So just back off, boys!'

All that his outburst accomplished was to change the happy group around him into an angry anti-American mob. The GI was quickly relieved of a pair of exquisite pearl-handled revolvers, which no doubt added considerably to someone's Bangkok fund, and he was told in no uncertain terms that the trade in parachute cloth would continue for as long as Uncle Sam allowed it to float down from on high.

Australian planes also flew over the camp, delivering food and medicines. The men recognised the DC-3s because they flew with their doors open; the crew could be seen kicking the packages out. One day a DC-3 came in really low, with its doors open as usual. When the men looked up, they saw a girl in the doorway. She was being held tight by three airmen to prevent her from falling out, and she lifted her skirt and danced and pranced about, waving to her very appreciative audience below.

'Christ, she's got no knickers on!' said one soldier, his neck craned back.

'That's just your imagination working overtime,' someone shouted back.

But there was more hollering and whistling than had ever before been heard on the railway. The men could not have wished for a better present.

In early September 1945, the Australians left the Nakhon Nayok camp early one morning and travelled by truck to Nong Pladuk, and then continued on to Bangkok. There, they were taken to the Chamber of Commerce building.

Digger and Max had discussed in detail what they would do when they got to Bangkok, and they decided there and then to put their plan into action. They took one look at the palliasses so thoughtfully supplied for them and decided that this did not meet their expectations of civilisation after three and half years of slavery. They had a better idea.

They took off into the town. They had very little money and were clothed in American cast-offs, but they had determined that, after their experiences, they were owed a great deal of money by the Japanese.

There were Japanese camps all over Bangkok; it was clear they had intended to be there for a while. It had been their head-quarters for the whole of Thailand, and now it was the centre of the Allies' attention. All Japanese within the city had been disarmed.

Max and Digger knew, from their experiences of the last few weeks, that the Japanese attitude to Australians, Americans and all Allied personnel was now strictly subservient – particularly if they were approached with a confident and dominant swagger. The boot was simply now on the other foot. Digger and Max had talked long and often about this; now they hoped like hell that they were right.

Spotting a Japanese camp, Digger and Max did not hesitate. They confidently marched through the gate without a word being exchanged. The Japanese guards were avoiding eye contact – a very good sign. They walked around the camp for a while, getting their bearings. They were particularly interested in transport and office buildings – there were plenty of both.

They very soon found what they were looking for: a medium-sized truck, easy to drive. They climbed into the truck and – after getting it started with a little difficulty – drove it up to the door of the nearest office. Just as confidently, they got down from the truck, opened the office door, and with gestures and in commanding voices began ordering the Japanese soldiers about. 'Get the furniture on the fucking truck – speedo, speedo!' They pointed to chairs, desks and tables. Within a few minutes, the truck was loaded and ready to go.

Digger and Max climbed back into the truck and drove it and its load past the guards, who again looked the other way. They headed into the heart of Bangkok, driving around until they found a busy street market. Finding an area that did not hinder the flow of the passing traffic, they stopped and placed a 'for sale' sign, in English, on a piece of cardboard on the side of the truck.

We sat down, lit a smoke and only then had a good look around. The first thing we noticed was that we were not the only ones at this caper. We could see four or five others of our kind – mostly Australians, by the look of them – doing exactly as we were. We could see tyres, typewriters, carpets and much more being sold by members of our long-suffering but eventually victorious Allied force. *Well*, I thought, *good on you, boys*. To Max I just said, 'I think we get first prize for a truckload of furniture.'

Max laughed and left me there as chief salesman, and he took off to chat to the others scattered around the market. He returned after about twenty minutes and explained that one was an American, but all the rest were Aussies. They were all just looking for the price of a good root. Max and I, on the other hand, were looking for a bit more – in addition, of course!

Stealing from the enemy and selling their gear was illegal, according to some rule or other. Max and I knew that – we weren't stupid. The British were probably too bloody scared of their officers to try such a trick, but we just didn't give a rat's arse. These Jap bastards owed us so much, we figured, so we were just taking a little on account. No bugger was going to stop us.

We were prepared to stay by the truck for as long as it took – well into the evening, at least – but within an hour a Thai bloke approached us. It was difficult because he spoke little English and we knew just a few words of Thai. He offered us a ridiculously low price – hardly enough for a couple of days in a hotel, as far as we knew, and we wanted at least two weeks' accommodation and enough pocket money for a great time.

It took a good ten minutes for the buyer to realise that we were selling the truck as well as the furniture. When we all realised what the problem was, we had a good laugh and soon struck a deal.

Digger and Max left the market with pockets full of *tical*. Their next goal was to find a hotel that offered something better than straw palliasses and the company of a few hundred other ex-POWs. They were over the moon.

Chapter 12
The On-on Hotel

'CHRIST!' SAID MAX. 'I'll swear there are cracks in your face I've never seen before, and that's a fact.'

Digger said nothing, but the broad smile on his face broke into laughter as he turned, punched his mate on the arm and ran ahead a few steps, jumping and clicking his heels in the air in sheer delight. He was free, with a mate, in a big city and with money in his pocket and the night was still young.

The local Thais and Chinese looked at them and smiled. Times were happier for them, too, since the surrender. Digger and Max responded, grinning cheerfully at the girls, who it seemed always smiled back. The hardships of the past were behind them, and only now did they realise the possibilities that freedom and a little money might bring, no matter how it had been obtained!

Three and a half years of imprisonment under a regime that demanded complete obedience, along with the continual nagging fear that any unwitting action might warrant a severe beating, had changed the attitudes and behaviour of most POWs. One major change in Digger and many of his mates was how they regarded army discipline. Never again would they do anything they did not want to do – in the army or not. Another was their utter contempt for the Japanese army. A truck and a few sticks of furniture did not even make a dent in what they were owed, Digger knew.

Digger was in no way fazed by what the Australian army hierarchy might think of his current actions. He remained a private, and proud of it, until the day he was discharged. By the time he was offered promotion, some time before his discharge, he had very little respect for the army as an organisation.

He now believed that young soldiers who joined up, as he had, did so through ignorance and stupidity. He had learned a lot since he joined. The manner in which the Allies had surrendered in Singapore, along with Digger's own observations of the behaviour of the 'officer class' at Changi, had permanently changed his thinking. Customs such as saluting and using the term 'sir' no longer concerned him. Along with all the other POWs he had associated with, Digger had not saluted anyone – except the Japanese, of course – since they had been captured in Singapore.

In general, the POWs had no regard for rank; they had all been treated exactly the same by the guards who ruled their lives. In Digger's eyes, all POWs were equal, and they should treat each other as equals. The fact that officers were not supposed to do physical work particularly bothered him.

There certainly were some officers who were natural leaders. Many had been spokesmen for their groups and had suffered because of this. There were others who were also held in high regard by everyone, particularly doctors such as Albert Coates, Kevin Fagan and Roy Mills. These men were all known to Digger and his mates, and were shown great respect because of their actions.

Max and Digger, as they wandered the streets of Bangkok, regarded themselves first and foremost as individuals, answerable to no one but themselves. They were free to do whatever they liked, and if any Jap bastard – or anyone else, for that matter – got between them and their intention, then look out!

'Okay, to business, then,' said Digger, gesturing across the street at a 'Hotel' sign with other words underneath in local characters. 'How about this? It's in the centre of things, not too obvious, in case anyone comes looking for us. We can easily get to the Chamber of Commerce for any mail.'

So Digger and Max settled into what turned out to be the On-on Hotel, which was owned by a Chinese couple. They had real furniture, a choice of Thai meals, Chinese meals, bacon and eggs, steak and chips or whatever they wanted – supplied on request and on real plates! There were also single beds, in the same room, but far enough apart to smell no bodies but their own. What a change – what a treat! It was fantastic to be alive. To them, this hotel was five stars at the very least.

But there was a small problem. Since the Jap surrender, the local Thais and Chinese had been at loggerheads. Gunfire and explosions across the city were not uncommon, particularly at night. In a city where ordinance of all kinds was available, this was not surprising.

Early in the evening of their second night at the On-on Hotel, Digger and Max were sitting in the hotel bar. They thought they might find some female company but were surprised – and not a little disappointed – that the place was strangely empty.

Suddenly, the sound of gunfire and explosions seemed very loud. Mr On-on, as they had christened the owner, came rushing in. He gestured to them to follow him up the stairs and into the main room on the first floor. He assured them in struggling English that they would be safe there; no one would be able to toss a grenade through the window because of the heavy window shutters.

It suddenly dawned on the two adventurers that this conflict between the Thais and the Chinese was really serious. Somehow they had landed in the middle of a local war.

'This is bloody terrible,' shouted Max across the room, above the noise of what they now knew to be a real battle. 'I was so sure that tonight was the night – you know? You saw the way that little waitress looked at me today. I'm not bloody dying here! This is not the fucking plan!'

'Just keep away from the window,' Digger shouted back, switching off the main light. 'And anyway, I think she was looking at me. What the hell's happening? I thought we were well out of it here.'

There was a commotion on the stairs, and Mr On-on and his wife appeared in the doorway with two wounded men. They were half carrying one man, who had a neck wound; the other was walking with difficulty and holding a blood-soaked cloth to his right leg.

Digger immediately went to work on the wounded men, just as he had been trained. Max did what he could, carrying water and making bandages. He also took charge of the pistol one of the men was carrying.

Digger and Max said little for the rest of that night, but both were thinking about the straw palliasses at the Chamber of Commerce building. Had they done the right thing by striking out so bravely on their own? Neither voiced his thoughts.

Gradually, the explosions grew fewer, and by morning all was quiet again. The man with the wound in his neck had died from loss of blood, but the other could walk. Soon he disappeared into the Bangkok morning.

'What should we do with this?' Max asked, showing Digger the pistol.

'That's our pay – for services rendered,' Digger replied. 'We might need it, so just put it in your pocket.'

It transpired that the cause of the small but very serious local war was that, after the Japanese surrender, the local Chinese residents had dared to fly their flags, and the Siamese had resented this. Perhaps they'd had enough of foreign flags. Why the Chinese Thais were flying their flags, Digger and Max neither knew nor cared. The good news was that this war seemed to be fought only after dark; in the morning everyone busily went about his or her business. *If only the war between the Allies and the Japanese could have been conducted so civilly*, Digger thought to himself.

However, there was at least one Allied casualty. One ex-POW, who was manning a truck that was rounding up the drunks from the brothels, was killed by a stray shot. It was a pointless tragedy, especially since the man had survived three and a half years of brutal savagery.[1] It seemed a dreadful waste.

Over the next few days, Digger and Max remained at the hotel and enjoyed themselves in the city. They now knew that leisure activities had to be pursued in daylight hours, and they pursued them with vigour.

After three and a half years, they were sick of male army company and happy to meet and talk to Thais, Chinese or anyone else. Digger and Max inhabited the cafés and revelled in the company of all the women, who seemed delighted to talk to them. Digger had already worked out that their apparent popularity with the opposite sex was not so much due to their good looks, but more likely that they were Australians on their way home to a rich country. But who gave a shit about that?

'It's been a bloody long time since we experienced this, eh, Digger?' said Max, as two girls they had not seen before eyed them from a nearby table.

'You're right, mate,' said Digger. 'Just thank your lucky stars that now we know everything's still in working order, and concentrate on making sure we get in some more practice again tonight. Now, sit up and look as rich and Australian as possible!'

Digger signalled to the women that they were welcome to join them, and the four were soon deep in semi-English, semi-Thai conversation. Digger felt they were the only people on the planet who really understood the meaning of freedom. It was the sort of freedom that they had dreamed about for so long.

There were many brothels in the city, from clean-looking houses with attractive girls to squalid hovels, and business in all establishments was brisk. The city was full of ex-POWs who had all recently received a portion of their back-pay at the very least. The girls in the extensive red-light districts were kept fully employed night and day.[2]

Digger and Max were both medical orderlies, and since both had served in the blue-light depots in Singapore three and a half years previously, they were very well versed in the risks of contracting venereal disease. They were also well aware that the women they attracted were probably there because of the money alone, and they took all the necessary protections.

They occasionally ventured out in the evenings to the entertainments laid on by the British authorities for the thousands of ex-POWs in Bangkok. The concert companies had singers, comedians and many young women, who were all greatly appreciated by the men for their looks and because they had bothered to come so far to entertain them – who cared whether they could sing or dance?

At most of these concerts, the entertainers would involve the audience in the show. Once Digger answered a few questions correctly and was allowed onto the stage to claim his prize of a kiss from the entertainer Lynn Britton. The lights were extinguished and Digger willingly did what was expected of him. He was still kissing this girl as the lights came on again.

'So, do I sleep in the lounge tonight?' Max asked, as Digger returned to the audience.

'No, mate,' Digger replied. 'I didn't have the breath left to ask the question!'

They frequently looked in at the Chamber of Commerce building, taking care to be as inconspicuous as possible. Each had written to his family, saying he was free and well. They knew they were likely to be transferred to Singapore before being shipped back home; much as they were enjoying life now, getting home was still their top priority.

They were also careful to pay attention to the general orders posted on the noticeboard at the Chamber of Commerce building; the last thing they wanted was to draw official attention to themselves. They registered and filled in forms about the camps they had been at, and went to the records office in response to a general request to report what they knew about bad treatment by the Japs. They knew plenty, of course, as did all the ex-POWs.

Digger informed the authorities that, as bad as the treatment of the POWs at Kanchanaburi had been, the very worst treatment meted out by the Japanese and Korean guards was to the *romusha* — the native workers on the railway. These men were Tamils, Malays, Indians, Chinese and Thais, and many of them had originally worked on the rubber plantations of colonial Malaya.

Digger spoke about how the *romusha* had been treated, particularly when they were sick, and about the huge numbers who had perished. He had personally buried thousands at Kanchanaburi. He was then thanked for his story and politely informed that the office was interested only in the treatment of Allied personnel.

While visiting the Chamber of Commerce building one day, Digger received his first letter from home. His last mail had been in

Singapore before the Allied surrender. Digger had not known it, but he had been posted as 'missing in action' since that time.

Digger recognised his sister Iris's writing. He took the letter outside the building and found a corner away from a group of his mates, who were smoking, chatting and killing time. It passed through his mind that he now knew these men better than he did his own family.

He realised that his home life, with all its responsibilities, hopes and ambitions, which were once so important to him, had faded into the background of his mind. Sheer survival had taken all the effort he could muster, each and every minute of every day. He felt some guilt as he pondered this while sitting on a low wall and opening the letter slowly. His heart beat a little faster as memories of his family and Melbourne came flooding back.

He unfolded the pages and began to read.

Dear Digger,

Well thank God you survived. We were all so relieved to get your letter. We can't imagine what a terrible experience you have had.

Unfortunately I am very sad to tell you that our dear Mum . . .

Digger's heart skipped a few beats and he closed his eyes. He felt a pain in his chest, knowing what he was about to read, and he stopped breathing. After what seemed a long time, he took a deep breath and fought to gain control of his feelings. He opened his eyes and continued to read.

Unfortunately I am very sad to tell you that our dear mum passed away in September last year. We gave her a great send off and your father . . .

Again Digger stopped reading. He swallowed hard, stuffed the letter into his pocket and, avoiding any contact, quickly returned to the On-on Hotel. Max was out, which Digger was glad of. He lay on his bed and read the letter several times, and cried quietly before falling asleep.

Digger had never been close to his father but he had felt the closest of bonds with his mum. He could not shake the thought that if he had been at home to look after her she might still be alive. Digger had been very close to his mum. When he was young and things were really tough, his father had given his mother a hard time. Now, he found it unbearable to know that she had died in his absence and that his father was still living.

As far back as Digger could remember, it was his mum who had always looked after the family. She was a clever businesswoman who had survived and provided for them all through the difficult times of the Depression. To learn of her death now, so close to seeing her again, was just the very worst of news.

Digger woke next morning to hear Max telling him of his adventures of the previous day. They involved a girl, of course – otherwise, what was the point of telling your mate? – but Max quickly noticed Digger's lack of response and asked what was wrong.

'I just got my first letter . . . Mum died,' Digger explained as briefly as possible.

'Aw, shit. Sorry, mate. I'm really sorry and you so near . . .' Max's response faded out as they both sat on the edge of their beds.

That day was difficult for them both. They were used to death, of course, but the death of a mother was a very different matter. Yet Digger did not want to wallow in his grief. They had breakfast, which was delivered to the hotel lounge from their favourite local café, and planned their activities for the day.

That evening, Digger and Max were sitting in the hotel bar. The 'flag war' was still being waged; they could hear gunfire but the hotel area was obviously not the target tonight. Business at the hotel was slow, but suddenly they heard English voices at the doorway. Into the bar walked a lieutenant in British uniform. The quality of his uniform immediately told Max and Digger that he was a recent import. He was definitely no ex-POW.

'Is one of you chaps Digger Barrett?' the lieutenant asked in a distinctly upper-class English accent.

'Who wants to know?' Digger asked in return, remaining seated and withholding the obligatory 'sir' that was always expected by commissioned officers.

'I'm Lieutenant Eldridge from the Commonwealth War Graves Commission,' the man explained, 'and I've come to ask you a favour.' He removed his cap and offered Digger his hand.

This was not the usual gesture of an officer, and immediately Digger was reassured. For a minute he and Max had thought that the army had caught up with their escapades and decided to do something about it. He shook the offered hand and said that he was indeed Digger Barrett.

'So what the hell are you doing out on a night like this?' Digger asked. 'Don't you know there's a bloody war on here?'

'Well, we don't have much time, and it was essential that I contact you tonight. I got your whereabouts from some of your friends at the Chamber of Commerce building.' Lieutenant Eldridge went on to explain why he wanted to see Digger.

It turned out that the Commonwealth War Graves Commission was a combined organisation for the Allied countries that looked after the graves of all servicemen. It was essential that the gravesites of soldiers up and down the Thai–Burma railway were found, catalogued and cleared now; if the jungle reclaimed them, they would be lost forever.

Eldridge asked Digger if he would volunteer to join a small party that was to go back up the railway. Digger was as close to a doctor as the War Graves Commission could find in Bangkok at that time, and they needed him to serve as the party's medic. There were very few doctors to be found, and none who would volunteer for this job. Most of the Allied officers, including all the doctors, had already been repatriated to their home countries.

Digger didn't hesitate, and volunteered immediately. He now had no reason to go home. After Eldridge had left him and Max alone, Digger said, 'Anyway, I want to see the rest of that fucking railway!'

Chapter 13

Back to the Railway

ON THE MORNING of 19 September 1945, Digger and Max were enjoying breakfast at the On-on Hotel. Their standard order, which was delivered by the café next door, was for steak and eggs, together with local pawpaw and toast. Tea came courtesy of Mr and Mrs On-on. They had eaten this every morning since they had arrived at the hotel, and they were a long way from getting sick of it.

The pair rarely talked while they ate. Eating was without doubt the second-most important activity in their current situation. They simply relished every morsel and let their thoughts roam back to the previous night — and the number one activity.

As he chewed on a mouthful of toast, steak and soft egg, Digger looked up towards the dining room door. He saw Lieutenant Eldridge approaching their table. He said nothing as he savoured his food but motioned the lieutenant to join them.

'Just look at that,' said the Englishman, casting his eyes longingly over the steak and eggs. 'That's more than we get in the mess at Sathorn House, I'll wager.'

'Have some tea,' Max offered, and signalled the waiter for an extra cup.

The two Australians continued their breakfast as Eldridge explained what the expedition back up the railway involved. The members of the party were meeting at Sathorn House that morning. Several meetings were scheduled for the next day or two so that all members 'signed up' to the goals of the trip, although what this actually meant was not yet clear.

When Digger and Eldridge arrived at Sathorn House, the place was bustling. There were all sorts there but mostly British and Australian army officers. Some were sergeants, others warrant officers, but most had a shoulder rank signifying His Majesty's Commission. *So this is where all the bloody officers are hiding*, thought Digger.

The ex-POWs were easy to spot. They wore hand-me-down shorts and shirts that were reminiscent of army attire, but they did not proclaim regiment and rank in the usual loud manner. Digger preferred it this way. He was, as yet, not ready to join in any army games.

When Digger met his fellow volunteer adventurers, he was glad to see that most of them were ex-POWs. As it happened, he had not met any of them before but he still felt comfortable in their company. Their similar experiences made for easy conversation and the promise of good working relationships. Every man there was committed to doing the very best he could for the friends he sorely missed and would never see again.

The men talked on many subjects, but no matter what they discussed, every conversation always came back to the same subject: they were here to do what little they could for those who, through no fault of their own, had to stay here forever. For many, guilt probably played a part in their volunteering for the mission. After all, they were still going home – just not right away.

One of the members of the expedition was Padre Henry Babb, a British ex-POW. In his diary entry for that day, he recorded the names of the men who were there:

Lieutenant Joseph Albert Eldridge (British) – a member of the War Graves Commission

Lieutenant Jack Holder Leemon (Australian) – a member of the War Graves Commission

Sergeant Lloyd Rankin (Australian) – a member of the War Graves Commission

Lieutenant G. H. Schroder (Dutch) – a member of the War Graves Commission and ex-POW

Captain R. K. A. Bruce (Federated Malay States, British) – ex-POW

Captain Athol Roland White (Australian) – ex-POW

Padre Henry C. F. Babb (British) – ex-POW

Warrant Officer Les Cody (Australian) – ex-POW

Sergeant Jack H. Sherman (Australian) – ex-POW

Sergeant Torry Lee (Australian) – ex-POW

Leading Aircraftman S. O. Simpson (Australian) – ex-POW

Leading Aircraftman Rex (Mac) McGregor (Australian) – ex-POW

Leading Aircraftman Eddie S. Wheeler (Australian) – ex-POW

Private Hilton R. Lees (Australian) – ex-POW

Private G. H. Kindred (British) – ex-POW

Private David William Barrett (Australian) – ex-POW[1]

The expedition was also to include a Japanese interpreter, Lieutenant Nagase Takashi, who had been a member of the dreaded *Kempeitai*, Japan's military police, and twelve Japanese soldiers to protect the party against bandits. Lieutenant Nagase was in charge of these guards as well as of two Japanese train drivers.

Digger was assigned the task of 'looking after' Lieutenant Nagase. He was unsure why, because his main task on this trip was to act as its medical orderly. Perhaps the Allied officers did not want to associate too closely with a Japanese officer – particularly a *Kempei* – but Digger took on the job willingly.

Over the next two or three days, Digger visited Sathorn House as he was instructed. Between visits, he and Max continued to enjoy their very well-earned break at the On-on Hotel. Digger thought he knew what had happened on the railway pretty well. However, as he talked to other ex-POWs, he learned about their experiences, the conditions in different camps, their friends who had died and those who had survived to be free again.

Those in certain areas, such as at the Sonkarai camp, near the border between Burma and Thailand, had suffered particularly bad treatment at the hands of the Japanese guards. A Japanese officer at Sokarai, Lieutenant Abe Hiroshi, was one of the most brutal officers on the railway. Many remembered this particular lieutenant for his cruelty.

The following extract was written by Carol Cooper:

> . . . the conditions there were probably worse than [at] any other [camp]. Engineer Officer Lt. Abe made no attempt at any time to try and stop the brutal treatment by his men, even in his presence. Hundreds of men are reported to have died in the Sonkarai camp from May 1943 and during the following months.[2]

The ex-POWs' shared sense of anger, resentment and intense hatred for the guards, whom they blamed for the deaths of their friends, drew the War Graves Commission group together. Many stories were related of friends who had died, whether from beatings or diseases such as malaria, severe ulceration of legs or feet, dysentery or just starvation. The IJA's policy of half-rations for the sick had hastened the deaths of many men. No doubt the officers in the group also harboured these feelings, but army protocol precluded the intimacy of conversation needed to share true feelings between officers and men, even in the Australian army.

Digger shared his stories too, but at the back of his mind he knew what had kept him alive. It was his hatred for all things Japanese, and his passionate longing to be able – somehow, sometime – to even the score. In the meantime, he was content to help to bring what little dignity he could to the dead by ensuring that they got a decent gravesite.

At this time, immediately after the surrender, the IJA in Siam and in Burma remained as it had been. The soldiers were still armed and occupied the same areas, all the way up the railway. The only difference was that their orders now came from the Allied forces under the command of a British officer. This was, no doubt, a terrible blow to Japan's officer soldiers, who had been taught to believe that the Japanese army would be victorious. Those Japanese who did not take their own lives rationalised their situation by arguing that they were still obeying their Emperor, albeit via the victorious Allied army.

It was with some trepidation, therefore, that the War Graves Commission party prepared for their expedition. They had no real notion of the reception they would get from the thousands of IJA soldiers who were still in the area and armed. They would also have to depend and rely totally on the cooperation of the Japanese, who were still in control of the railway operations.

The areas north of Bangkok were also inhabited by the infamous *dacoits*. These were armed gangs, some of whom may have acted as guerrilla forces against the Japanese, but who were now working only for themselves. They were menacing hundreds of small villages in Burma and Thailand at this time.

To protect themselves from these threats, the Commonwealth War Graves Commission search party was to be well armed. They would be kitted out with Thompson submachine guns, Sten guns, rifles, sidearms and grenades.

At Sathorn House before their departure, Digger and the rest of the group were assembled in an area with individual desks and chairs. It was for all the world like a classroom, Digger thought. All members were required to sign a document, but first they were briefed on the purpose of the expedition.

Padre Babb, who was charged with keeping a diary of the expedition, summed up this briefing in the introduction to his report:

> As trainloads of ex-prisoners came into the capital of Thailand on their way to the evacuation airport, many senior officers and warrant officers were carrying Death Records of either their regiments or the Groups in which they worked as prisoners. Some had rough sketch maps of cemeteries, and the best effort was made by Sgt. Kemp of the R.A.O.C. who was in Group 2 [a Japanese-organised grouping] as a prisoner. He had been working in the Nip office and collected information about every group – how he did it will always remain a mystery. His maps and cemetery plans are excellent.
>
> All the records [of ex-POWs] were collected into Sathorn House and everything was prepared by the ex-prisoners to hand over to the Graves Commission.
>
> Then came the appeal, 'Who will volunteer to go back along the railway line to show the Graves Commission the positions of the cemeteries?' It was necessary to have fit men and those who knew the areas concerned. A party of 13 ex-prisoners volunteered [plus three who were not ex-POW] in spite of the fact that they could hear the aeroplane engines roaring which were taking their fellow ex-prisoners home.[3]

As Digger learned that day, the reason for this expedition was not simply to locate and document the gravesites but also to recover evidence of atrocities that had been buried with the bodies. The Japanese and Korean guards had taken no interest in any POWs once they were dead, so the graves of Allied servicemen had become hiding places for all manner of information, including details of atrocities and who was responsible for them.

Captains Bruce and White, the senior officers in the group, delivered a lecture to the group. They reminded the men that since the Japanese surrender the Allied forces were now in charge – and being in charge carried with it heavy responsibilities. One of those responsibilities was to respect the property of others, including property owned by the defeated Japanese army and its members, regardless of how they had treated their prisoners in the camps.

There was much muttering and swearing from the group at this point, but Captain White, while expressing his sympathy with their feelings, insisted that these principles be agreed to. He asked all the men to complete and sign various documents.

Just the usual army crap, thought Digger. As he signed the form, however, he couldn't help wondering again whether his and Max's activities had reached the ears of the Sathorn House hierarchy. Could that be the reason for this lecture?

Finally, early on Saturday 22 September 1945, Digger set off with most of the party in two trucks. First they were to travel to Nakorn Pathom, a station on the railway around fifty-six kilometres north-west of Bangkok and just twenty-three kilometres from Nong Pladuk junction. From there, they would take trains north-west along the railway to Thanbyuzayat, in Burma.

It was a long and boring day, not just because of the distance but because one of the trucks kept breaking down. At times Digger wished he had just said no and stayed with Max at the On-on Hotel. The previous night, Max had told him that – at long last – transport had been arranged for their group. He would be shipping to Singapore soon. And here was Digger, stuck on the back of a bloody truck, nursing a Thompson submachine gun and going back up the railway!

As the trucks pulled up at the station, they were met by a rather anxious Captain White. He had travelled ahead earlier in the day with a small advance party. The trucks were three hours late.

Digger and the group now met Lieutenant Nagase Takashi and the twelve Japanese guards who were to accompany them. Nagase was deferential and polite in manner towards Digger. Despite his feelings about the Japanese in general, Digger was determined to do his job, so he kept his feelings in check and greeted Nagase as politely as he could. He was a little bloke, not a lot more than five feet tall, but he was smart, as were most Japanese officers. Nagase said little at their first meeting, but Digger noticed that he spoke near perfect English.

Digger was alarmed when he saw a steam engine hitched to two enclosed steel rice trucks. They were exactly the same as those into which he and his mates had been crammed for five long days on their journey from Changi to the railway. As he forced himself to look inside, he felt that he could smell the shit and the misery of that journey; the feelings of that experience would not leave his mind.

The other train consisted of a large diesel truck with converted wheels to fit the rails pulling two *attap*-roofed and open-sided wagons. Here, the party would live, cook and sleep for the duration of the trip. *Thank God for that*, thought Digger.

Nagase began ordering the twelve Japanese guards to work. They did all the heavy lifting, getting the stores and ammunition aboard the wagons. This was a marvellous turn-around, Digger thought. He was lounging back and the Japs were working hard. *As it should be*, he thought.

Chapter 14

The War Graves Commission

THE NEXT TWO days were spent travelling up the railway, and the group arrived at Thanbyuzayat at three p.m. on 24 September 1945. Their plan was to search for the graves and then record their findings on the return journey.

They had travelled during the day, spending their nights at camps and villages along the way. They slept on palliasses next to the armaments store in one of the *attap*-palm-covered trucks. The Japanese had guarded the party from dusk to dawn from attack by the *dacoits*, who would have dearly loved to get their hands on these supplies, particularly the weaponry.

Several times along the way, the guards had prepared baths for the officers on the War Graves party, and had even entertained them at what had, until recently, been a Japanese 'comfort house'. No such luxuries had been offered to the other ranks, of course. *Usual officer perks*, Digger had thought. *Mind you, if I need anything from these bastards, I'll just take it!*

Digger had been surprised at how quickly he'd adapted to being waited on and having to do no manual labour whatsoever. At the different camps along the railway, the local Japanese had cooked for the whole party.[1]

A problem awaited them at Thanbyuzayat, the Japanese base camp at the Burmese end of the railway. It was only three weeks since the Japanese surrender, and there were still thousands of IJA soldiers in the area, all fully armed. Many were milling around on the area, curious at the party's arrival, but no salutes were on offer here. This was in great contrast to the warm and deferential welcome from the Japanese at the rest stops during the journey.

Lieutenant Nagase was sent to the local Japanese headquarters to confirm that full cooperation from the IJA command in this area would be forthcoming. In the meantime, the rest of the party did not know quite what to expect. All were very conscious of the fact that they numbered just sixteen, with only thirteen Japanese guards. And they, Digger realised, might well choose to side with the IJA, if a conflict erupted.

The Japanese camp was a kilometre or so from the railway, so the War Graves party expected Nagase to return within two hours at the most. Their trains were moved to two parallel railway tracks in the yards at the end of the line. Captain Bruce was determined that nothing was going to keep him from searching for graves; all he required to proceed was confirmation from Nagase that the Japanese command here would cooperate.

Four hours passed, and still Nagase had not returned. Captain Bruce decided to be patient and give Nagase time to accomplish his task. If the Japanese here had not received orders to cooperate, he realised, it would take some time to get a radio message to the right people, for decisions to be made, and to receive the orders back again.

As darkness came, there was still no sign of Nagase. Now the War Graves party had no option but to wait and see what the morning would bring. This night, six of the Allied men, as well as the twelve Japanese, stayed on guard while the others tried to sleep.

Early in the morning, Nagase finally returned to the train. He did not look well and appeared very nervous. He reported that the local command had no knowledge of this mission. No orders had been received to cooperate with the War Graves Commission party.

Captain Bruce bristled at the news. He had been patient and reasonable, but this was not good enough. Here they were, on important War Graves Commission business – which would not even have been necessary had the Allied POWs been treated as they should have been – and now these bastards were refusing to cooperate! The one good thing, Captain Bruce figured, was that if the local Japanese command had wanted to be obstructive, they would have taken action. This had not happened, so he decided to ignore the Japanese and proceed with the mission.

Captain Bruce, Digger and three others set off in the jeep for the cemetery. The Thanbyuzayat cemetery was only a few kilometres from the station, and quite close to the road. It took the group only ten minutes or so to find.

Digger was left to guard the jeep, while the others disappeared through two-metre-high tiger grass along a path at right angles to the road. *Well*, he thought, *it's me against the Japanese army – that's about the right odds!* So he just relaxed, sat in the jeep and let his mind wander.

After about half an hour, Digger began to nod off from the heat and the boredom. He suddenly realised that he could hear the sound of marching feet – many of them – together with the bark of commands in Japanese. He immediately stood up in the jeep and looked down the road to his left, towards Thanbyuzayat. He could see only empty road to the first bend, about a hundred metres away, but men were definitely approaching.

Digger looked back to the path on which Captain Bruce and the others had set off and immediately considered abandoning the jeep before he was seen. Bruce reappeared from the tiger grass just as a Japanese battalion of about 1000 men appeared around the bend, six abreast and led by a high-ranking officer in dress uniform.

Captain Bruce reached the jeep just as the soldiers approached. The battalion kept marching. As they passed, the Japanese officer raised his sword in salute and gave a smart 'eyes right' to Captain Bruce, who responded with a casual salute in return.

Digger realised that this soldierly routine obviously meant that cooperation would be forthcoming in future. Still, the method of conveying this information had obviously been intended to intimidate and create inconvenience. Captain Bruce resolved to report this faithfully. At present, however, he had to be content to order a complete clean-up of the area around the cemetery.

After spending a couple of days identifying graves in the Thanbyuzayat area, the party gradually worked its way back down the railway line, stopping to look for burial places and noting the position of each and every grave of any Allied soldier. They found many, many graves, of Australians, Americans, Britons and Dutch.

Where possible, individual graves were identified. The party left orders with the Japanese in each area to keep jungle vegetation clear, to maintain paths and gravesite crosses, and to retain and care for any other specific identification markers. In many places the Japanese had already received these orders, and local cemeteries either had already been cleared or were in the process of being cleared. In some areas the cemeteries had recently been decorated with crosses, flowers or shrubs. It appeared that orders were certainly being obeyed.

Padre Babb noted in his diary how cooperative the Japanese were in maintaining the gravesites, and how courteous they were at the places where the War Graves party's trains stopped – apart from at Thanbyuzayat.

It would be unfair to conclude this diary without saying a word of praise for the Japanese cooperation. The 'Civilian railway Nips' both those in positions of authority and the rank and file, have obeyed orders implicitly and helped us more than we could have hoped for even in our wildest dreams. They saved us hours of toil and labour and were at all times polite and eager to do their best for us. If the same type of man had been dealing with us as prisoners, I am convinced that our lot would have been a happier one and many lives would have been saved.[1]

Digger, however, did not agree with Babb's interpretation. He believed the Japanese were indeed the same men in both situations – brainwashed to be totally obedient to the Emperor. This is why they had been so brutal as guards and why they were so helpful now. As Digger said to his mates in the group, 'The same bastards that were belting the shit out of us one minute are wiping our arses the next!'

At many of the cemetery sites along the railway, records were recovered that had been hidden in the graves. These documents invariably contained evidence of atrocities. There were diaries, drawings, photographs and even film, which had been secretly buried with the bodies of fallen comrades. The officers in the War Graves party had evidence of where this treasure was buried; indeed, some of the party had been present when these materials were buried.

There were some amazing finds. Padre Babb wrote about a rubber plantation to which they were guided by Eddie Wheeler on 25 September 1945.

We drew into the plantation and LAC Wheeler went off like a hare.
The other members of the party followed with spades and cameras,
he led us through the rubber trees and stopped at one tree and said,

'here is the spot'. A cube of earth, size 2 ft, was dug, and bang in the centre of the base was the top of a small metal drum. We gaped with surprise for here was a fellow without maps or sketches hitting right on the exact spot of his buried treasure more than two years after he buried it! The drum contains 16 mm Cine films of conditions etc. of our prisoner of war life. We all hope they will develop well, for our people at home will be able to see and judge for themselves how we were treated since 1942.

The Japanese were amazed, and no doubt a little worried, about the evidence the party was gathering about the conditions in the POW camps. Padre Babb noted that one officer's 'eyes almost shot out of his head' as he watched the Allied team recover a four-gallon tin of records from the grave of Private M. W. Fraser of the 2/4th Machine Gun Battalion at Angannan Cemetery on 24 September 1945.[3]

Digger gradually got to know Nagase, and discovered that he was also very worried. Being a *Kempei*, Nagase had attended many interrogations as interpreter and had witnessed some horrific tortures. He seemed eager to tell Digger of these experiences, although Digger did not really want to listen. It turned out that Nagase was very worried about being charged as a war criminal.

At this time, Digger, like most ex-POWs, was completely incapable of forgiving any Japanese, especially any member of the *Kempeitai*. However, Nagase managed to explain that he had taken no part in any torture and had only been present as an interpreter. Digger had grave doubts about the truth of this. After all, the *Kempeitai* had held great authority, and others in the IJA feared them intensely.

Even at this early stage in their acquaintance, Digger felt there was something different about this man. Rather guardedly, he advised Nagase that there was no way he could help him, but that helping the War Graves Commission should work in his favour. This advice seemed to do little to calm Nagase's nervousness.

When the party was searching for gravesites in the area around Nieke about 28 September 1945, they uncovered evidence of a particularly nasty incident, which Padre Babb reported in his diary.

> It was here a spot of bother reared its ugly head. For one Australian had died on July 22nd (1945 just 3 months previously) as a result of a hammer blow on the head, and Capt. White is determined to find out the Nip responsible for this. Capt. Omatsu who is i/c of this area was with us – a cruel looking fat faced Nip, the type typical of our POW days. He told us that the prisoners in the area in July 1945 had worked on air raid shelter construction and camp work. Capt. White asked him who was in charge of the camp and after much contradiction he said a cadet officer Tsono, who had since died of malaria.[3]

Captain White's determination to find the perpetrator of this crime was well documented over three pages of Padre Babb's diary. Babb described the very thorough interviews that were conducted with anyone who could possibly have been involved in, or who might have known about, the incident. Unfortunately, he could not determine who the criminal was. White therefore decided to photograph possible suspects or witnesses, intending to show the pictures to ex-POWs from this area who might recognise the offender.

Every member of the expedition had a job to do. Digger set up local clinics at all the stops along the railway. Word of these soon spread, and he was kept very busy with ulcers, malaria and the very common diarrhoea. He enjoyed what he was doing simply because, at long last, he had the necessary medicines. The local people were hugely grateful. He also treated members of his own group; a few still suffered bouts of malaria and the odd case of diarrhoea.

Digger's workload did not stop him from enjoying his newfound freedom, however; the novelty of being at liberty had not yet worn off. He and his new mates had plenty of opportunities to go exploring, which they often did early in the morning. Each man took a Thompson submachine gun, and off they went to explore the local area. They would wander into villages, talk to the kids who flocked around them, tramp through the bush and of course look out for anything they might be able to shoot or scrounge for the cooking pot. A favourite place to explore was any local Japanese camp, where they would go for the very simple but satisfying feeling of being in charge.

If anyone asked where they were going, they would invariably reply, 'Just tiger hunting.' Their roaming around the local areas had not been envisaged by the War Graves organisers and may not have been within the rules of the expedition, but no one stopped them. Digger's behaviour, manner and attitude on the trip had been enough to let everyone else know that he was his own boss, and would not take kindly to being told what he could or could not do. He saluted no one, spoke to the officers on an equal basis and just got on with his job of attending to the sick.

Quite a few others in the group appreciated Digger's way of thinking, which fitted in exactly with the way they felt. After so many years as POWs, they rejected all authority, including that of their own officers. And, as Digger explained, exploring was some reward for having given up their time to this War Graves Commission activity. Most of the officers would be rewarded through enhanced reputations. They would be mentioned in reports and perhaps promoted because of their work, but other ranks were generally excluded from this sort of recognition. In their minds, something more immediate was required. A little 'tiger hunting' fitted the bill nicely. They went 'tiger hunting' on 1 October 1945.

I remember at Brenkasi, early one morning, 'Sos', 'Mac', the train driver, another couple of Japs and I went fishing. But we had no rods or lines – all we had were our Thompsons and a few Jap grenades. So the tigers were safe enough that morning. We wandered down a steep jungle track next to the railway, and out onto the east bank of the Kwae Noi River. There were great swimming holes and great fishing spots all along the bank.

We came to a beautiful large pool that looked really deep. We all agreed it would be a beaut spot for fishing. So we just let the Nips get on with the job. But we had to take some precautions because we all knew about these Jap grenades. We took cover behind a big tree on the bank. I then signalled to the Japs to get on with the job.

The driver, I think it was, just very casually stood on the bank at the edge of the water and pulled the pin on the grenade. Then he lifted one leg and banged the grenade on the heel of his boot before tossing it into the middle of the pool.

Apparently, these grenades did not have a good reputation. They only operated correctly if they were struck after the pin was drawn – something to do with the mechanism, maybe, or perhaps it was just bravado on the part of the Japs. Of course, the gossip was that there were a large number of one-footed Japanese soldiers as a result, but I never saw one.

The explosion wasn't loud but it was very effective. A shower of water rose about four metres above the surface, and then slowly we saw the result as dead or stunned fish floated to the surface. The Japs stripped off and swam out to collect the fish of reasonable size.

There was one beauty about two feet long. I borrowed the camera and took a photo when we got back.

That same afternoon, Digger persuaded Sos and Eddie Wheeler to accompany him to a local Japanese camp. For Digger, baiting the Japs had become a sport. Sos and Eddie however, while agreeing with Digger's attitude, could not completely shake the feeling that any contact with the Japanese military could earn them a beating. And they knew that every time they encountered Japanese troops, Digger would push the boundaries. But as mates do, they went along anyway.

They entered the local Japanese camp through the gate with the familiar terraced guard post, which for so many long months had symbolised their complete lack of freedom. There was no challenge and they continued on to the main offices. It did not appear to be a very large camp, Digger noticed. As they came to the offices, a group of three men came out. When they were about ten metres from the Japanese, the middle one – a captain – held up his hand in what may have been a half salute or an aborted signal for them to halt.

Digger picked up on the captain's momentary hesitation. He walked straight up to him, stopping less than a metre away. He used his Thompson submachine gun to point to the camera that was hanging around the captain's neck. As he lightly poked the man in the chest with the barrel of the gun, he said in a loud, clear voice, 'I'll have that – it's my camera.'

Whether the captain understood English or not, there was no mistaking what Digger wanted. The man simply unslung his camera and handed it over. In the background, Digger could hear Eddie Wheeler swearing under his breath: 'For fuck's sake, Digger!'

Digger smiled at the captain and said, very politely, 'Thank you very much.' He turned around and led his mates out of the camp.

As soon as they passed the guard post and were out of earshot, Sos looked earnestly at Digger. 'You'll get us all court-martialled, you bastard. What the hell did you do that for?'

'For Christ's sake, calm down,' Digger said. 'There's nobody going to court-martial anybody now. They're all too busy cleaning up the fucking mess here. Anyway, how would it look in the local papers back home: "Heroes find graves and are charged with pinching a Japanese camera"! Whose side would everyone be on? Just forget it.'

But Sos couldn't forget it, and he kept on about it all the way back to camp.

Digger explained as best he could that, at Changi, all the POWs had lost their possessions. 'Did you lose your kit, Sos? Yes, of course you did. We were all sent up the railway and never saw our kits again – and we never will! Is that right?'

Digger again looked at Sos, and before he could answer, Digger almost shouted, 'Of course it's bloody right! So this camera is my camera. It's the camera that I left in my kit in the store when we all went to Changi, and I've just recovered it. I tell you what – if you had a camera in your kitbag, we'll get it back tomorrow.'

'Oh, just forget it,' Sos at last managed to reply.

They walked the rest of the way back to the camp in silence. When they arrived, Digger showed his camera to others in the group, and soon everyone had heard the story. Naturally, it reached the ears of Captain White and Captain Bruce.

Early in the evening, Captain Bruce approached Digger for a word. As they wandered down the track, Bruce explained very clearly that Digger would be court-martialled for his offence unless he returned the camera. He explained that there was no way he could do anything else. The Japanese officer had been to see him, and that made the complaint official.

Digger then explained his reasoning and why he regarded it as his camera. There was obviously a Japanese somewhere walking around with his original camera – very probably a senior officer.

Digger appreciated the way that Captain Bruce had spoken to him, without any of the usual crap connected with official army investigations. It was just as well, because Digger would have rebelled against any attempt at a formal process. He insisted that he still regarded it as his camera and that therefore he would keep it. He didn't believe a court martial could possibly result from this.

A night's sleep is a great thing when important decisions must be made. In the morning, Digger went to Captain Bruce and gave him the camera. Bruce said nothing other than 'thank you'.

Digger had reasoned that if he did not return the camera, Bruce would have been forced to report the matter on their return to Bangkok. An official inquiry might also involve Sos and Eddie, who, of course, had had nothing to do with it. Lastly, he had of course signed that bloody piece of paper promising not to do this very thing. It was clear that hanging onto the camera would be more trouble that it was worth.

The POW camp at Kinsaiyok was their next stop on the way down the railway. It was set in a beautiful area, with tropical jungle vegetation and hills with deep valleys, rivers and waterfalls. But this had made it very difficult terrain through which to build a railway; Digger knew the POWs must have had a terrible time working here.

The group arrived at Kinsaiyok on 2 October 1945. They investigated and recorded two large cemeteries in the area, with a total of 347 graves, and a large 'cholera grave' that contained an unknown number of bodies. All those who died of cholera had been cremated and the remains buried together.

In the five days they were based at Kinsaiyok, some of the War Graves party used the diesel train to go up and down the railway line, looking for various cemeteries. Others used the jeep to explore gravesites in places that could not be accessed from the railway.

One reason they based themselves at Kinsaiyok was because of an incident that had occurred at Hintok a week or so before. A railway bridge had collapsed when a train was crossing on its way up the line; the driver and two others had died. When Digger and a few of the others got this news, they resolved to walk over all the bridges on their return journey.

Lieutenant Leemon wrote about one of these crossings in his diary.

> Crossing the 'pack of cards bridge' past Hintock — some of those with us had been at the building and told stories of cutting off the ends of the supporting beams so that there was no support under the soil and shovelling in buckets full of white ants. All were nervous at the crossing. So was I.[4]

Digger held clinics for the local people at a few places around Kinsaiyok. He had no knowledge of the graves in this area and so had little else to do. He had spoken to Captain Bruce and Captain White about the graves at Kanchanaburi, but they had seemed preoccupied with their current tasks.

Early one morning at Kinsaiyok, Digger was able to persuade Sos Simpson and Eddie Wheeler to accompany him on yet another 'tiger hunt'. He promised that he would in no way get them into any bother. In fact, there had been many reports of actual tigers in this area. The local Japanese were apparently terrified of them but Digger and his mates had never seen one before. Anyhow, there were three of them and they each had their trusty Thompson gun.

They walked along a narrow track though light scrub. They were about three kilometres away from the Japanese camp that they were making for when they heard a voice in the distance – a man was obviously in distress. They came to an open area that had recently been cleared. They saw a bloke about 150 metres away who appeared to be stuck up a large tree. As they got a little closer, they recognised the language he was speaking.

'It's a fucking Nip,' said Eddie. 'What's up with him?'

No one answered. None of them instinctively wanted to help this man, as they might have in different circumstances. They laughed and thought about how they might turn this to their advantage, and moved to a spot where they could not be seen from the tree.

Sos's eyes suddenly widened. He grabbed Eddie's arm and pointed in the Japanese's direction. 'Look! Look at that big patch of grass to the left of the tree – it's a fucking tiger!'

The tiger could be seen only if they stared intently at the grass patch, so well did its colours blend in with the dead grass. As they stared at it, they saw that the tiger was crouched down on all fours. Its tail flicked from side to side, and its gaze appeared to be fixed on its prey – the man up the tree.

The sun was rapidly rising behind them, and the breeze – if there was one – was in their faces, so it was unlikely that the tiger would detect them.

Sos had recovered from his surprise. 'Well, it must be happy if it's wagging its tail, eh?' he said.

'Don't be such a fucking idiot,' Eddie whispered back. 'It's dogs that wag when they're happy – cats wag when they are concentrating on something.'

'Okay, okay, let's just shut up and think about what we're going to do,' Digger said.

'Maybe he's happy because he's going to eat a Japanese,' Sos continued. 'I wonder what Japanese taste like, anyway. Like shit, I bet!'

The group shrank back further to make sure they would not be seen. Digger later realised that they had remained remarkably cool, considering the situation. They knew instinctively that the tiger was too far away for an accurate shot from a Thompson submachine gun. Should they try to get close enough to kill the tiger? How dangerous would this be? Should they get help for the poor bloke or just let him stay there? Sos joked that maybe they should shoot him and let the tiger have him.

Finally, they decided to back off as quietly as possible and get the hell out of there. They agreed that, in the circumstances, nature should just take its course.

On their return to camp they said nothing, even when Lieutenant Eldridge asked jokingly how many tigers they had bagged that morning. They just went about their normal duties, keeping their ears open for any news of tiger attacks.

On 5 October, Padre Babb reported the conversations he'd had that day with local people.

> . . . we were excitedly told more Tiger stories. A tiger last night had kept four Japanese soldiers up a tree all night. A tigress and one cub had entered a Tamil camp and taken off one coolie who was just outside the entrance to a hut: a tiger had struck another coolie who was near a 'window' of another hut and the unfortunate fellow bled to death. Nagase was positively greyish green with fright – he has had three sleepless nights in succession.[5]

The whole camp was talking about tigers that evening, but the three 'tiger hunters' did not mention their experiences of that morning.

On 7 October the War Graves party left Kinsaiyok for Wanpo station. When they arrived, someone in the group carelessly left a pistol on the floor of one of the *attap*-palm-covered wagons. It lay in full view of the many locals who were milling around the area.

Digger was busy treating a couple of locals beside the railway track, and a few others had also gathered, obviously hoping for some medical help. Digger noticed the pistol as he moved to get some more gear from the wagon, but before he could retrieve it he saw a young local, probably in his teens, pick it up and run off down the shallow embankment.

Digger didn't hesitate and immediately set off after him. Before he knew it, he was on a bush track with jungle on both sides. It wasn't long before he was gaining on the boy.

Suddenly the youth stopped running and turned around. It took Digger a fraction of a second to process the image of this young boy pointing the pistol directly at him. He instantly decided that discretion was the better part of valour, so in one fluid motion he turned around and ran as fast as he could in the other direction. He was back at the train within a minute.

They would all have to be more careful in future. Digger was very thankful that the young man had decided not to fire at him during his very hasty retreat.

The only major location that remained for the group to visit was Kanchanaburi. Digger had lived – or, rather, existed – here for many long, hungry months. He knew where each and every grave was located because he had dug many of them. Mostly they'd been for the *romusha*, who died at twice the rate of the Allied POWs, but Digger also knew where other graves were.

It irked Digger somewhat that, even now, the leaders of the War Graves mission seemed to dismiss his attempts to provide information about the gravesites at Kanchanaburi. As soon as he brought the subject up, he was told that they had all the information they needed and were sure they would be able to locate everything. It crossed Digger's mind that perhaps the camera incident had soured his relationship with the leaders, but that was no skin off his nose. Then he thought of all the men he had known at Kanchanaburi whose graves he had dug. He resolved to continue offering all the information he had.

After the party had logged over 500 graves in the area, Digger's pestering could no longer be ignored. Captain White organised for him to accompany Lieutenants Leemon and Eldridge to show them a few more graves. Padre Babb reported on the day's findings.

16.30 hours and the lorry had returned: 'Doc' Barrett had done his stuff with a vengeance. Near Kanchanaburi No 1 Cemetery, as close as 100 metres behind what the Nips had said was a Coolie Cemetery is a large cemetery with British, Australians and Dutch buried in it – the cemetery had been cleared but not railed off. The mounds had been made up and some of the original crosses are still standing. Names were taken down. There are 276 graves in this No. 2 Cemetery. Adjacent to this one was yet another cemetery – No. 3, and 128 graves are there. 'Doc' said there is another just here, and through a bit of scrub he led the way to an area where 130 lads are buried. This last cemetery has no number. So once No. 1 Cemetery is located the rest is easy in that area ... It was poor work on our part to have missed 3 cemeteries near No. 1 Cemetery and we were far too easily 'put off' by the Nips when they said that there were no more thereabouts. We were silly not to have taken 'Doc' Barrett with us in the morning – for he had actually dug many of the graves and carved some of the names on the crosses. Had he not quite openly and repeatedly said 'I do know where there are more cemeteries; I ought to for I have dug some of the graves and was stationed here for 18 months' – anyhow he has played his part and but for him we would have missed 534 graves . . . I had heard of the high death rate in this area in 1943 and early 1944 – very sick men were being evacuated from up country. Now I can see by the huge add up of graves what a terrible time this must have been for all concerned.[6]

This view was confirmed by Jack Leemon, who reported that Captain Bruce had refused to listen to what Digger had to say about gravesites at Kanchanaburi, but that he and Eldridge had listened and so they took Digger out on his own. They had found a further 534 gravesites.[7]

Digger was also concerned about the terrible fate of the native labourers, the *romusha*, who had died on the railway by the thousands – about 100,000, Digger guessed. He had tried to explain this to the authorities in Bangkok before the trip, but they'd dismissed him – they were only interested in Allied POW graves. This was probably why, a number of times during the expedition, the War Graves Commission officers had been persuaded by the Japanese that some graves were 'just' *romusha* graves.

Digger slept well that night, knowing that – at last – he had been listened to and his mates would be honoured and remembered. It was a satisfying feeling.

The party arrived back at Nakorn Pathon on 10 October 1945. The expedition had lasted eighteen days. Padre Babb recorded his thoughts about the success of the mission.

Our work for the Graves Commission is now completed and our hard working little party tried to point out 10,549 Allied war graves on and near this 'Railway of death'. We failed to locate 152 of these, and I am sure that all will agree that we have done well. There are 144 cemeteries in which are buried young British, Australians, American and Dutch sailors, airmen and soldiers of all ranks. This Railway is certainly not mis-named.

With proud thanksgiving, like a mother for her children, the home countries will mourn for those who have died as prisoners of war out in this far distant land – they were our friends and our fellow comrades. 'They went with songs to the battle – they were young, straight of limb, true of eye, steady and aglow' when they were captured. As such let us remember them. It is true that they will not, on this earth, mingle with their laughing comrades – they will not see their native lands again – they gave everything they had; their lives, for us and their dear ones that we might all be free.

'They shall grow not old, as we that are left grow old; age will not weary them nor the years condemn; at the going down of the sun and in the morning, we must remember them – we must not break faith with them.'[8]

Chapter 15

Transition

WHEN THE WAR Graves Commission expedition concluded, the party was disbanded and the authorities made arrangements to send all the ex-POWs home. Digger was promised a flight home from Singapore – a most unusual circumstance in those days – which he expected was partly a reward for his volunteering for the War Graves work.

By now, Max Wall had been shipped home. Digger found himself billeted at the Oriental Hotel for a few days as arrangements were made to send him to Singapore. The Oriental was considered the best hotel in Bangkok in 1945. It was certainly a vast improvement on the On-on Hotel. Everything was paid for by the War Graves Commission – even down to the girl that Digger discovered in his bed after he had checked in.

> She was beautiful and even spoke a little English. She appeared to be clean on first inspection, and she smelled great, so I kept her. It was a strange but convenient circumstance. We would spend the night together, and in the morning she was always anxious to leave the hotel before breakfast. I never asked her what she did all day and she never told me.

I had things to do at Sathorn House, organising to get paid and so on, and I just generally took in the sights, ate well at every meal and had a great time throughout the daylight hours. She would be back again in the evening, and we would eat together, go out for a few drinks and get back to the hotel – pretty early, usually! That was how it was for all the time I was there. I never paid her anything and I never asked if someone was paying her. I presumed someone was. It was an excellent arrangement.

Digger had little money left, having spent most of his share of what he and Max had gained by their entrepreneurial activity a few weeks earlier. Within a day or so, however, he received his pay from the British for his time with the War Graves Commission: an amazing £500. Why they paid him this much, Digger had no idea. He immediately went on a shopping spree, buying presents for all his relatives and friends at home.

At Sathorn House, he was interviewed by a new organisation, the Recovered Allied Prisoners of War and Internees (RAPWI), about his time at Kanchanaburi and Lop Buri. Again he tried to impress on the authorities the degradation and misery suffered by the *romusha* at the hands of the Japanese. He tried to explain how it had generally been much worse than the suffering of the POWs. He described the cholera ward and the death house at Kanchanaburi's No. 1 Coolie Hospital, and he impressed on those interviewing him the numbers he had buried every day. But, as before, it felt as though he were talking to himself. The interviewers didn't even have the courtesy to pretend to take notes.

About a week later, Digger reluctantly said goodbye to his new friend and was flown by DC-3 from Bangkok to Singapore. Unfortunately, the promise of a flight home had vanished, and in late

October Digger found himself, along with about a hundred others, aboard HMHS (His Majesty's Hospital Ship) *Karoa*, a 10,000-tonne rust-bucket that set sail for Australia from Keppel Harbour. Digger found an old mate, Vern Hansen, from his early AIF training days. The two spent a very boring twelve days at sea before docking at Fremantle in Western Australia.

Only a few hours later – and without any shore excursion – the *Karoa* set off again, bound this time for Albany. It turned out that the dockworkers at Fremantle had gone on strike. Vern and Digger were furious and had plenty to say about the difference between those who had volunteered for the war and those who had stayed at home. Once they arrived in Albany, however, they forgot all about the dockers.

At very short notice, the welcome that had been planned for them in Fremantle was transferred to Albany, thanks to that town's mayor. And what a welcome it was.

The real reason for docking at a West Australian port was probably so that we could refuel, but apparently when the local people of Albany heard that we were a few hundred returning soldiers they put on a huge welcome for us. There was a brass band playing, flags flying and the mayor was there shaking hands and offering us the freedom of the city. We were there for the weekend.

It was a miracle that they could have organised all this in such a short time. The whole town appeared to be on the wharf, including hundreds of young and very friendly girls. We couldn't wait to disembark. Vern and I had hardly descended the gangway when twin sisters grabbed us and hustled us away from the crowd and into the town. We spent the whole day with them. They showed us the city sights, took us to cafés and then to their home for dinner.

We had a terrific two days. It really felt good to be in Australia again. I took photographs with the camera I had acquired from the American at the Nakhon Nayok camp.

The welcome at Albany was in stark contrast to that at the port of Melbourne a few days later. Digger had a feeling in the pit of his stomach that his reunion with his family was going to be difficult.

As the *Karoa* docked, Digger saw his sister, Iris, her husband, Clive, and his father, David Barrett senior, waiting to meet him. Seeing his family there without his mother brought his grief at her death back to him. They waved and shouted to him, and Clive threw a bottle of beer up to the ship, which Digger deftly caught. The beer was warm; this was not how he had imagined his first taste of a Melbourne brew.

Digger could not shed his sadness that his mother was not there to welcome him. Somehow, he felt, this was his father's fault. Digger managed to contain his feelings of anger, especially when he saw that his father was not as he had remembered him. He was pitifully older, and remained quiet. The bully that Digger knew him to have been was no longer there.

The family's greetings at the dockside were limited to handshakes and polite conversation about the business of collecting baggage and the like. Digger had three pieces of luggage: two kitbags and a haversack. The group waited while the soldiers' kitbags were offloaded, but Digger's were nowhere to be seen. The authorities assured him that they would be forwarded on to him. Digger again found himself cursing the dockers, but this time in Melbourne. The presents he had bought in Bangkok and Singapore were gone, and Digger now had nothing but the clothes he stood in.

The Red Cross had organised a fleet of taxis for the returned soldiers and their families. Vern and Digger exchanged their details and said goodbye. On the way home, Digger's father produced Digger's bankbook, which contained very good news. The army had been regularly banking his pay all the time he was in captivity, as had the Australian Glass Factory in Melbourne. Along with the money Digger had been paid by the British for his War Graves Commission work, this made Digger a relatively rich young man. *Some good news at last*, he thought as he pocketed his bankbook.

But the greatest disaster that weekend for Digger was to come. He discovered that all his possessions – his keepsakes, his guns and even his clothes – had been discarded or given away to friends. After he was reported missing in action, his family had presumed the worst. His father had vacated the family home and now lived with Digger's sister and her husband. Gradually, Digger realised that his mother's death had also hit his father hard, but still he was unable to forgive him or sympathise with him in their common loss.

For almost five years, Digger had longed to get home to the house he had grown up in. Now, even though his sister was making him welcome in her house, it was not the same.

Later that weekend, he received a call from Vern, whose homecoming had also not been as he expected. He was upset and wanted Digger's advice. When Vern had got home, he'd been greeted by his nine-year-old daughter, who had said she was so glad to see him because now 'that other man' would go away.

Vern's wife had admitted that an American soldier had been living with them. She had begged his forgiveness, but all poor Vern could think of doing was to phone his mate. Digger simply told him that if he loved her then he should forgive her. The war had done terrible damage, not only to those in the fight.

On his first Monday at home, Digger reported back to his unit. He was immediately transferred to the 115th Heidelberg Military Hospital, in the Melbourne suburb of Heidelberg West. He knew he had malaria, but it also turned out that he had amoebic dysentery and hookworm. He was not a bed patient, though, and so he was free to enjoy life in Melbourne.

He bought himself a motorcycle – a Velocette 500 cc – which was every young man's idea of the best mode of transport. One morning, he was sent for by the hospital commandant, who complained of his absence during doctor's rounds. He told Digger that while the hospital didn't wish to place any restrictions on his movements, he should at least be present during ward rounds in the mornings. Digger agreed that he would.

Not long after, he had a visit from an officer who asked him to stay on in the army with the War Graves Commission. He was promised immediate promotion, and it was also hinted that he would receive a commission. But by now Digger had had enough of the army and so he refused the offer. He just wanted to get on with civilian life.

Digger was discharged from the army on 16 January 1946. He collected his demobilisation pay, added it to his bank account and went back to work at the Australian Glass Factory. He continued to stay with Iris and Clive, sleeping on the floor. He had been offered a bed but could not get used to its softness, having slept on hard surfaces for so long. He also had great trouble sleeping and found himself pushing his bike down the road, away from the house, before starting the engine and driving around for a couple of hours to clear his mind. There were times when he wished he had not come home.

A few weeks later, the army got in touch with Digger and demanded that he pay back the money he had received from the British in Bangkok. He figured they had probably paid him too much for his work, but Digger just told them to stick it. He never heard from them again.

On 18 February 1946 – Digger's twenty-fourth birthday – he enrolled in the Commonwealth Reconstruction Training Scheme at Melbourne Technical College, earning a Certificate in Painting and Decorating. He then applied for and got a job in charge of the crew painting the wings of the Mustang fighter planes at the Commonwealth Aircraft Corporation at Fisherman's Bend. It was a great place to work. The workers held a raffle on payday every fortnight, and the winner got a girl for the night.

Digger gradually recovered from his postwar blues. He had made his mind up to get on with life and make a success of it. He sold his motorcycle and bought himself a car. He had a near spill on the bike, which persuaded him that he needed a method of transport more suitable for an adult. By the end of March 1946, he had left the Commonwealth Aircraft Corporation and started a painting and decorating business, in partnership with Clive. Digger also bought himself a house, at 109 Severn Street, Yarraville.

Finding a home was a priority, because little more than three months after returning from Thailand, he had fallen in love with and, on 30 March 1946, married Betty, his first wife.

PART 4

A Final
Accounting

Chapter 16

The Business Life

AFTER HE MARRIED, David Barrett was determined to forget about the war and concentrate on achieving success in his business and family life. He dropped the nickname 'Digger', which reminded him too much of the past. For two years, he worked hard and built his painting and decorating business with Clive, but by 1948 he was restless for a change. While he and Clive were successful business partners, they were never close friends.

David's closest mate at this time was Ron Lucas. The two would talk regularly about where there was money to be made and where there were exciting times to be enjoyed. Both fancied working in Queensland. Over time, they talked themselves into believing that they should move to Queensland, enjoy more sun and have a great life.

David never talked about the past, but he knew within himself that his positive attitude had allowed him to learn many lessons at Changi and Kanchanaburi. With great excitement and anticipation for the future, he and Ron moved their families to Queensland. David simply gave his half of the painting and decorating business to his brother-in-law.

Ron and David sold their Melbourne homes and together bought a block of four units at Hawthorne on the Brisbane River, complete with its own tennis court. They never doubted they would both get work, and within a few days David was a salesman with Brittains Pty Ltd, a wholesaler that supplied every kind of hardware imaginable. He loved it and reckoned that as a salesman he had really found his niche.

They did have one small problem. One of their tenants in the units was a solicitor and had a contract that stipulated he should pay only a nominal rent. They could not budge him or put his rent up, and he would not see reason. But David had a plan.

Over the course of about six months, he and Ron befriended the tenant. Eventually, they were able to persuade him to move to the other unit in the property, which was better. When he agreed, Digger and Ron's lawyer immediately explained to this fellow that his original contract was no longer valid. The tenant left when Ron and David outlined the amount they were now asking in rent.

After about two years of their new life in Brisbane, Ron's wife was killed in a car accident. David bought Ron's share in the units, and Ron and his child returned to Melbourne.

In 1950 David joined the company James Campbell & Son. The company sold 'everything for better building', as its slogan claimed. This included hardware as well as all the tools of the trade, and the company reputedly had the largest wholesale warehouse in the southern hemisphere.

David was required to relocate to Maryborough, around 250 kilometres north of Brisbane. He sold the block of units and moved his family into a house in Maryborough that had been built by a customer of his, Max Lohse, who was also a very good friend.

Every five or six weeks, David travelled up the east coast to Rockhampton, then home via the Dawson Valley, through Mount Morgan, Monto and Gayndah, selling building supplies. He loved meeting different people, building relationships and seeing new places. He made many friends.

David remembers playing poker with some of these mates. Sometimes they played for days at a time. Regulars included Ron Bromley, an optometrist, and Bill Lehr, the local publican. They played in Bill's pub, so there was always beer on tap. The gambling skills David had learned from Coy York at Changi, years earlier, stood him in good stead.

David's other passion at this time was rally cars. Being a successful salesman, he was able to persuade Campbell's to sponsor him in this hobby.

Our deal was that they would receive all the advertising and publicity, and in return they would pay all my expenses. I would get to keep whatever it was that I might win, so winning was very important to me. As I became known as a driver, young blokes would keep challenging me to race. I brushed these off as much as I could, but some were more insistent, so to those I demanded that they put up at least a hundred pounds to race against me – winner takes all! We would race between neighbouring towns – thirty or fifty miles, for example – and I never lost a race.

David also won many Apex rallies in and around Maryborough in the 1950s.

While David's business career was going from strength to strength, his marriage was not. He had reasoned that being a travelling salesman might be good for him and Betty – that absence might make the heart grow fonder – but after eight years with Campbell's it was clear that their marriage was failing.

In 1956 David got a job as a salesman in Brisbane with International Majora Paints, which sold industrial and marine paints to shipping companies, the Australian Navy and the Department of Aviation. He was able to put his people skills to work in this job like no other.

In those days, Majora competed with other suppliers of paints, including Berger, Dulux, Taubmans and British Paints. There was a system in place in the Cairns Cross Graving Dock – a dry dock on the Brisbane River – by which a ship might be halved or quartered for painting purposes. Different paint suppliers would be awarded different fractions of a ship for anti-fouling paints and the like.

I was supposed to be responsible for how the paint was applied, for reasons of efficiency. But this proved bloody impossible. I would go down to the docks and tell the work gangs what they were doing wrong in applying the paint but they would just tell me to fuck off. My boss said not to worry, that I should just ensure that we got our share of the order, because nobody could tell these unionists what to do. But I thought, *Bugger it, I'll fix them.*

So I went down to the dock one Saturday before knocking-off time, and I told all the painters that I would meet them in the local pub after work. I went there early and told the manager to give the twenty or so painters all they could drink when they arrived. I said I would pay for the lot. They came in and began drinking schooner after schooner. Some managed to survive till closing time, and they were all well and truly pissed.

I never had a problem with them after that. Our share of sales soared. We never had less than half a ship, and the painters would do exactly as I told them. The other paint companies had a bit of a problem; occasionally the unions would simply refuse to use their paints!

Another customer was the Department of Aviation, which bought paint for the acres and acres of lines and markings on its airfields.

In the late 1950s we were in competition with Berger and a couple of other companies for an order from the Department of Aviation for 5000 gallons of marker paint. What was used on the runways then was a product called Cataphos, an oil-based paint that needed turps for thinning. All the tools, markers and brushes also had to be cleaned in turps.

Unfortunately, Berger had the upper hand because they could source Cataphos at a better rate than Majora could. My mate at Berger was pretty cocky about this; he was very sure they would get the next order. But we had a new water-based paint that we had just produced. I went to great trouble to make sure it was approved for use on the airfield by the Department of Aviation. It was a real hassle keeping this secret from all my competitors.

I had already made a friend of the airfield manager, and when I told him I had got the approval to use our water-based paint, he was all for it. But he explained that I would still need to submit the lowest tender. With that, he excused himself to go to the toilet for a moment and left all the other tenders open on his desk!

In due course, we won the tender. My mate from Berger was on the phone to me immediately. 'You bastard, Barrett,' he said. 'Do you know how much bloody Cataphos we have on hand just now?' And my boss was also very stressed because Majora had to suddenly fulfil this huge new order.

I knew that it wasn't what we were selling that was important, but who and what we knew. That was great fun!

By 1960, David had left Majora Paints and become a representative for the Industrial Public Relations of Australia (Queensland) organisation. There was very little difference between sales and public relations, as far as David was concerned. Both depended on knowing people and being able to persuade them to do what you wanted them to do.

Despite the fact that David was now becoming a very successful businessman, he and Betty had been unable to reconcile their differences. They separated and were divorced in 1965.

With his home life unhappy, David concentrated harder on his work. His job was to organise conventions, all in connection with any aspect of commerce or business. These could take place anywhere in Queensland but were mostly in Brisbane.

One evening, David joined John Reid, the company's managing director, and another sales rep, Doug Pipe, for a drink. They had been drinking for an hour or so when John asked David what his ambitions were. David answered that it was to take over his position as director of the company, and as quickly as possible. The director laughed, but what he did not know was that David was serious. And within six months David was indeed the director.

John Reid started the Brisbane Ideal Home Show in 1965, and the next year David was in charge of it. David delighted in organising large shows and exhibitions. The company organised all the advertising and the necessary publishing, persuaded all exhibiters to take part, and sold the tickets. David hired squads of students to undertake the heavy work of setting up, running and dismantling these trade events.

Around this time, he also helped organise the Sydney International Trade Fair. It hosted stands from all over the world. France donated its stand to the company at the end of the show.

In 1968 David became the Queensland sales manager for Peter Isaacson Pty Ltd, which produced a host of industry magazines in areas such as fashion, aviation, travel, tourism and the arts, as well as industry directories and registers. Its main source of income was the advertising in its publications.

David was charged with compiling a list of all companies with five or more employees for the Queensland section of a publication called the *Kompass Register of Australia*. Today Kompass is a worldwide business-to-business computer search engine, but in the 1960s Peter Isaacson produced the print version.

David had to find, meet and persuade every business owner he could to list their companies in the register. The only tools he had were a phone book, a telephone, a car and his skill in getting further leads from those he talked to. For a full four months, David travelled all over Queensland, staying in some of the best and worst hotels around.

Peter Isaacson and David became good friends, and after publication of the *Kompass Register* David became the company's trouble shooter, charged with increasing the advertising revenue from its publications. This meant travelling a great deal between Brisbane, Sydney and Melbourne, so eventually David decided to base himself in Sydney.

Just occasionally David would visit old mates if he just happened to be close to where any of them lived.

One time I was driving from Coffs Harbour to Newcastle, and since I was in no particular hurry, I had the notion that I should look up one of my mates with whom I had spent over a year burying thousands of *romusha*. Gloucester took me off my route a little but I was looking forward to seeing him; the last I had heard of him was about five years previously. I knew his brother had a shop in the town, and I didn't have any trouble finding it. I got his address, which was a mile or so out of town at a caravan site.

When I got there I found him living on his own, although I remembered he'd had a wife at one point. I was in the same position, of course. But that was where the similarities ended. The poor bugger had no teeth, and he'd been such a good-looking bloke in his youth. He didn't invite me in but suggested we go down the road to the pub instead. *Fair enough*, I thought. He hadn't known I was going to call.

At the pub, my mate downed only one schooner and was obviously seriously affected by it. He gave me a long story about the pension people refusing to give him more teeth because he kept losing or breaking them. I asked him how I could help, and then he started arguing with me. Why would I want to help the likes of him?

I bought him a few extra bottles and took him home. It really upset me, especially because I knew there were many others in very similar positions.

In the early 1970s David began to feel the need to get back into sales. Yaffa, a Sydney company similar to Peter Isaacson, was very progressive; it produced the most important publication for the advertising and marketing industry, *Advertising News* – the forerunner of today's *AdNews*. David joined Yaffa as a salesman for *Advertising News*.

He had a little trouble with two salesmen colleagues, who accused him of poaching on their territory. They apparently had a comfortable arrangement about how the client territory was to be shared. This excluded David getting business from existing clients and left him only able to get new business. David was happy to develop new business for the company but was most unhappy about this cosy arrangement among the sales team.

This problem was solved when the two other salesmen invited David for a drink at the local hotel after work. A few drinks into the session, David suggested that they go outside to settle their differences. He was serious but, like all intelligent people, he agreed that first they should have a few more drinks. By the end of the evening, the three salesmen had become the best of friends. And all of them were now clear about how David could work with them. Just a few months later, David was appointed sales manager and got on well with all his staff.

The circulation of *Advertising News* was limited to the industry itself, although it also sold commercial television advertising. David did his best to increase advertising in the publication but it was challenging.

One day, David Yaffa, the owner of the business, called David into his office. 'I'm not happy with the recent sales figures, David,' Yaffa said.

'Well, neither am I,' replied David. 'They could certainly be much better.'

'So what's stopping you?' Yaffa asked sharply.

'Right, let me tell you.' David sat forward in his chair. 'First, we have to take all restrictions off telephone calls. No more logging of calls and getting permission to make calls. And that's just for starters. I have to put up with staying in second-rate hotels when I travel — I'm too ashamed to invite any potential client back to my hotel to entertain them. I want to stay in the best hotels. I have to be able to make a good impression. Lift those restrictions, and I promise you sales will improve.'

'Okay, David,' Yaffa said eventually. 'But they had better improve.'

A few years later, David's entertainment expenses were so great that the Department of Taxation queried them. But as he had predicted, the resulting sales were also far higher than they had been.

For more than a year, David had been trying without success to get some business from television's Seven Network. He had been dealing with upper management, and while everyone had been polite and cooperative, a substantial account always evaded him. It seemed that every time he managed to come to an arrangement with the managers of various departments, the Seven Network's director always had the final say. Invariably it was no.

Having spent a fortune on entertainment while trying to get this account, David decided on an all-or-nothing approach. He invited the director of the Seven Network to lunch at the Menzies Hotel in Sydney.

David made polite conversation until the director was in the middle of the main course. He then asked, 'Are you not curious about why I asked you to lunch today?'

'Yes, I am,' replied the director. 'I presume it is because you have some special deal to offer us?'.

'Well, you're wrong,' said David. 'I just thought I'd ask you out to tell you're that you're the biggest bastard in the industry!'

The director burst out laughing. No one had ever had the courage to tell him that before, he said. He knew that David had been trying to make a deal with Seven for a very long time. By the time the lunch was complete, he had a better understanding of what *Advertising News* was offering and eventually David got the account.

It was at about this time that David first met his future wife, Greta.

In 1977 I was at a Christmas party put on by a couple of newspapers in Parramatta. I was with Frank Dormer, one of our salesmen, in this lovely garden setting. The party progressed into the early evening, and Frank and I were standing around and talking to people when suddenly I saw this beautiful girl. She was accompanied by two men, one of whom appeared to be her boss.

Before I'd had the chance to approach her, I noticed that she was about to leave. So I went up to her, tapped her on the shoulder and, as politely as I could, said that I would like to see her again and could I please have her phone number. Thankfully, she gave it to me. This was Greta.

David took Greta out to dinner at the Menzies Hotel shortly afterwards, and they were together from that time on. They were married in 1980.

David's last position before he retired was as manager of the Yaffa Group in Melbourne. His main job was to network and entertain, so that the company's clients were satisfied and continued to provide their business. He was well suited to this lifestyle. One Yaffa employee later told the tale that when David retired, all they found in his desk was a list of phone numbers and hotel and restaurant brochures. As David explained, 'Well, they were the tools of the trade!'

David had led a very successful business life, and he'd enjoyed every single minute of it. Although, like many other men, he'd had a terrible time as a POW, in many ways it had strengthened his character. On 15 March 1946, Major Dr Kevin Fagan, a hero of David's, had delivered a lecture about POWs to the New South Wales Branch of the British Medical Association. His words apply very aptly to David.

. . . the returned prisoner of war is in most cases not only a normal man, except for some temporary physical disability, but one who has had intellectual and emotional experiences which give him a decided advantage over his fellows. He has learned to appreciate the minor pleasures of life. He knows the essentials of existence.

He has a high threshold to the pin pricks of ordinary life. He knows man for what he is – his courage, his cowardice, his limitless generosity, his gross selfishness, his nobility and his utter meanness. And if he tends towards cynicism at the discovery of the relation of man's best qualities to his intragastric tension, he is robbed of all bitterness by the memory of the heights to which he has seen some men rise in spite of starvation, of illness and of every degradation which a malignant enemy could put upon them.[1]

After David retired, he and Greta bought a four-wheel drive and a caravan. They made plans to tour Australia, but fate intervened and they had to stop when they reached the Gold Coast, where Greta needed to care for her mother.

They found they both loved the Gold Coast, especially its hinterland. In the end, they decided to stay, and they built a beautiful new home at Tamborine Mountain.

Chapter 17
Fighting Again

'HAVE A LOOK at this, mate!' The tall figure of George Stevenson strode across the lounge bar area of the Holiday Inn Hotel on the Gold Coast. He joined David and Greta at their table and handed David a piece of paper. 'It's from the *Vancouver Sun*, and it's not that old.'

David read the article, which had been published on Friday 20 June 1986. It stated that Canadian survivors of the Japanese POW camps, who had formed a group called the War Amps (Amputees) of Canada, were filing a claim with the United Nations against the Japanese government, claiming reparations for war crimes and gross violations of human rights suffered during their captivity.

David and George were members of the Australian Ex-Prisoners of War Association. They were two among two and a half thousand, including wives, who had gathered on the Gold Coast. Some had come from around Australia and others from Canada, the USA, the UK, New Zealand and Hong Kong, although there were fewer of them than at the last gathering two years earlier, in 1984.

Everyone in this club was at least sixty-three years old, and some were much older. Those still standing were truly remarkable men, and there were also some remarkable women, including a few nurses who had managed to survive their captivity. They had lived through the rigours of war and had suffered particularly brutal treatment as POWs; some had contracted medical conditions as a result, which generally shortened their life expectancy.

The week-long reunion lasted from 12 to 19 October 1986. The Queensland state organisation, and its Gold Coast branch in particular, had worked hard to bring the ex-POWs together. David had recently joined the Gold Coast branch. He had the required qualifications. It was a standing joke among members that no one could buy their way into this club.

The Ex-POW Association had members who had served in all the theatres of World War II, including Europe, Singapore, Thailand and Burma, Indonesia and Hong Kong. Like David, George had been a captive on the Thai–Burma railway.

David had never been an active member of the association. He tended to stay away from meetings, annual get-togethers, the RSL, Anzac Day marches and anything associated with armies, war and the past. He hated war, continuing to see those who joined up as naïve young adventurers – just as he himself had been in 1940. He did not want to be reminded of it.

In David's opinion, war was an activity controlled by politicians and prosecuted by individuals too stupid to think things through for themselves. When he was discharged in early 1946, he swore he would never do anyone's bidding under such circumstances again. Any organisation that he might have joined – including the Ex-POW Association – had links to the forces, uniforms, marching, officers and hierarchy, and he loathed all of that.

It was Greta who had urged David to get more involved with the Gold Coast branch of the Ex-POW Association. She knew that he thought a lot about his many less-fortunate ex-POW mates. David had been successful in business and had survived the war with little worse than crooked teeth from his broken jaw.

His general health remained good and he knew how to look after himself.

The same could not be said for the majority of others who had survived their captivity. Many had returned home so traumatised that their only escape was through alcohol; as a result, many ex-POWs had died in their forties or fifties. Others had severe mental problems or dietary problems, or combinations of illnesses. They had returned from the war experiences to a society that did not recognise the illnesses – mental, physical and physiological – that had resulted from their prolonged starvation, abuse and torture.

David found it very hard to talk about the men he knew who had died since the war. Many had passed away long before their time. Many had experienced problems that resulted in divorce and estrangement from family. David himself had been divorced. He knew that, for ex-POWs, family problems could be attributed directly or indirectly to what they had suffered during their imprisonment. Talking about mates who had experienced such hard times since the war was extremely difficult – even harder than talking about those who had died in the camps.

Despite his reticence to get involved, David had always approved of the actions the Ex-POW Association took to help their less well-off members. These men needed all the backing they could get, and so too did the association as it fought for better government support. Greta encouraged David to join in the fight, knowing that he was happier when he was busy.

'This is great news, mate,' David said, raising his eyes from the article George had given him. 'The only question is why we aren't doing the same thing.'

'Exactly,' said George. He took back the cutting from David and passed it to Greta. 'Surely if the Canadians think they are owed reparations, then we are too.' Greta read the article. 'So what do you reckon?' he continued.

'What would it involve?' she asked, before making a suggestion. 'The first thing you could do, right here and now, is find out what the rest feel about making a claim.'

The rest of the reunion that week was filled with discussions about gaining more support for health issues, with meetings with old friends, with story-telling, and with speeches paying respect to those who did not survive the POW camps.

David and George now had another important objective. They probed for opinion and discussed with as many people as possible how they might organise a claim against the Japanese government. By the end of the reunion, they were convinced that most members were in favour of claiming reparations for all Australian ex-POWs of the Japanese, and they had convinced themselves of the worthiness of the action.

George and David persuaded the executive members present at the reunion to hold an informal discussion on the question of reparations for ex-POWs. The result of this meeting came as a shock to them both.

It transpired that the executive of the association was not in favour of claiming reparations. Although rank and file members, almost to a man, supported the move, not a single executive member could be persuaded that it was a good idea. They all had a remarkably similar position about the proposal. Too much time had passed, they said. It would be very costly to emulate the Canadian action; in fact, only the Australian government could make such a claim against another government. Amazingly, they even argued that the push for reparations would not get the support of the association's membership.

Sir Edward 'Weary' Dunlop was the best known member of the executive at the reunion. He was president of the Victorian State Council of the Ex-POW Association. He summed up David and George's proposal as 'simply pie in the sky'.

For David, the attitudes expressed at this informal meeting were like a red rag to a bull. As he said to George as they left the meeting – loud enough so that others could hear – 'If these bastards won't do anything, then we'll do it ourselves.'

David realised that Weary Dunlop was the leader of the 'anti-reparations' group. Always one to meet a challenge front-on, David invited him to meet with the Gold Coast branch members before he flew back to Melbourne. Confident of his ability to argue and persuade, David hoped that by getting Weary among a group of enthusiasts, he might change his position. He expected that Weary would be up for the challenge but was disappointed when Weary explained that his 'busy schedule' prevented him from accepting the invitation.

In 1986 the Gold Coast was the place in Australia where one was most likely to meet a Japanese person. Japan was growing wealthier, and Australia, particularly the Gold Coast, was fast becoming its people's favourite holiday destination. Many Japanese were investing in real estate on the Gold Coast, and Japan had been Australia's major trading partner since the early 1970s.

Any participant at the Ex-POW Association reunion who took a walk among the beachfront shops not only saw many Japanese tourists but also noticed that a fair proportion of shops were staffed by Japanese and probably owned by them. Many ex-POWs resented this. They had spent more than three years being starved, bashed and brutalised – not by these individuals, of course, but perhaps by their fathers or uncles.

One member at the reunion was arrested that week for lashing out at a young Japanese man. The Japanese, who was less than half the Australian's age and much fitter than his older attacker, was unharmed and had apparently done nothing to provoke the assault. Perhaps he resembled someone from this ex-POW's past. The incident illustrated the depth of anti-Japanese feeling held by many ex-POWs.

Prime Minister Bob Hawke – who, incidentally, was David's first cousin on his mother's side – had come to power three years previously, in 1983. His government had taken great pains to encourage Japanese investment in Australia and maintain good relations with its premier trading partner.

Most Ex-POW Association members who were in favour of claiming reparations from the Japanese did not, of course, have Australia's relationship with Japan as their first priority. Even those who had taken the trouble to consider the value of Japan as a trading partner – and this included David and George – believed that Japan still owed them a great debt. They intended to shout long and loud about it.

A few members appreciated the Australian government's efforts to maintain a good relationship with Japan, and perhaps believed that a group of agitating and crusading ex-POWs could prove an embarrassment. After all, the subject of compensation for what happened to Australian POWs had, to all intents and purposes, been settled at the San Francisco Peace Conference between the Allied governments and the Japanese. Article 14 (b) of its treaty, signed on 8 September 1951, seemed to put an end to any hope of further compensation from the Japanese. It stated that:

Except as otherwise provided in the present Treaty, the Allied Powers waive all reparations claims of the Allied Powers, other claims of the Allied Powers and their nationals arising out of any actions taken by Japan and its nationals in the course of the prosecution of the war, and claims of the Allied Powers for direct military costs of occupation.

What the treaty did provide for was described in Article 14 (a):

It is recognized that Japan should pay reparations to the Allied Powers for the damage and suffering caused by it during the war. Nevertheless it is also recognized that the resources of Japan are not presently sufficient, if it is to maintain a viable economy, to make complete reparation for all such damage and suffering and at the same time meet its other obligations.
Therefore . . .
2. (I) Subject to the provisions of subparagraph (II) below, each of the Allied Powers shall have the right to seize, retain, liquidate or otherwise dispose of all property, rights and interests of
    (a) Japan and Japanese nationals,
    (b) persons acting for or on behalf of Japan or Japanese nationals, and
    (c) entities owned or controlled by Japan or Japanese nationals . . .[1]

In essence, the Allied countries agreed that Japan had no money to pay compensation in 1951, so they settled for the value of whatever property Japan had left in the countries it had occupied. This included the Thai–Burma railway, on which so many Australians laboured and died.

The money available was paid into a fund organised by the Australian government, 'The Enemy Property Trust Fund'. In 1952 the government made an initial distribution of £32 to each ex-POW, or to dependents of deceased POWs . In 1956 a further payment of £54 was made, followed by a final payment of £16.10s in 1963. The total, then, was £102.10s.[2]

All ex-POWs knew they had been paid this minimal compensation in the past, but in the thirty-five years since the treaty was signed, Japan's riches had been greatly restored. The Gold Coast members of the Ex-POW Association were ready to fight for compensation again, no matter what the government had negotiated in 1951.

David and George received great support from members at the reunion. They knew they would probably enjoy similar support from the rank and file members of all of the association's branches, as well as from ex-POWs who were not members. But they would have to lead the movement themselves. David felt completely confident that he had the experience and the determination to do this, without relying on the executive of the Ex-POW Association.

He was ready for the fight, having regularly taken on the establishment since his days at Changi. In his opinion, the executive of the Ex-POW Association should have been leading the fight. Had they done so, he would have been their greatest supporter, but since they refused to lead, he would take the job on. He felt as though a bulldozer could not have stopped him.

David was aware that the executive most likely thought that a small group of ex-POWs on the Gold Coast would soon fall by the wayside, particularly when they had to find hard cash for their campaign. David, too, knew that his enthusiasm was always likely to be greater at the annual get-together. Back at the branch meetings it might be more difficult – but he had plans to overcome this.

All David's working life, he had brought people around to his point of view. He was well aware of the value of publicity, and had plenty of contacts in the newspaper industry. He knew that his knowledge, his skills and his contacts would serve him well.

From that moment on, David became an active and committed member of the Gold Coast branch of the Ex-POW Association. By the end of November 1986, he had been appointed secretary and treasurer of the branch, and he had persuaded the branch president, Harry Nesbitt, to support the fight for reparations. By December, he had persuaded Peter Collas, an ex-POW himself (in Germany) and a solicitor with Collas Moro – to join the reparations claim group. Peter kindly volunteered to work free of charge.

The small reparations group now met regularly to plan and make decisions. David, George, Greta and Peter had now been joined by Gordon Jamieson, an ex-POW and friend of Peter Collas, and Joy Cox, the wife of an ex-POW. This small group of committed and passionate individuals was determined to extract from the Japanese government what they regarded as the right of every Australian prisoner of war. Beneficiaries would include the next of kin of those who had died in captivity during the war and of those who had died since. The task was really one for the national government, but the small Gold Coast branch took it on willingly.

The group knew that its chances of success would be greatly increased if it had the support of the national executive of the Ex-POW Association. Despite the poor reception he had received from the executive at the Gold Coast reunion, David put forward the following four-part motion to the Gold Coast branch meeting on 7 December 1986.

This association of Ex-Prisoners of War is concerned that the heinous, inhuman, brutal and completely unlawful treatment imposed upon Australian prisoners of war by the Japanese military authorities during World War Two has not received the recognition or acknowledgement in terms of reparation or in any other way on the part of the Japanese nation.

That this association is of the opinion that the bashings, the tortures, the starvation and murderous atrocities imposed upon Australian prisoners of war, which brought about the premature death of some 7,700 of them and broke the health of the remaining 13,800 who managed to survive, deserve condemnation of the Japanese by the world community of nations.

That with this objective in mind, this Association does, on behalf of all Australian prisoners of war who underwent captivity by the Japanese in World War Two, inclusive of next of kin of those who in captivity or who have died since, embark on the necessary action to claim reparations from Japan for the unlawful acts so wilfully perpetrated.

Furthermore, in pursuance of this objective this Association investigate the feasibility of enforcing such reparation claims in the international arena, including utilising, if thought fit, the instrumentalities of the United Nations Organisation, the Sub Committee of Human Rights at Geneva; and implement the necessary action as may be feasible and lawful to enforce such reparation claims accordingly.[3]

The branch members voted in favour of the proposal, and the Reparations Committee was born.

David knew the protocols for creating and executing new policy in the Ex-POW Association. Proposals were first put at branch meetings and, if passed, were then proposed again at higher levels of the organisation until they reached the national executive. This ensured that the majority of grassroots members supported the motion. Members knew that if a proposal reached the national executive, it should be acted on in good faith. However, David also knew that the executive could also use the system to block policy that it did not agree with, against the wishes of its members. The process was also very slow, since the state and federal councils of the association met infrequently.

David was well aware that the executive was against his proposal. It would be very easy for them to ensure that the motion got bogged down and forgotten, or even deliberately sabotaged, so he decided to take some preventative action.

He put the motion out as a press release and ensured that it was circulated as widely as possible. His proposal was news on morning radio, and even the federal executive of the Ex-POW Association – in faraway Victoria – immediately became aware of the plans of a small group of ex-POWs on the Gold Coast to launch an action against the Japanese government.

David's next goal was to obtain the approval of the Queensland State Council of the Ex-POW Association, and for this he had another plan.

His first move would be to persuade the largest branch of the Ex-POW Association in Queensland, in metropolitan Brisbane, to support the Reparations Committee's proposals. David believed this would be possible as he had many friends among the rank and file members of the Brisbane branch, although he knew that George Beard, its president, and Clarrie Wilson, its secretary – both of them loyal disciples of Weary Dunlop – were against the proposal.

David organised for a motion in support of the action of the Gold Coast branch to be submitted to the executive of the Brisbane branch in time for its next meeting. The proposal would be announced at the meeting, debated and voted on, just like any other item on the agenda. David confirmed that all this was in order with Clarrie Wilson.

The meeting was held at the Bookmakers Club in Wharf Street, Brisbane, early in January 1987. The meeting room was packed – members were even standing at the back. The branch officials, including George Beard and Clarrie Wilson, sat behind a table on a small stage at the front of the room. David had ensured that all his mates, and their mates, were there. He'd even smuggled Peter Nally, a reporter friend from the Gold Coast, into the event.

The meeting proceeded with its routine items. Suddenly, David realised that Beard was winding the proceedings up – the motion in support of the Reparations Committee had not even been mentioned. He immediately stood and objected loudly. The motion had been submitted according to the rules, he said, but it was being ignored. He continued to complain as the chairman rose to his feet.

'Order, order,' shouted Beard. 'Could you just sit down and shut up for a bit?'

David continued complaining, and soon voices could be heard from all around the room. The loud objections gradually formed a chant by the whole audience: 'Read the motion! Read the motion! Read the motion!'

'Okay, okay, just sit down and listen,' Beard shouted. He held both arms above his head, requesting silence from those on the floor. He conferred with Wilson as the ruckus gradually died down.

Moments later, Wilson got to his feet, cleared his throat and started to explain why the proposal had not been put to the meeting. 'Unfortunately,' he began, 'the papers proposing the motion were not submitted to the executive on time, so the motion . . .' His voice disappeared under a new uproar from the floor.

At that moment, David knew he had the Brisbane branch on his side. After several calls for silence, a face-saving procedural motion from the executive was put to the meeting and passed. Finally, among much shuffling of paper, the motion in support of the Gold Coast branch's Reparations Committee was produced and read. It was overwhelmingly approved by the members.

A few weeks later, on 22 February 1987, the Queensland State Council in turn approved the Reparations Committee's four-part motion to work towards claiming reparations from the Japanese government.

Now, David and his hardworking helpers had to persuade every Australian ex-POW of the Japanese, whether they were members of the association or not, that the Reparations Committee needed their support. For this, David had a twofold strategy: he would design publicity to inform the public of their cause – and to embarrass the Japanese – and he would campaign to win the support of the other State Councils and the Federal Council of the Ex-POW Association.

By now, David recognised a passion building within him that he had almost forgotten. He first had these feelings on the night that freedom had arrived at the Lop Buri POW camp in Thailand. It was an intense hatred, combined with a need to dominate and debase the Japanese, just as he and his mates had been dominated and debased. It was a need to tear from their torturers, by any means possible, at least some payback for the massive hurt and humiliation inflicted on them for three and a half years.

David had satisfied these feelings in late 1945. Now, he truly believed that, if he worked hard, they could be satisfied once again.

Chapter 18

The Fight Continues

IN EARLY 1987, the Reparations Committee began providing stories to every reporter who would listen. Given David's background, he had many contacts he could call on.

The information from Canada about suing the Japanese was like the light at the end of a tunnel for us. I had reporter mates in Melbourne and Sydney who I'd worked with before I retired, and they gave me the names of a few more journalists who they thought would be sympathetic to our cause. I knew the Australian government hated the publicity because Japan was its main trading partner. I also knew the Japanese were embarrassed by our campaign, and of course I knew Weary Dunlop and his mob were furious.

We sent out press releases bloody everywhere. We took care that they were always factual – we didn't have to exaggerate. The truth alone was horrific enough. These stories certainly denigrated the Japanese, but then that was the point of the whole business.

We told the papers that we were suing for $500 million, that the Japanese behaviour in the war had been barbaric, and that we could never forgive and forget. Bruce Ruxton was behind us. He said that former Nazis were being chased all over Europe for what they did but that nobody was saying boo about the Japanese war criminals.

Now, making public any action that needs bureaucratic approval from an organisation or association is often frowned upon. Bureaucracies generally like to consider proposals without the pressure of publicity. The federal level of the Ex-POWs Association was, therefore, not amused when the Reparations Committee of the small Gold Coast branch broadcast to the world that it intended to go after the Japanese government – via the United Nations – for reparations, especially since it stated clearly that it expected the support of all other state branches and the federal executive. By publicising the cause, David had ensured that the committee's intentions could not be ignored.

David very much wanted the support and the authority of the Federal Council. As it was, the Reparations Committee was acting under the authority only of the Gold Coast branch, and with the tacit support of the Queensland State Council. David did not believe that the 1951 San Francisco Peace Treaty had put an end to any hope of compensation. He had sought some expert opinions on this from the lawyers who were working on the Canadian claim. He knew he had to inform the rank and file of the movement in order to gather their support. Newspaper articles were one of the best ways to achieve this.

David knew that some ex-POWs believed that this effort would be all too late and therefore hopeless.

People often asked me why we were taking action at this late stage. I'd say to them, 'Well, what about the Jews?' They had been bringing World War II holocaust criminals to justice for years after the war.

In Japan, hundreds of war criminals were still living a peaceful existence because the Allies hadn't meted out the same justice to those who had mistreated and tortured us. Every POW who didn't come back died in his own kind of hell. Many might have welcomed a quick death, but thousands died clinging to the belief that life was better than death. We who survived believed that no amount of money could compensate us for that pain. However, I thought that what little we might get would be of some comfort to survivors and widows, and I was determined to get it for them.

The year 1987 was a busy one for the members of the Reparations Committee. In addition to publicising their cause through newspapers, they corresponded with the ex-POW associations in Canada, Britain, Holland and New Zealand. They worked hard to gain support from the other higher levels of the Australian Ex-POW Association, the government, the RSL and the Red Cross.

After the Queensland State Council approved the Gold Coast branch's reparations proposal in February 1987, it was sent to the Federal Council with the request that it also give approval. As the committee chairman, David asked that a poll be organised of all members of the association, Australia-wide, to ascertain the feelings of grassroots members. David doubted that this would be as straightforward as it appeared, but the process had to be followed.

Greta supported and helped David throughout this very busy time. She typed and organised and made their house at Mount Tambourine available as the committee's headquarters. David, George Stevenson, Peter Collas and Joy Cox planned, wrote letters and developed an application form with which Ex-POWs could register their support for the compensation bid. A $10 registration fee was requested from each claimant to fund all the administrative work.

David continuously lobbied the various state councils of the Ex-POW Association, informing them of what the committee was planning and what it expected of the Federal Council. Everyone knew what was happening. The committee was determined to succeed. Even at this early stage, as a result of the publicity and their committee members' letters, applications began to trickle in, along with donations to the cause.

By the end of April, there had still been no response from the Federal Council. The committee resolved to take the initiative and hurry things along a bit. They sent a document with much information to all the main office-holders of the Federal Council and all the state councils. They also requested that information be published in *Barbed Wire and Bamboo*, the official magazine of the Ex-POW Association. The article never appeared; David was sure that the Federal Council had blocked it.

I figured that if the members of the Federal Council were unsure of how to go about their business, with regard to the claim for reparations, then we should set them right! I reminded them again of our activities and enclosed copies of everything they needed to understand our position. Even at this stage, I was quite willing to hand the whole kit and caboodle over to the Federal Council, if this was what they wanted, but I didn't believe it was.

I knew that the state representatives on the Federal Council, including George Beard and Clarrie Wilson from the Queensland Council, were still voting with Weary at the Federal Council meetings. I'm bloody sure they had their eyes on other prizes; they just wanted to keep sweet with their pals in the government. I knew that many of the office-bearers in the various state councils and the Federal Council had received government awards – usually as a result of proposals from other state or Federal Council members.

No doubt all were well deserved, but I could not help wondering
if a sense of obligation kept them from supporting an organisation
whose actions tended to embarrass that government by continually
insulting its chief trading partner.

As a result of the Reparations Committee members' publications in
various newspapers, they gained a great deal of feedback and were
able to gauge the general feeling for their cause. Bruce Ruxton wrote
that 'support for the reparations committee at RSL meetings has been
overwhelming'. J. L. Fitzgerald, the secretary of the Victorian Ex-
POW Association, wrote: 'I personally fully support your effort, and
will do everything possible to bring about a satisfactory result.' He
was from Weary's own branch. Similarly, George Morgan, President
of the Wollongong branch, wrote that 'you have my fullest support
and again I thank you for the great work achieved'.[1]

But of course there were also some detractors. Jim Boyle,
secretary of the Federal Council, wrote to Ralph Coutts, secretary
of the Queensland Council, saying, 'I think that their [the Reparation
Committee's] enthusiasm far outstrips their discretion but let's
wait and see what transpires'.[2] By far, however, the feedback was
positive.

Between early June and the end of November 1987, there was
frequent correspondence between officials of the Reparations
Committee and both the Queensland State Council, on the one hand,
and the Federal Council, on the other. The main protagonists in
these discussions, at either end, were David and Sir Edward 'Weary'
Dunlop.

In a series of letters, Weary argued — mostly in exasperation,
judging from their tone — that 'there is a repugnance among many
members about approaching the Japanese on this matter'. He stated
categorically: 'Do not raise the hopes of unfortunate people by

premature glowing newspaper articles about receiving reparations money . . . It is a lightweight approach to seek reparations without Government support . . . It would be too difficult to collect and collate claims without Government participation and support.'

He even seemed to be unwilling to take any action to find out what the rank and file felt about claiming reparations: 'We should let the Canadians do the hard work and see what happens . . . Too many years have passed to make a claim now . . . Just leave it to the states to vote yes or no.' The final blow for the Reparations Committee came when Weary informed it that 'South Australia, Victoria and New South Wales are all against the proposal and West Australia needs more time before making a decision.'³

The Reparations Committee members were very disappointed with Weary's comments, but David argued back with polite enthusiasm. 'We can't let the Canadians down,' he wrote. 'We too should do some of the heavy lifting . . . My committee believes that any problems of communication and funding can be overcome by good leadership and by being single-minded of purpose . . . We do not think that our costs will diminish through ongoing delay.'

The committee members were shocked by some of Weary's comments, and David's responses conveyed this:

We were surprised that a "repugnance" exists among ex-POWs in respect to this claim because our enquiries reveal the exact opposite . . . Some German war criminals are only now being brought to justice in Europe so in no way are we behind in our actions . . . You will doubtless agree that all ex-POWs practiced optimism to see us through our darkest years, so surely optimism in this matter is more likely to bring a successful conclusion.

David also included what he considered practical advice in his responses: 'Let us consider motions from the branches without delay and encourage members to express views freely and without influence . . . [We should] conduct a referendum using a coupon in *Barbed Wire and Bamboo* that would cost nothing.' Finally, he added, 'I hope that I am mistaken in thinking that individual thoughts and feelings of the executive are taking precedence over the needs and wishes of the rank and file.'[4]

Despite these practical suggestions by the Reparations Committee, Weary's final communication on the matter was military in tone and straight to the point:

> State Branches were asked to vote and they have done so . . . Please take note that any further action by you or your committee in relation to the question of reparations which involves this association or its Branches throughout Australia must cease forthwith.
>
> By order of the Federal Council.[5]

Now David's back was really up. It was like the 1986 conference on the Gold Coast all over again. Most of the state executives were led by men of the same mind as Weary. The rank and file of the association had basically been ignored.

Some people in these circumstances might have been persuaded to give up, but the response just made David and his committee more determined than ever. They could not accept that they 'must cease forthwith'. The mood at the next Reparations Committee meeting was dark.

'Who the hell do they think they are?' one member asked.

'Are we still in the bloody army?' said another. 'Is this an order from Brigade Command?'

'Fuck 'em! Let the mutiny begin!'

David had never kowtowed to any officer while he was in the army, and he was not about to start now. He could not understand why Weary, who had looked after his men so well when they were prisoners – and indeed had suffered alongside them – could possibly think of letting these bastards off the hook now that they had a chance to do something about it. David was sure that most POWs felt as he did; the general enthusiasm for the reparations movement proved it.

David had got in touch with Bill Holtham, the chairman of the Japanese Labour Camp Survivors Association in Britain. He had informed David that in Britain they too had a great deal of opposition from the headquarters of their association. Bill was sure it was because many of them had been awarded honours of one sort or another from the Queen; therefore they simply refused to support anything that would upset the government.[6]

David had been wondering for a while whether this was indeed the case with the Federal Council of the Australian Ex-POW Association.

When we got that reply from Weary telling us to 'cease forthwith', I saw red. I could feel all the old hatreds and the anger come flooding back. I really thought we had been positive and had responded to his points calmly and reasonably; to be ordered to 'cease forthwith' was unbelievable!

Anyhow, we stayed polite. We should probably have written back saying 'stick it up your arse' or something similar, but we didn't. We just said that we would carry on with the authority from our own Gold Coast branch and the Queensland State Council. I did make some comment about him not being able to read properly. And then, would you believe it, we had another order telling us once more that we 'must cease'. So that was it. We just ignored him after that.

The Reparations Committee met and discussed at length what they would do from here on. They were agreed that the rank and file of the association, except for those in Queensland, had not yet had a say in all of this. Secondly, they knew that there would be many ex-POWs of the Japanese who were not members of the association but who would be eligible to apply for reparations money. The obvious solution was simply to appeal to ex-POWs and their families directly. They also reckoned that so long as the Reparations Committee kept up its pressure, the state councils would eventually come around.

On 19 June 1988, the Queensland State Council of the Ex-POW Association passed the following official motion:

(a) That a committee be formed to take all the steps necessary on behalf of this Council to prepare and submit a claim to the United Nations Sub Committee on Human Rights, to be called the Queensland Reparations Committee.

(b) That the Committee already appointed by the Gold Coast Branch, namely D.W. Barrett, Chairman, P. I. Collas, Secretary and G. Stevenson be authorised to act as the Queensland Reparations Committee with power to co-opt other members to assist.

(c) That the Queensland Reparations Committee be authorised to raise funds to meet all the expenses of taking the necessary action, such funds to be controlled by the Gold Coast Branch in a separate account under the control of its treasurer.

(d) That the said Committee report to this Council at its regular meetings and from time to time as requested as to progress made.[7]

By this motion, the Reparations Committee was empowered and expanded considerably. They now had the necessary authority to pursue their claim on the Japanese government through the United Nations.

> We redoubled our efforts and used every means possible to publicise the mission. It was a terrific committee at this time. We got the addresses of every Ex-POW Association branch, every Battalion Association and every RSL club. We wrote articles to be published in every magazine. I got on to all my old mates at Yaffa who had close connections with all the newspapers. We advertised the fact that every ex-POW (Japan) could apply for reparations money, provided that he complete a form, and we let it be known that we would also accept donations.

Soon the completed forms came rolling in, along with their $10 registration fee. Usually an additional donation was included too.

In October 1988 the Federal Council of the Ex-POW Association appointed a new executive. The president was now Bill H. Schmitt, and with this change came the acceptance of the Reparations Committee.

David received a letter dated 26 October 1988 from Clarrie Wilson, who remained the Queensland delegate to the Federal Council. Wilson explained that the Federal Council now accepted the fact that the Reparations Committee was under the control of the Queensland Ex-POW Association; it was thus entitled to continue its claim for reparations from the Japanese. Furthermore, they could now have access to the association's magazine, *Barbed Wire and Bamboo*.[8]

At this time, a mate of mine in the real-estate industry was selling blocks of land on Russell Island off the Gold Coast. I asked him if I could have a good block and he said sure, and he quoted me a very attractive price. 'No, no,' I said. 'I need it for free, and I'm going to raffle it.' I told him not to worry, that there would be so much publicity, Australia-wide, that he would have to buy more development land to take advantage of the demand. I got the block for free.

The newly renamed Australian Reparations Committee was well on its way.

Chapter 19

The Health of the Ex-POW

THE REPARATIONS COMMITTEE was not David's only interest at this time. For many years, he had been concerned by the plight of fellow ex-POWs who, unlike him, had been unable to make a good life for themselves on their return from the war. Many were heavy smokers or drinkers, or both.

David was convinced that their failure to secure their futures was largely due to the suffering, both physical and mental, that they had endured as prisoners of the Japanese. Many men had died young, often from afflictions exacerbated by alcohol or from the residual effects of diseases suffered during their imprisonment. The Australian government's Department of Veterans' Affairs, David believed, had failed to recognise that the plight of these men was as a result of the service they had given to their country, and not through any fault of their own.

David's aim was to secure improved legislation that would look after ex-POWs of the Japanese, and that would provide them with pensions or disability payments. In the mid-1980s, these pensions were very difficult to get; the ex-POWs and their medical advisers had overcome almost impossible hurdles to qualify. In David's view, all ex-POWs should receive the maximum pension. He had been able to obtain this for himself, but it had been a long and hard battle. He now resolved to help others in this endeavour.

He was not alone in this, since all the ex-POW associations across the nation were also fighting for this cause. Chief among the proponents was Weary Dunlop. In late 1987, he had written to Prime Minister Bob Hawke and explained very clearly what the situation was for an ex-POW (Japan).[1]

David was not a doctor, as Weary was, but he had always had a great interest in medicine. He was as keen as anyone to get the best possible deal for his fellow veterans. He and Weary were of exactly the same mind on this subject. Typical of David's efforts was a letter he sent to the Minister for Veterans Affairs, Ben Humphreys, in May 1989:

Dear Mr. Humphreys

Australia is a reasonably rich, productive and probably one of the best-fed countries in the world today. It is not surprising that chronic deficiency diseases and their residual effects are rarely diagnosed in this country . . .

Seeing thousands of Australians with far-advanced acute and chronic deficiency diseases is an experience unknown to most Australian physicians, unless they were so unfortunate as to have been incarcerated in the Orient when the Japanese Imperial Army overran the Far East . . . Australian physicians are often difficult to convince that the former prisoners have sustained permanent and service-connected disability as a result of wartime experience.

This experience began in 1942 for those Australian troops who were stationed in Malaya and Singapore . . . Hence began every gradation of acute dietary deficiency disease known to medical science . . .

In the next forty months, thousands of Australian and other Allied prisoners died in Prisoner-of-War camps throughout South East Asia and Japan as a result of starvation, disease, overwork and the brutality of their guards. Those who survived were scarred for life and in most cases their life expectancy was shortened by many years.

The 'typical' prison camp diet varied little from day to day. At the very best, the diet composed a poor grade of rice and watery greens, a half full cup of thin rice gruel or pap (about 8 oz or 160 calories) twice a day was standard. The rice was of the polished variety, containing much foreign material such as maggots, weevils and dirt. There were days when no food was issued at all. Meat of dubious origin would supplement the diet from time to time, no more than a few grams of protein for each prisoner.

During the first few months of captivity [at Changi] a number of prisoners died each day and were buried in common graves. After that, prisoners were permitted to purchase extra food from a small canteen, however this was limited. Some of the healthier prisoners planted small vegetable gardens, but they had to guard them carefully since vegetables frequently disappeared before they were ready.

Most of the prisoners suffered from amoebic or bacillary dysentery, or both, consequently their bodies could absorb very little of the food they were able to get. Prisoners on working parties were fortunate because they could steal extra food.

After the liberation of Allied Prisoners-of-War in 1945, an adequate diet supplemented by the required vitamins and minerals rapidly improved most of the acute symptoms, but many of the individuals who were prisoners of the Japanese of 6 months or longer (most 3½ years) were left with one or more . . . permanent residual effects.

After returning home, many of the former Prisoners-of-War vowed they would never 'go without' again. They over-ate, over-smoked, over-drank, over-medicated and just as detrimental to their health, under-exercised . . . They preferred diets rich in fats, cholesterol and salt, and they drank lots of coffee.

Unfortunately, the many ex-Prisoners who have chain smoked since the end of the war have complicated their residual diseases with tobacco-related diseases . . . Some have become chronic alcoholics, further damaging their brains, hearts, livers, stomachs and nervous systems. A few became addicted to drugs.

One sad result of these added complications is that some former Prisoners-of-War have difficulty persuading the Veterans' Administration that their disabilities are service connected. Most of the ex-prisoners are suffering from one or more of the residual conditions and are fully entitled to disability under the appropriate Act, yet cases are still being brought to the attention of the DVA where such individuals have been unable to convince the Department of the validity of their applications . . . As a result, their post war death rate is up to seven times higher than other war veterans'.

It is the considered opinion of eminent and medically qualified ex-Prisoners-of-War that anyone who was a Japanese Prisoner-of-War for 6 months or longer, who survived the trials and tortures of imprisonment in the Orient, should be considered for disability pensions.

I sincerely hope this will give support to all ex-Prisoners-of-War, who in serving their country, sustained the terrible hardships of Japanese incarceration and are still suffering from the after effects.[2]

About the time I wrote to Humphreys, I began to think more deeply about my own health and state of mind. The more I studied the health of Ex-POWs in general and the effects that their treatment so long ago had on their present state of health, the more clearly I understood my own condition. I was gradually able to accept that I too was not as whole as I had always regarded myself.

It had taken me a lifetime to begin to understand my own condition. I knew that I had been in denial for most of my life, and of course I also realised that this was probably one reason why so many ex-POWs found it so difficult to apply for a pension. To help solve this problem, I wrote and distributed among the ex-POW community what I had discovered about myself. I thought long and hard before I decided to make it available to everyone.

War and Post War: The Ex-POW Japan

I was captured at the Fall of Singapore and held prisoner in Changi, the Siam/Burma railway and various Japanese Army projects in Siam for three and a half years. The Japanese were brutal captors. During most of that time, we were starved, overworked and deprived of medical treatment, clothing, footwear and anything resembling hygiene. The Japanese guards treated us as expendable slave labour, and the threat of death was a daily prospect, whether by accident, execution, casual brutality, illness or starvation. Only the atomic bomb saved us from certain death, either by pre-invasion execution or by starvation during death marches.

The prison camps taught us certain survival skills. One of the first lessons in survival that we learned was to show no resistance and to hide all expressions of anger or disapproval. We learned to be docile and uncomplaining in the face of extreme provocation. Where the normal human reaction to a blow is to strike back, we learned not only to repress that reaction but also to repress the emotion that would prompt such a response. Where it is only natural to show anger when one is abused unjustly, we learned to accept indignities, even pain, without displaying any emotion. We found reason to practise this deceptive behaviour daily throughout the years of our captivity. We came to be so adept at these life-preserving suppressions of our natural feelings that eventually the behaviour became an automatic response. We found ourselves enduring discomfort and physical punishment without even thinking about the need to blank out our feeling. We became accustomed to behaving in ways that were not normal until the abnormal became our norm for survival.

To an outsider, we appeared to be subhuman creatures, acting as automatons in such circumstances where ordinary men would have been rebellious, angry or hostile. This does not mean that we did not feel the blows and that we did not resent our unearned punishments. Did we come to accept the cruelties of our guards as right and proper? My own recollection is that we were just as enraged at injustice and sadistic cruelties after three and a half years as we had been after one week of captivity. We were no longer surprised by it and we were better prepared to survive such a regime than we were at the beginning of our ordeal. But we still felt the hurts and we still resented them as deeply as before. We never considered the starvation, overwork and the beatings as normal and acceptable behaviour. I do not remember becoming so inured to the brutality that I did not from time to time entertain myself with fantasies of revenge.

We eventually arrived back in Australia after spending almost five years overseas and receiving little notice, and no special attention was paid to our adjustment problems. In my own case, I recall that horrifying nightmares, nervous tremors, generalised paranoia, acute depression and crying episodes caused me to seek medical advice when I returned to Heidelberg Military Hospital after weekend leave. I was hospitalised for observation because of my complaints and later discharged from the Army as unfit for further military service. I was then awarded a 10% disability pension. One of the disabilities mentioned was anxiety neurosis. Today, those symptoms would be diagnosed as Post Traumatic Stress Disorder.

Anxiety neurosis is a common affliction of former Prisoners of War (Japan). Many of us with that diagnosis do not understand the illness. We are not able to say just what is wrong with us, and we do not know why we have the symptoms associated with that type of illness. Most of us would, I suspect, deny that we are particularly anxious or that we are neurotic. For several years after liberation, I did have problems of adjustment. By 1960, however, fifteen years after the war, I was able to put aside my identification as an ex-POW and to see myself primarily in terms of my work role. I thought then that my behaviour was normal, and I believed that I no longer had adjustment problems.

Like most of us, I convinced myself that I had no grudge against the Japanese. Whenever questioned about it, I would absolve the Japanese people for the crimes committed by their military leaders. In my efforts to come to a peaceful resolution of my past, I acted sincerely. I believed that I was doing what was both right and necessary. So far as I could tell, I had no problem coming to terms with my prison camp experience.

It was in 1968 that I first began to suspect that I might have a more serious problem than I realised in shedding my prison camp history. On attending my first Anzac Day march and wearing my war medals for the first time, I found to my dismay that a few yards down the road I started to weep uncontrollably. I started to shake and became disorientated. I then broke away from the group I was marching with and made my way home. I have never marched or worn my medals since.

Later, it occurred to me that, during the march, memories had started to flood back of those horrendous years, memories that I thought had been put out of mind or in perspective. When I related the incident to my wife, I tried to tell her about the way the Japanese had treated us in captivity. I again broke down and wept, unable to continue.

In retrospect, I reasoned that I had denied myself the right to have normal human emotions about what had been done to my comrades and me by the Japanese. It was only natural that I should be angry with the Japanese guards. Instead of recognising and admitting my anger, I had denied my feelings because they conflicted with my social training. I had been taught as a child and counselled as an adult that it is wrong to hold a grudge, and that it is right to forgive one's enemies. I did the dutiful and correct thing, dealing with the issue rationally and free of emotion. For the most part, I thought I was successful in forgiving the unforgivable and in forgetting the unforgettable experiences of my captivity.

It made me see that I was, first of all, a human being and not some kind of forgiving angel. I was able to live with my anger only because it had been so deeply buried in my subconscious that I was not aware of the burden I carried . . .

The joy, the easy and spontaneous happiness that I witnessed in others, I could not emulate in my own life. My ability to feel strongly and to care deeply about many things had been dulled. My life was much more serious and less fun than it might have been.

It affected my work life in ways that I did not realise for many years. My behaviour progressively got worse: bouts of emotionalism that at times left me shaking and near to tears. I would rant and rave at people I respected or loved, for no real or obvious reason.

What this tells me is that all of us, normal human beings, were deeply offended and terribly angered by what the Japanese did to us and to our helpless companions. We hid that anger in order to survive and we controlled it for so long a period that we buried it out of our consciousness. This numbing of feeling and burial of anger became necessary adaptations because there is no other way that we could have functioned in that setting. Today, these many years later, we live with the physical and mental consequences of that suppression of strong emotions. Fatigue, restlessness, depression, irritability, crying, insomnia, nightmares and shaky hands are some of the symptoms that point to the anger within each of us today. We have demonstrated a tendency to direct this latent anger toward members of our families and to blame them for our emotional problems instead of the war years.[3]

The laws regarding pensions for ex-POWs (Japan) changed very little as a result of all this effort by Weary, David and many others. However, David's self-analysis revealed to him exactly why he was so determined to make the Japanese government accept, apologise for and pay for their soldiers' past behaviour.

George Beard and Clarrie Wilson, the chairman and secretary of the Queensland State Council of the Ex-POW Association, continued to make things difficult for David and the Reparations Committee.

George Beard kept referring to our Australian Reparations Committee as a sub-committee of the State Council. Perhaps we were, but he certainly knew that it would annoy the hell out of me. We had got this far despite his activities, not because of them. Here was someone who in the recent past had done his best to stop the Reparations Committee and had gone along with everything Weary said about the impossibility of the task. Now, when he could see how successful we were, he wanted to take control. Not on your bloody life! If we had to report to the State Council, fair enough, but I wasn't having George run the show – no way!

George had various concerns about our activities and always wanted to meet and discuss them at a moment's notice. I refused to play his game. Every request he made was of vital importance and urgent, according to him, so the first thing I'd do was take my time. Even although we reported regularly, openly and honestly, he was never satisfied and always wanted to run the committee his way.

He wanted to control where the money was invested, where the bank statements were kept, what our travel expenses were, what the quorum for a meeting should be, what the criteria for accepting claims were, what the taxation implications were, and so on. We told him that his claims were frivolous and mischievous, and that quieted George down – at least for a while.

Some registration forms from members came with the minimum of information, but others were accompanied by horrific stories of suffering under the Japanese. The committee recorded all of them, of course, and used some stories as evidence of suffering in their claim documentation.

One example of an understated claim form came from the very well known nurse, Sister Captain Vivian Bullwinkel, a survivor of the sinking of the SS *Vyner Brooke* in the Banka Strait in February 1942. She stated simply that she suffered from 'malaria, dysentery, tinea, Banka Island fever and malnutrition'. And in answer to the question about sadistic treatment, she wrote: 'Shot in the back, only survivor of 21 nurses on beach, Banka Island, Japanese machine-gunned us from behind as we were forced to walk into the sea.'[4]

David also made direct contact with the Japanese government, through its Australian ambassador. He tried to persuade him that the best course of action for the Japanese government – to prevent further embarrassment – was to apologise and pay reparations for the wrongs it had inflicted on Australian POWs, just as other countries such as Germany were doing. He explained the Reparation Committee's mission, and detailed how it had gathered extensive evidence of horrendous Japanese war crimes. Japan had to demonstrate 'her genuine desire to make amends to former Australian POWs', David wrote, which 'would also help to restore Japan's national honour in the eyes of the international community'.[5]

The Reparations Committee encouraged all those who had registered a claim to write to the Japanese embassy in Australia. They should explain their position, describe the harsh treatment they had received from the Imperial Japanese Army and ask when the Japanese government would pay reparations. All who did this received a standard reply, along the lines of that which the Reparations Committee itself eventually received:

> The question of reparations to Australian nationals caused by the action taken by Japan or its nationals has already been settled between Japan and Australia, one of the allied powers, by Article 14(b) of the San Francisco Peace treaty of 1952.[6]

David decided that letter writing was getting them nowhere with the Japanese Embassy.

> We made little headway with the Japanese through correspondence, so I decided to go to see them personally. I took Greta along to the embassy in Canberra on two occasions. We were always received very politely and shown every courtesy. However, the result of

these meetings was no better than what we had achieved by sending letters.

We always met with the First Secretary at the embassy and several officials. All the questions I asked were answered only after the officials had a discussion in Japanese in front of Greta and I, and after they had consulted this huge bloody book. I have never seen such a big book. Apparently, it contained all the answers to every question they were ever likely to be asked about anything!

One of the officials was not as polite as the others. He looked like the worst type of railway guard, just as I remembered from all these years ago. He was in his mid-twenties, a squat, muscular little bastard, and he hated the questions about torture and starvation that I was putting very directly to the First Secretary.

I could always feel this guy's anger, although he never said a word. I just smiled at him because I knew that would annoy him even more. I could feel Greta's hand on my arm, pulling me back slightly as if to say, 'Please don't annoy that man any more.' I really felt like thumping him but he was forty years younger than me so I resisted.

David arranged for Japanese newspapers to have access to the stories of Australian ex-POWs: what they felt about the Japanese and what they were preparing to do about it. The greater the embarrassment to the Japanese government, David reckoned, the more likely they were to pay reparations. It seemed likely that this was why the executive of the Federal Council of the Ex-POW Association had been so against claiming reparations. They didn't like upsetting the Japanese government because that would upset the Australian government.

David's strategy seemed to be working well, as evidence was emerging that the Japanese were worried about their relationship with Australia.

David never missed a chance to correspond with the media in Japan. He was even interviewed by the Japanese press, always emphasising that Australian POWs were owed compensation for the horrendous treatment they had suffered.

By mid-1989, the funds held by the Reparations Committee totalled approximately $77,000. The raffle for the block of land was expected to bring in another $30,000. Much of the money was lodged in term deposits, which at the time were paying interest rates of up to seventeen per cent.

The committee employed a writer, James Essex, to develop the claim documents and conclude the project's draft stage. They hoped to have the final copies of the claim printed by September 1989.

Chapter 20

To Geneva

DURING THE SECOND half of 1989, the members of the Reparations Committee prepared for their trip to the United Nations in Geneva, Switzerland, where they would lodge their claim against the Japanese government. They knew, as always, that publicity would be important.

This was foremost in their minds as they met, on 7 July 1989, at the offices of their solicitors, Collas Morro, on the Gold Coast. The more international publicity they could generate, the better chance they would have of shaming Japan into action. It was agreed that David and Peter Collas would travel to Geneva via Canada, the United States and Britain.

David's attention was drawn to an article in Sydney's *Daily Telegraph* of 24 July 1989. It reported on atrocities witnessed during the war years by a former intelligence officer of the Japanese army by the name of Nagase Takashi, who was visiting Australia. David immediately recognised the *Kempeitai* officer with whom he had worked during the War Graves Commission trip back up the railway all these years before.

David had suspected then that Nagase probably was guilty of war crimes, but he was apparently a completely different man now. Even then, David had not disliked him. Now he was, by all accounts, a respected former officer who had some influence in Japan, and he had admitted being ashamed of the atrocities he had witnessed against Allied POWs. That was enough for David to recommend that the Reparations Committee should approach him.

Nagase Takashi had come to Australia at the behest of one Don Kibbler. He was a builder who had worked with the Japanese architect Ken Nakajima to construct the Japanese Gardens at Cowra, which commemorated the 234 Japanese POWs and the five Australian soldiers who had died during the breakout there in August 1944. Kibbler also had extensive business connections in Japan.

A meeting with Don Kibbler in Sydney was arranged, which was attended by David, Gordon Jamieson, the Reparations Committee's secretary, and George Morgan, the NSW Reparations Committee's representative.

After the group had briefed Don on the Reparations Committee's mission, he proposed a strategy of more direct negotiations with the Japanese government, with Nagase Takashi acting as the middleman. Nagase's views were well known by the public in Japan, and it was likely that he would be keen to help with their efforts to gain reparations. The mayor of Kyoto had also publically apologised to Don on Japanese television, and he thought there was at least an opening for them to approach the Japanese government directly.

Don explained that he thought it more likely that the Japanese government would respond to an intermediary such as Nagase because they would feel less intimidated. In his view, the Japanese would be less likely to agree to compensation if they felt threatened. David was not so sure but was willing to give it a go.

Don then went on to explain how they might propose a foundation that would benefit ex-POWs and their families. He argued that this might be more likely to win the Japanese government's favour, rather than a straightforward claim for an amount of money based on the number of claimants.

The claim could be set out as a proposal to fund some institution, association or service that would promote greater understanding between the people of Japan and Australia. The claimants' requirements could then be recognised in a trust deed, and a figure of $25,000 could be paid to each, at the discretion of the trustees. Don had some experience in setting up this type of trust: he had been chairman of the Cowra–Japan Memorial Foundation, which could serve as a model for the Reparations Committee to follow.

Don said he could discuss all this discreetly with his contacts in Japan, including Father Tony Glyn, a Catholic priest working there, and several Japanese politicians. While David was glad to have Don's enthusiasm and advice, he was still unsure how effective such an approach would prove to be.

I was not comfortable with these ideas from Don Kibbler. He was all charm, and although I voiced my view that hard and embarrassing publicity against the Japanese would be the way to wear them down and eventually get reparations for all our claimants, the others on the committee were suddenly enthusiastic about Don's proposals. So we went along with it.

Suddenly, everything had to be secret. We didn't want anyone to know about this foundation plan until the Japanese had agreed to it. My immediate thought was: what about our claimants? Did we have a right to keep from them what we were planning? Until then, the claimants had been able to read in every Ex-POW newsletter, in every battalion magazine, in *Barbed Wire and Bamboo*, and in their local newspaper exactly what we were up to.

Towards the end of 1989, the Reparations Committee had their claim documentation organised. They had also organised for Booralong Press to publish a book, *Nippon Very Sorry: Many men must die*, which contained all the details about their claim.

David wrote the letter to the Secretary-General of the United Nations that accompanied the Reparations Committee's two-volume claim document with them to Geneva.

Dear Sir

Re: ECOSOC RESOLUTION 1503

The above mentioned committee being duly so authorised lodges herewith on behalf of ex-prisoners of war (Australian) of the Japanese Theatre of War in World War 2 a claim for reparations for the extreme and barbarous violations of human rights suffered by them at the hands of the Imperial Japanese Army during that time.

The claim is set forth in 2 volumes. Volume 1 contains a summary of the claim, the legal basis of the claim plus an account of the historical facts on which the claim is based.

Volume 2 lists the names, addresses and particulars of the actual claimants. There are 6057 separate claimants listed in this volume . . .

It is anticipated that the total number of claimants . . . will eventually be between 8,000 and 10,000 . . .

On behalf of my committee and on behalf of the claimants my committee represents I respectfully request that the United Nations Office of the Centre for Human Rights will give due and proper consideration to the claim now made.

David Barrett

Committee Chairman

Justice Marcus Einfeld wrote the preface to the submission document in Volume 1.

> Between 1942 and 1945, 22000 Australian service personnel were prisoners of war of the Imperial Japanese Army. Over 7000 of these men and women died while captives . . .
>
> This very high death rate is in stark contrast to the number of POW deaths of Australians held by the German and Italian Armies
>
> International law makes clear that persons in declared armed combat commit no crime per se. When captured such persons are entitled to decency, dignity and respect. Yet in one regard after another the Imperial Japanese Army breached what have long been regarded as the customary rules of war. It is hard to believe even now when provided with irrefutable evidence, the inhuman treatment and slave labour, which was the lot of POW. There can be no excuse for or rationalisation of these atrocities and acts of brutality committed by the Japanese Armed Forces and their commanders in the name of Japan and the Emperor . . .
>
> We now make a plea to the United Nations to ensure that these Australians are properly compensated by requiring the Japanese Government to pay compensation to the claimants . . .
>
> Such a response will powerfully mark the Japanese people's regret at what occurred and will signal Japan's determination that such evil will never be allowed to happen again.

At this time, the committee decided to consult with Weary Dunlop and gain his perspective on the form that a foundation might take. Peter Collas wrote to him on the topic. It was also an attempt to bring him into the Reparations Committee fold. Peter's letter explained exactly what was being proposed by Don Kibbler.

Dear Sir Edward

I write to you as vice-chairman [of the Federal Ex-POW Association] and on behalf of the Queensland Reparations Committee, and at the committee's request, to draw your attention to a new twist in this matter which the committee believes may be of interest to you.

As no doubt you are aware, the prime object of the committee is to prepare and file a reparations claim in the human rights division of UNO in Geneva. The work is well in hand, and the claim backed by over 6,000 separately signed authorities by survivors and next of kin is in the course of completion. The claim is for $25,000.00 for each claimant, which means that if the claim is successful there will be a payout by the Japanese of $150M approximately . . .

However I can confirm that in addition to the work of preparing the claim, the committee is also through an intermediary negotiating on this matter directly with members of the Japanese Government. These negotiations have been made discreetly for obvious reasons . . .

The object of these negotiations is to endeavour to persuade the Japanese government to finance the setting up of a foundation to the value of $500M. If the negotiations are crowned with success, then of course the proposed UNO claim will become redundant.

The object of the foundation will be firstly to pay claims for reparations as may be filed with the reparations committee, and this will take up approximately $150M or thereabouts, and secondly with the balance funds to set up some sort of permanent and practical memorial establishment which can in some way symbolise not only the horrendous hardship and suffering underwent by Australian POW at the hands of the Imperial Japanese Army, but also to symbolise a manifestation by Japan of its recognition of the injustice so imposed and its atonement in regard thereto.

The purpose of this letter is to invite you to give consideration to the question of what form such memorial should take. My committee has yet to formalise its ideas on this topic. One suggestion made so far is to set up a research hospital in tropical diseases and inclusive of psychiatric research, these being matters closely associated with the POW experience . . .

My committee would value highly any suggestion you may care to offer in this issue . . .

We look forward to receiving your favourable response.

Peter Collas[1]

David and Peter were now ready for their trip 'around the world in twenty-one days', as David referred to it. They were due to set off on 12 March 1990. They would stop over in Los Angeles and then fly on to Toronto, Ottawa and London. After London, they would fly to Geneva, back to London and on to Osaka via Singapore. They would eventually leave Tokyo on 2 April and fly back to Australia. The trip was eventful, to say the least.

We met with the Canadians, who explained that their organisation had now been recognised by the UN as a non-government organisation (NGO). Australia's claim and claims from the British, the New Zealanders, the Dutch and the Americans could now all be submitted to the United Nations under the umbrella of the Canadian NGO.

In Britain we were met by Bill Holtham, the man in charge of the British claim. He was a great guy. Bill and his lawyer, David Lloyd Jones, an expert in international law, were very interested in our submission. They took us to the House of Commons to meet Sir Bernard Braine MP, who was their hero. Sir Bernard took us into his very tiny office at parliament and talked to us very enthusiastically about claiming reparations from the Japanese.

It was a different story in Geneva, but the Australian embassy helped us greatly. We met with a UN Human Rights officer. She was very understanding of our mission and gave us information about how the process worked. She explained that the claim first went before a five-nation panel, who could accept or reject it. If it passed, it went to the government against which the claim was made – Japan. The claim could be rejected or accepted at any stage, without immediate notification to the applicant, apparently. That process could be repeated *ad infinitum*. We were not very pleased.

In Japan we were met by Don Kibbler. 'Feted' would not be too strong a word to describe our treatment. It was as if everyone we met was in favour of paying reparations to Australia. But I wasn't naïve enough to believe this. However, there was obviously a large section of the Japanese people who were in favour of recognising their wartime atrocities.

The press was there and we were interviewed. I held nothing back. They got both barrels about how we had been treated. We met with Tony Glynn, who read and spoke Japanese fluently. He acted as our interpreter. We also met politicians and public servants, all of whom were sympathetic to our claims for reparations. And, of course, I met Nagase Takashi.

Nagase didn't recognise me at first, and I had to describe what we had experienced together on the War Graves Commission trip before he suddenly remembered. His eyes opened wide as he smiled and bowed yet again, and he shook my hand vigorously for the second time.

We were wined and dined constantly, and taken to places such as the Hiroshima Peace Culture Foundation, always with the press in attendance. Nagase had arranged this in order to build a good image of us for the Japanese people.

I was delighted with these developments. At last, we had our foot in the door with the Japanese media. But my ideas of how we might use the media to our advantage were very different from those of Don Kibbler.

Over the next few months, the idea for a foundation was developed. The committee decided to involve Professor John McCaffery of James Cook University, who promised to prepare a proposal for a tropical diseases research facility based in Townsville.

Arrangements were made for further meetings in Japan. David and Gordon Jamieson also met with the new Japanese ambassador in Canberra, in a bold effort to try to set up a meeting with the Japanese prime minister, Toshiki Kaifu, in September.

By mid-1990, David was becoming less and less enthusiastic about the foundation proposal, and about the way in which most members of the Reparations Committee wanted to proceed with this idea. One proposal from Father Tony Glynn was that an exchange of paper cranes – a symbol of peace in Japan – should take place in Nagasaki's town hall in the presence of the mayor of Nagasaki, Hitoshi Motoshima, who was apparently a very outspoken gentleman critical of the behaviour of Emperor Hirohito and his failure to stop the war before the atomic bombs were dropped. David politely turned the offer down, on the grounds that that it was irrelevant to the reparations cause and a gross misuse of committee funds. But Gordon Jamieson saw it as a chance to visit Japan and make progress with the foundation idea. He accepted the invitation, with the support of others on the committee.

Nagasaki was the city where the Allies had dropped the second atomic bomb, on 9 August 1945. An exchange of peace symbols at this place would certainly be interpreted by the press as a two-way apology. David knew very well that most of the ex-POW claimants would not support such an action from their Reparations Committee. Most regarded the atomic bombs as the act by the Allies that had saved their lives. Ex-POWs knew very well that, had the alternative plan of invading the Japanese mainland taken place, their captors would have followed orders and executed them all.

It was very obvious by this time that most of the Reparations Committee was hooked on the foundation idea. I did not like it one little bit. Firstly, the $25,000 for each and every claimant now hardly rated a mention, and Don Kibbler kept advising that we cut back on our negative Japanese publicity. This was totally against my opinion. According to Kibbler, our publicity should now be of a 'philosophical nature' and not designed, as it had been in the past, to directly embarrass and shame the Japanese.

I knew that we were letting down our Canadian, American, British, New Zealand and Dutch comrades, who were still in favour of using embarrassing publicity against the Japanese to support the UN claim. Nagase Takashi was most certainly on my side in this. We could see that a secret approach, which Kibbler also insisted upon, was going to cut the claimants out of the picture altogether. Our claimants – who now numbered around 8000 – would be suspicious as hell. They would think we had all run off with the money. And to crown it all, it was bloody ridiculous to think that the Japanese would bother to settle the Australian claim to the exclusion of the other five claimant countries.

On 31 August 1990, David tendered his resignation to the Reparations Committee.

The constant work with the committee since 1986 had taken a toll on David's health. He was advised to slow down, and Greta had been advised to move to a cooler climate. All in all, then, David did not regret his resignation. He had founded the Reparations Committee despite strong opposition, he had raised more than enough money to assure its continuity, he had assembled and presented Australia's submission of claim against the Japanese to the Sub-Committee of Human Rights of the United Nations in Geneva, and he had published the submission in book form, with all royalties going to the welfare of ex-POWs or their families.

David and Greta bought a house in Launceston, Tasmania. Once they had settled in, David joined the local branch of the Ex-POW Association. Very soon, he began thinking again about how the Japanese could be shamed into paying compensation.

He wrote to Cliff Chadderton of the Canadian War Amputees Association, explaining the position of the Australian claim, as he now saw it.

My view now is that the UN has proved the wrong tack for us . . . The Japanese regard it as a 'victors organisation' and have no respect for it . . . The UN itself seems pedantic and not actively motivated by our claim.

I agree, we could sue our own governments for reparations, letting them recover these from the Japanese government, or we could go to the International Court of Justice.

My suggestion is for the six nation claimants to immediately initiate a combined international media campaign deliberately designed to shame Japan. In Australia we started this two years ago, but since my resignation the committee have abandoned it . . .

My contacts in Japan have told me that the Japanese government
was greatly relieved when our publicity campaign quietly died.[2]

Over the next year or two, David became increasingly concerned about
how the members of the Reparations Committee were conducting
their business. As he saw it, the committee had an agreement with
those who had paid their $10 registration fee. That money had been
donated to fund the claim for reparations, not to set up a foundation
or a research organisation. The deal was that each claimant would
receive $25,000 if the claim was successful. It was very doubtful
that claimants would be willing to swap hard cash for a foundation,
however grand it turned out to be.

David began bombarding the Reparations Committee with letters,
letting them know that, in his opinion, what they were doing was
illegal. They had a duty to inform the claimants of what was going
on, he argued. The claimants had heard nothing except rumour.

By early 1993, the Reparations Committee had set up the
Asia-Pacific Foundation Trust with only one trustee, a company
it had registered – the Asia-Pacific Foundation Pty Ltd – with all
the directors and shareholders being members of the Reparations
Committee or their wives. Their intention in all this was becoming
very clear.

They also developed a top-secret brochure containing all the
details of their proposal, including a schedule of work and costing,
a location map and plans for proposed buildings. These documents
expressed the hope that if the Japanese accepted and funded the
proposal, these projects would be complete by 1995, to celebrate the
fiftieth anniversary of the end of the war in the Pacific.

All this documentation was sent to the Ex-POW Association's
Federal Council by Clarrie Wilson, the secretary of the Queensland

State Council. The confidential nature of the proposal was stressed repeatedly. In conclusion, it stated:

> Without malice we request that the knowledge gained through this letter and enclosures, not be imparted to our Ex-Chairman, Mr. David Barrett, for fear of media exposure.[3]

But David was already a step ahead. He had all the information, courtesy of friends such as Dave Hassett, from Bundaberg, who regularly kept him informed of what the Reparations Committee was up to. In turn, David tried his best to keep the claimants informed.

Over the next two years, Resolution 1503 – the claim submitted to the United Nations Economic and Social Council (ECOSOC) by the Reparations Committee while David was chairman – ploughed on without result. By this time, the Canadians, Americans, New Zealanders, British and Dutch claimants were considering suing their own governments for failing to hold Japan to account during the 1951 San Francisco Peace Treaty conference. Some also took the Japanese government to court in Japan. The Australian Reparations Committee was not in favour of either of these actions and took no part in them.

The Australian Reparations Committee was the only one that was continuing on a course that did not promise to reward claimants a sum of money. In fact, by February 1994 the Reparations Committee had spent most of its claimants' money, without informing them of what was happening. Now it asked the Australian government for money for the continued promotion of the Asia-Pacific Foundation proposal.[4]

In 1996 the Reparations Committee met and considered all aspects of its claim. The committee members came to the conclusion that the Japanese government would never pay compensation to individuals, nor would it fund the proposed tropical diseases foundation. They voted to disband the committee and transfer its assets to the Queensland State Council, for disbursement to all the state ex-POW associations.[5]

The court case that some countries had pursued in Japan also came to nothing. If it had been successful, the Australian Reparations Committee would have been in real strife, because it had chosen not to join the action.

In 1997, Greta, David's wife since 1978, died of lung cancer. She had been the love of his life, and he was devastated. This was the lowest point in his life. He didn't even care that the reparations project appeared to have failed.

David had stayed in touch with Nagase and had visited Japan on many occasions. Nagase had also visited Australia, accompanied by his wife. When he heard that Greta had died, he invited David to come to Japan with his daughter, Denise, and insisted on paying for the whole trip. Being surrounded by such concerned and friendly Japanese people aided David's recovery. It also helped him to appease the deep-seated anger that had driven him all these years.

During the last years of the twentieth century, most of the governments of the countries with POWs claiming reparations from the Japanese had considered paying these claims themselves. They had certainly let the Japanese off lightly in the 1951 San Francisco Peace Treaty, and very gradually they became convinced that the only way to stop continuous action against Japan would be to pay the reparations themselves. The first country to award payment to their ex-POWs (Japan) was Canada, and the others quickly followed suit.

In Australia, each and every ex-POW of the Japanese – if they were still surviving – received the sum of $25,000, as did surviving widows. The money went into bank accounts around the nation in mid-June 2001. The payments were free of income tax and did not affect other benefits that an ex-POW or his widow was receiving.

It had been a long haul. In David's opinion, the POWs should have had the previous ten years to enjoy this money. But it was better late than never.

Chapter 21

Reconciliation

DAVID IS STILL a frequent visitor to Japan. He returned from a recent visit in early December 2011, having gone at the invitation of the Japanese Ministry of Foreign Affairs as part of the Japanese POW Friendship Program. He was one of five Australian World War II ex-POWs on the trip.

It is difficult to talk about the Imperial Japanese Army's brutality on the one hand, and sincere reconciliation on the other, but David and his Japanese friends have been discussing these issues since 1990, when he first visited Japan. In those early days, David thought more about brutality and reparations, but gradually he got to know and respect more and more younger Japanese people. He has found them to be very different from the guards on the railway. Those with whom he has associated have been very knowledgeable about the behaviour of the Japanese military during the war and very eager to apologise for the past deeds of that generation. They have always been quick to assure David that Japan no longer thinks and acts as it did during that time.

Most of the people David talks to now believe that Japan should pay reparations. Many, like Nagase Takashi, have helped David in his attempts to achieve this goal. David has accepted many apologies, and Prime Minister Tomiichi Murayama even offered an apology on behalf of his government in 1995. But of much greater importance were the apologies David received directly from Japanese people he knew as friends. During David's 2011 visit, some twenty-five years after he founded the Australian Reparations Committee, it was now more appropriate to talk of reconciliation.

The media followed the Japanese POW Friendship Program members at every turn during their most recent visit. The ex-POWs in this group laid wreaths at the Commonwealth War Cemetery at Hodagaya, and inspected and took photographs of the records of Allied war dead kept at the Ryozen Kannon Memorial Hall in Kyoto. David also met with many of the Japanese friends that he has made over the years.

At all times, the officials organising the arrangements were very conscientious and went to great lengths to accommodate David's requests to meet up with his friends. Unfortunately, he was unable to meet with his oldest Japanese friend, Nagase Takashi, who died on 21 June 2011.

David first met Nagase Takashi – 'Nagase-san', as he came to call him – in 1945. Since then, Nagase probably worked harder than any other Japanese that David knew, both for his own forgiveness as a member of the Imperial Japanese Army and on behalf of all Japanese, for what the army did to the peoples of all the countries they occupied in South-East Asia in the 1930s and 1940s. Nagase worked particularly hard to achieve reconciliation with the Thais and with the Allies, particularly the Australians.

Although David had only been a private in the Australian army, Lieutenant Nagase had often sought his company during the War Graves Commission trip, probably because some on the expedition wanted to avoid talking to an officer of the *Kempeitai*.

During the War Graves trip, as I looked at Nagase, I thought, *Poor little bastard*. He was in the uniform of those who had been our judges, but now that uniform gave him no authority. He was a pathetic figure. But he wanted to talk to me. Since he was a *Kempeitai*, I was very interested in what made him tick, so it was a kind of a mutual thing. I would ask him why the Japanese were such bastards – I never minced my words – and he would agree with me that they were. By way of explanation, he would talk of duty and the Emperor.

I think I probably had an influence on him. I remember Nagase came to Sydney on one occasion in the early 1990s, and people booed him off the podium and would not let him speak. I felt so concerned for him because I knew how devastated he felt at this reception. I knew how much he was doing in Japan to promote our cause. I wanted to protect him, and I wanted all my colleagues to hear what he had to say, but it was impossible because the anger against Japan and the Japanese was so great in the ex-POW community.

Nagase first started returning to Thailand in 1963. He spent millions over the years, building Buddhist temples to those Allied soldiers who died on the railway, and also repatriating the *romusha* workers on the railway who had never been able to return to their native countries. He not only paid for their fares but also accompanied some of them home. As David learned, Nagase had returned to Thailand and the site of the railway more than 130 times.

Nagase once explained to David how the Japanese soldiers – including him – were what he termed 'cultists', under the spell of the Emperor Showa (in his lifetime known as the Emperor Hirohito). They were brainwashed as young men into a way of life in the military that required strict obedience, regardless of what the orders were, because all orders stemmed from the Emperor.

Nagase came to believe that the way Japan had conducted the war was foul and cruel, and that the Emperor Hirohito should have taken responsibility for it. He was very brave to expound this point of view in Japan, because there were – and still are – many in Japan who believed that their military leaders during World War II were heroes. Nagase was a great, generous and brave man.

I have met many Japanese who have never apologised – or never apologised sincerely – for the behaviours of their military during World War II. One of them was Abe Hiroshi, who never apologised with sincerity. He was the famous engineer officer in charge of the railway track at Sonkurai during the *speedo* time in the months before October 1943, when the railway was completed. Thousands of British and Australian POWs died through disease, lack of food, beatings and overwork at Songkurai. Abe was tried as a war criminal and sentenced to death, but the sentence was later commuted to several years in prison.

I've been at conferences attended by Abe Hiroshi. I have heard him agree with the opinion that all the prisoners ever got by way of discipline on his section was 'a bit of a slap'. This is far from the truth. My friend Bobby Small survived at Songkurai for many months, and he was sick for most of the time. I held him in my arms on the ground at Kanchanaburi, where he died from a combination of bashings, sickness and prolonged starvation at a Songkurai camp. So I knew that they suffered a lot more than 'a bit of a slap'.

In the late 1990s, I was at a meeting on the railway organised by the Japanese POW Research Network at Kanchanaburi on what is now known as the 'Bridge Over the Kwai'. The old ex-guards walked towards us ex-POWs to shake hands in a gesture of reconciliation and forgiveness on the bridge. I could see that Abe Hiroshi was headed towards me with his hand outstretched, so I grabbed it. I held onto it and abused the bastard for a full minute before letting go. There was no reconciliation felt by me at that moment, I can tell you, even though the cameras were rolling at the time.

Cameras were also rolling during David's recent visit. On Friday 2 December 2011, he met with around twenty university students and their professor, Tomoya Nakao. The students had been learning about the building of the Thai–Burma railway during the war, and about how the Japanese had treated the POWs.

It was the first time these students had talked to an Australian who had been a POW under Japanese military rule. David stayed with them for about an hour, answering their questions. He was amazed at how keen these students were to know more about him and the war. He doubts very much that Australian students of the same age know much about what happened on the Thai–Burma railway.

David has many other close friends who have all played a part in gradually persuading him to reconcile with Japan and its people. He met a few of them on this recent visit. One was history professor Toshiyuki Tanaka. David has known Yuki, as he calls him, for many years and is familiar with his writings about the wartime behaviour of the IJA. Yuki is a tireless researcher and peace activist in Hiroshima.

In 1998 David had been invited to a seminar Yuki had organised in Hiroshima. The topic was whether the dropping of the atomic bombs in 1945 was an act of terrorism.

There were about 200 Japanese there, as well as history professors from London, Tokyo, New York and Melbourne. They were all giving papers. Towards the end of the meeting, during discussion time, everyone had agreed that yes, dropping the bombs were acts of terror. Anyway, Yuki then introduced me to the audience and said that perhaps I, with my POW experience, could give my point of view.

I thanked him for inviting me, and the Japanese audience for accepting me. I just said that in the fourteen years from 1931 to 1945, the Japanese performed cannibalism, raped, tortured, starved and murdered more than 30 million people. In comparison, in my view, dropping the atomic bombs was not an act of terrorism. It had saved the lives of all the Allied prisoners of war. That ended the seminar and they all trooped out quietly.

Yukako Ibuki, whom David knows as Yuka, is another person for whom he has great respect. They met again during his recent visit. Yuka is a teacher, journalist and translator, and is an activist for those who suffered under the oppression of the IJA during World War II.

Yuka was six years old when World War II finished, but she has learned a great deal about the war experiences of various people over the years.

'My heartfelt apology as a Japanese goes to the people victimised by fanatic brutality caused by the Japanese,' she says.

Currently, she is Tokyo's representative at the US–Japan Dialogue on POWs, a bilingual website dedicated to the 27,000 American soldiers and 14,000 civilians who were imprisoned by the IJA. Many died as a result of the inhumane treatment they suffered. The website's aim is to promote understanding and dialogue among and between the people of Japan and the United States.

Perhaps the most important organisation for David, and for all Australian ex-POWs of the Japanese, is the Japanese POW Research

Network. David has known and respected its two founders, Taeko Sasamoto and Yoshiko Tamura, for many years, and he met them both during his 2011 visit.

The aim of the POW Research Network is to work to 'dig out' the buried historical facts about all that happened during World War II, particularly information relating to Allied POWs, civilian internees and the trials of war criminals. After the end of the war, the IJA destroyed as much documentation relating to the POW camps as it could. Sasamoto and Tamura feel it is important that Japan's younger generations learn about the truth of what happened in World War II, so that they will not make the same mistakes in the future.

Queen Elizabeth II honoured both Taeko Sasamoto and Yoshiko Tamura with MBEs for their excellent work with this organisation. These were presented by Australia's Minister for Foreign Affairs, Alexander Downer, at the Australian Embassy in Tokyo in 2006.

> The POW Research Network is still working hard to help ex-POWs and their families and friends. It seems to be an obligation that they feel. It is more than a hobby. A lot of Japanese feel very obligated because they know what happened to us during the war, and they feel a very strong impulse to make amends. The POW Research Network knows better than anyone else what the IJA was guilty of, and they cannot do enough for us. These women are great. I admire them both very much.

David fought for years, through the Reparations Committee, for an official apology and for monetary compensation from Japan, but had little success. But on his many visits to Japan, he always came away with pleasant thoughts and new friendships.

I think perhaps reconciliation was first sown in my mind by the actions of Mariko Matsuo. She introduced me to her young students at the railway at Kanchanaburi in Thailand in 1995.

It was the first time I had met Mariko. The children were delightful. Every child there presented me with a card that they had made themselves, each saying how sorry they were for what had happened to POWs during the war. And yet all were different!

It was probably the fact that they were so young and so innocent, and yet here they were apologising for the actions of their grandfathers or great-grandfathers. I defy anyone not to be moved and impressed by such actions.

This gradually convinced me that there was another way to think about the whole thing. That visit enabled me to separate the brutal wartime Japanese – including the Emperor – from the new generations of beautiful Japanese people. I love them all.

Mariko is now a teacher at Kamisaibara Junior High School, and during David's 2011 visit she again brought him a letter from every student in her current class. He has now replied individually to each and every student.

Mariko has been teaching for many years, gradually contributing to the change in Japanese knowledge of the war.

Think how many children Mariko has influenced, how many have now learnt about the futility and evils of war, and how many this will ultimately influence, through their children and grandchildren. This is how great changes happen.

Over the years, the actions of all these people influenced David greatly. His attitude gradually changed from anger and hatred to an acceptance of things past, and to a love and respect for the great many Japanese who have not only apologised on behalf of their countrymen but who, in so many ways, through their activities and their writings, now live their lives as an act of apology. David senses that these are acts of atonement, on behalf of the Japanese men of his own generation.

In 1995, Japanese Prime Minister Murayama did apologise on behalf of his government for the way the IJA treated people in South-East Asia during World War II. It was right that he did so, although there were many in government at the time who disapproved. Yet apologies from concerned individuals and from the children of a country are of even greater worth, in David's view. Their apologies are most certainly from the heart, and in many cases they are backed by personal actions.

And what is reconciliation?

It has a lot to do with forgiveness but has nothing to do with forgetting. It is about acceptance, new experiences and getting on with living.

I no longer have any hate or thirst for revenge in my heart. I carried that with me for far too many years. I am very glad that I can now say that I have gradually found reconciliation with the people who are the present generations in Japan today.

Endnotes

CHAPTER 1

1 Robert Likeman, *Men of the Ninth: A history of the Ninth Australian Field Ambulance 1916–1994*, Slouch Hat Publications, Rosebud, 2003, p. 119.

CHAPTER 2

1 Likeman, *Men of the Ninth*, p. 120.
2 Likeman, *Men of the Ninth*, p. 120.
3 Bill Flowers, *A Recollection*, from a personal copy given to David Barrett, p. 3.
4 Peter Thompson, *The Battle for Singapore: The true story of the greatest catastrophe of World War II*, Portrait Books, 2006, p. 43.
5 The *Vyner Brooke* was sunk by Japanese bombs in Banka Strait. Twenty-two of the nurses made it to Banka Island, where they were ordered back into the sea by a Japanese patrol, and machine-gunned from behind. The only survivor was Sister Vivian Bulwinkell, who, after hiding for two weeks in the jungle, caring for an injured British soldier, gave herself up and joined a different group of thirty-one nurses from the ship. Only twenty-four of the sixty-five nurses survived the war. (See the Australian War Memorial's Encyclopedia entry 'Nurse survivors of the Vyner Brooke', available at www.awm.gov.au/people-1906.asp.)
6 Flowers, *A Recollection*, p. 3.
7 Thompson, *The Battle for Singapore*, p. 47.
8 In the copy of a paper supplied by David Barrett via A. D. Clark, Werribee RSL, and titled 'Lecture on Malayan Campaign 1941–1942' by Lieutenant-General Sir Lewis Macclesfield Heath (no date).
9 Likeman, *Men of the Ninth*, p. 127.

CHAPTER 3

1 Elliott McMaster, 'Malaya peninsula', *A Prisoner of War on the Burma Railway*, available at http://greatlakeshistorical.museum.com/burmarailway/index.html.
2 Elliott McMaster, 'Contact with Japanese', *A Prisoner of War on the Burma Railway*, available at http://greatlakeshistorical.

museum.com/burmarailway/
index.html.

3   '2/18th Battalion', *Australian War
    Memorial*, available at www.awm.
    gov.au/units/unit_11269.asp.

4   'Battle of Gemas', *Wikipedia*,
    available at http://en.wikipedia.
    org/wiki/Battle_of_Gemas

5   'Australia's War 1939–1945',
    available at www.ww2australia.
    gov.au/japadvance/malaya.html

6   'The Parit Sulong Massacre –
    World War 2 Talk', available at
    www.ww2talk.com/forum/war-
    against-japan/9688-parit-sulong-
    massacre.html.

CHAPTER 4

1   Elliott McMaster, 'Singapore
    Island', *A Prisoner of War on
    the Burma Railway*, available
    at http://greatlakeshistorical.
    museum.com/burmarailway/
    index.html.

2   Thompson, *The Battle for
    Singapore*, p. 265.

3   Corporal William Parker, 2/20th
    Battalion, 'Prisoners of War of
    the Japanese 1942–1945', available
    at Lieutenant Colonel Peter
    Winstanley's website, at www.
    pows-of-japan.net/articles/67.
    htm.

4   An account from Lieutenant
    Colonel Thomas Hamilton, 'A
    Japanese tribute to 2/4 Machine
    Gun Battalion men – Prisoners of
    War of the Japanese 1942–1945',
    available at Lieutenant Colonel
    Peter Winstanley's website,
    at www.pows-of-japan.net/
    articles/50.html.

5   Jeffrey English, *One for Every
    Sleeper: The Japanese death
    railway through Thailand*, Robert
    Hale, London, 1989, p. 12.

6   Thompson, *The Battle for
    Singapore*, p. 424.

7   *Report by General Sir Archibald
    Wavell*, September 1942, first
    released in 1993.

CHAPTER 5

1   Elliott McMaster, 'Tanglin', *A
    Prisoner of War on the Burma
    Railway*, available at http://
    greatlakeshistorical.museum.
    com/burmarailway/index.html.

2   David Barrett holds what looks
    to be the original of this poem,
    written on a very old envelope
    and bearing the name 'Alec
    Bourne (8th Division Signals)'.
    Bourne may be the author or
    may have copied it from
    somewhere.

3   From the website of the
    Australian War Memorial
    Encyclopaedia, Changi page,
    available at www.awm.gov.au/
    encyclopedia/pow/changi.asp.

4   Author unknown. This poem
    is from the 2/26th Battalion's
    website, www.2-26bn.org/
    poems_page_4.htm.

CHAPTER 6

1   Flowers, *A Recollection*, p. 12.

2   Flowers, *A Recollection*, p. 12.

3   James Le Fanu, 'Fighting off evil
    with grass soup', *The Sunday
    Telegraph*, 5 February 1995.
    Available at www.jameslefanu.
    com/articles/history-of-

medicine-fighting-off-evil-with-grass-soup.

4 Clifford Kinvig, *River Kwai Railway: The story of the Burma/Siam railroad*, Conway Maritime Press, 2005, pp. 121–123.

5 Peter Winstanley, 'Prisoners of War of the Japanese 1942–1945', available at www.pows-of-japan.net/articles/58.htm.

6 H. C. Benson, *Report on the History of "L" Force POW Thailand*, Imperial War Museum, London, 28 October 1945, p. 1.

CHAPTER 7

1 Benson, *Report on the History of "L" Force POW Thailand*, p. 3.

2 Kinvig, *River Kwai Railway*, p. 162.

3 Benson, *Report on the History of "L" Force POW Thailand*, p. 2.

CHAPTER 8

1 Paul H. Kratoska (ed.), *The Thailand–Burma Railway, 1942–1946*, Vol. 4, Routledge, Abingdon, 2006, p. 109.

2 'Experiences of a Prisoner of War in Jap Hands', lecture given by D. Gauldie, I.A.C.C. to officers of the Lahore Area in Garrison Theatre, 13 March 1946 (copy held by David Barrett).

3 Benson, *Report on the History of "L" Force POW Thailand*, p. 8.

4 Benson, *Report on the History of "L" Force POW Thailand*, p. 9.

5 Benson, *Report on the History of "L" Force POW Thailand*, p. 3.

CHAPTER 9

1 Benson, *Report on the History of "L" Force POW Thailand*, p. 6.

2 Major C. H. Wild, 'A Report of "F" Force on Thailand, April–December 1943', available at www.cofepow.org.uk/pages/asia_thailand6.htm.

3 Russel Braddon, *The Naked Island*, Penguin, Melbourne, 1993, p. 103.

4 Peter Winstanley, 'Prisoners of War of the Japanese 1942–1945', available at www.pows-of-japan.net/articles/6.htm.

5 Ronald Searle, *To the Kwai and Back: War Drawings*, Souvenir Press, 1986, p. 128.

6 Searle, *To the Kwai and Back*, p. 110.

7 Benson, *Report on the History of "L" Force POW Thailand*, p. 7.

8 Benson, *Report on the History of "L" Force POW Thailand*, p. 11.

CHAPTER 10

1 Information found after the Japanese surrender proved that the suspicions of the prisoners were correct. IJA orders for disposing of the POWs were as follows:
The time and method of the disposition are as follows:
(1) Time.
Although the basic aim is to act under superior orders, Individual disposition may be made in the following circumstances:
(a) When an uprising of large numbers cannot be

suppressed without the use of firearms.

(b) When escapees from the camp may turn into a hostile Fighting force.

(2) The Methods.

(a) Whether they are destroyed individually or in groups, or however it is done, with mass bombing, poisonous smoke, poisons, drowning, decapitation, or what, dispose of them as the situation dictates.

(b) In any case it is the aim not to allow the escape of a single one, to amilhilate [sic] them all, and not to leave any traces.

[Source: Supreme Commander Allied Powers Legal files, RG 331, Preliminary list developed for war crime trails proceedings, available at www.mansell.com/pow_resources/Formosa/taiwandocs.html.]

CHAPTER 11

1   Frederick Noel Taylor, 'Railway of Death', available at www.far-eastern-heroes.org.uk/private_5776807/html/railway_of_death.htm.

CHAPTER 12

1   Jack Leemon, Betsey Leemon and Catherine Morgan, *War Graves Digger: Service with an Australian Graves Registration Unit*, Australian Military History Publications, 2010, p. 86.

2   Leemon, *War Graves Digger*, p. 86.

CHAPTER 13

1   Henry C. Babb, 'Searching for Graves Near the River Kwai: Diary of a unique journey in 1945 on the Burma–Siam Railway'. This diary is unpublished but David Barrett has a copy and permission from Padre Babb to quote from it. Much of the detail about times and places in this chapter and the next is taken from Padre Babb's diary, to give context to Digger's own memories of this trip. The diary was very useful in this regard, and I am very grateful for its author's cooperation.

2   Carol Cooper, 'The "F" Force: The Endurance of 7,000 POWs in Thailand', available at www.cofepow.org.uk/pages/asia_thailand_f_force.htm.

3   Babb, 'Searching for Graves Near the River Kwai', introductory note.

CHAPTER 14

1   Babb, 'Searching for Graves Near the River Kwai', p. 50.

2   Babb, 'Searching for Graves Near the River Kwai', p. 4

3   Babb, 'Searching for Graves Near the River Kwai', p. 13.

4   Leemon and Morgan, *War Graves Digger*, p. 87.

5   Babb, 'Searching for Graves Near the River Kwai', p. 35.

6   Babb, 'Searching for Graves Near the River Kwai', p. 46.

7   Leemon and Morgan, *War Graves Digger*, p. 106.
8   Babb, 'Searching for Graves Near the River Kwai', p. 49. This includes quotes from the poem 'For The Fallen' by Laurence Binyon, written in September 1914.

CHAPTER 16
1   K. J. Fagan, 'MJA Surgical Experiences as a POW', available at www.pows-of-japan.net/articles/6.htm

CHAPTER 17
1   'Treaty of Peace with Japan', signed at San Francisco by forty-eight Allied governments and the Japanese, 8 September 1951.
2   Letter to David Barrett from the Honourable Robert Ray, Minister Assisting the Prime Minister, 19 January 1989.
3   Motion by the Reparations Committee at the Gold Coast branch meeting of the Ex-POW Association, 7 December 1986.

CHAPTER 18
1   Letter to the Reparations Committee from J. L. Fitzgerald, secretary of the Victorian Ex-POW Association, 11 May 1987; letter to the Reparations Committee from George Morgan, president of the Wollongong branch of the NSW Ex-POW Association, 20 May 1987.
2   Letter to Ralph Coutts, secretary of the Queensland Council, from Jim Boyle, secretary of the Federal Council, 28 May 1987.

3   Letter from Sir Edward Dunlop to Peter Collas, 2 June 1987; letter from Sir Edward Dunlop to David Barrett, 10 June 1987.
4   Letter from David Barrett to Sir Edward Dunlop, 20 July 1987.
5   Letter from Sir Edward Dunlop to Mr Simmonds, president of the Queensland State Council of the Ex-POW Association, 26 August 1987.
6   Letter to Cliff Chadderton of the War Amputations of Canada from Bill Holtham, chairman of the Japanese Labour Camp Survivors Association (UK), 6 June 1988; copy held by David Barrett.
7   Resolution passed by the Queensland State Council of the Ex-POW Association, 19 June 1988.
8   Letter to David Barrett from Clarrie Wilson, Queensland Council delegate to the Federal Council, 26 October 1988.

CHAPTER 19
1   Letter to Prime Minister Bob Hawke from Sir Edward Dunlop, 14 December 1987.
2   Letter to Minister for Veterans Affairs Ben Humphreys from David Barrett, 1 May 1989.
3   David Barrett, 'War and Post War: The Ex-POW (Japan)', 1 February 1990.
4   Reparations claim form of Sister Lieutenant Vivian Bullwinkell, 20 December 1989.
5   Letter from David Barrett to the Japanese Ambassador, 17 December 1988.

6   Letter from Hideaki Kobayashi, Counsellor at the Japanese Embassy, Canberra, to David Barrett, 26 April 1989.

CHAPTER 20

1   Letter from Peter Collas, vice-chairman of the Reparations Committee, to Sir Edward Dunlop, 7 December 1989.
2   Draft of a letter from David Barrett to Cliff Chadderton, War Amputees Association Canada, draft copy, no date (c. July 1991).

3   Documentation referring to the proposed Asia-Pacific Foundation sent to the National Secretary of the Ex-POW Association by the Queensland State Secretary, Clarrie Wilson, 26 March 1993.
4   Reparations Committee report to the Queensland Ex-POW State Council, 9 February 1994.
5   Reparations Committee report to the Queensland Ex-POW State Council President, 20 March 1996.